Story-telling is at the heart of what it means to be human, because stories give shape to what often seems shapeless. Here Deacon Gary Stone tells the story of his long years of service in the military and police, but also the story of his service to God. It is the story of God in the midst of the human mess, and it explains why now Gary Stone feels called to work closely with those who have known war and its aftermath. This book shows why he may be the man to help others to tell their own story and to see God at the heart of it.

Mark Coleridge
Archbishop of Brisbane

From time to time, service as an unarmed United Nations Military Observer can lead to enormous physical and emotional stress. In 1989 Gary Stone was at the centre of an extremely tense standoff between Iranian and Iraqi military forces, in no-man's-land and protected only by United Nations flags. This episode was only one from Gary's military career that began in 1970 at the Royal Military College. It was my privilege to train with him at Duntroon and to have seen his wonderful contributions to Peacekeeping, the Australian Defence Force and to our Nation.

Ian Gordon
Major General (Retd.)

To my wife, Lynne, and our children Catherine, Michael, Christy and Paul
- *thankyou for your love, support and understanding.*

Duntroon to Dili

Mayhem and Miracles
Traumatic Stress and Trust in God

Gary Stone

ECHO BOOKS

First published in 2014 by Barrallier Books Pty Ltd,
trading as Echo Books

Registered Office: 35-37 Gordon Avenue, West Geelong, Victoria 3220, Australia.

www.echobooks.com.au

Copyright ©Gary Stone

National Library of Australia Cataloguing-in-Publication entry.

Author: Stone, Gary, 1952—author.

Title: Duntroon to Dili : mayhem and miracles, traumatic stress and trust in God / Gary Stone, with Bob Breen.

ISBN: 9780992530112 (paperback)

Subjects: Stone, Gary, 1952-. Australia. Army--Officers--Biography. Australia. Army--Chaplains--Biography. Peacekeeping forces--Australia. Post-traumatic stress disorder. Veterans--Mental health--Australia. Military chaplains--Australia--Biography. Australia--Armed Forces--Operations other than war.

Other Authors/Contributors: Breen, Bob, author.

Dewey Number: 355.347092

Book design by Peter Gamble, Ink Pot Graphic Design, Canberra.
Set in Garamond Premier Pro Light Display, 12/17 and Sheila.

www.echobooks.com.au

Contents

Foreword	vii
Preface	xi
Map	xvi
Chapter 1, A Prologue	2
Chapter 2, Foundations	16
Chapter 3, Towards Higher Command as a Soldier of Australia	44
Chapter 4, Keeping the Peace on the Iran–Iraq Border, 1989-1990	84
Chapter 5, The Battlefield of the Mind	112
Chapter 6, Army Chaplain—Soldier of Christ	124
Chapter 7, East Timor—'Loving our Neighbour'	148
Chapter 8, Peacekeeping in Bougainville	172
Chapter 9, God's Call to Follow my Conscience	200
Chapter 10, Friends and Partners with East Timor	220
Chapter 11, Ministry with the AFP—Tsunami, Solomon's, Timor	234
Chapter 12, The President has been Shot—Please Pray for Him!	270
Chapter 13, Soldiering On	288
Chapter 14, Promoting Post Traumatic Growth and Maintaining Wellbeing	306

Contents (cont)

Epilogue, The Way Ahead	318
Appendix 1, Listening to God	322
Appendix 2, Hymn—*Soldiers of Australia*	332
Appendix 3, Homily—Private Grant Kirby	334
Acknowledgements	340
Glossary	347

Foreword

By José Ramos-Horta,
Nobel Peace Laureate
President of the Republic of Timor-Leste (2007-2013)

I have had the great fortune of getting to know Padre Gary Stone very well over recent years thanks to the Stone family's rich contribution in Timor-Leste. Gary is a man that represents the finest of human qualities and I am pleased to have the honour of introducing these memoirs of his life.

Duntroon to Dili is a compelling story of a man who has committed his life to the service of others: to his nation as a combat Soldier, Army and Police Chaplain, to our God as an ordained Deacon in the Catholic Church and to the people of Timor-Leste and many other countries as a spiritual leader, humanitarian and man of action. Gary serves people every day of his life, void of prejudice or self-interest. He has an impressive ability to bring joy and reason to every person and situation he engages, and is always smiling, though, as you will read, he is very aware of the gravity of every situation and personally committed to carry the cross, to take on other's pain and demons in every effort to help them and serve our God.

Gary's life journey began growing up in Brisbane in the fifties, joining the Australian Army Cadets at the age of thirteen, and on completion of school attending the Royal Military College, Duntroon in 1970. Upon graduating from Duntroon, Gary served as an infantry officer deploying to Malaysia as a Lieutenant, was selected to be an exchange instructor at the Royal Military Academy Sandhurst as a Captain, commanded an infantry rifle company as a Major, commanded the embarked Land Force Elements deployed in response to the 1987 Fiji Coup, and finally as a Lieutenant Colonel, commanded a Peacekeeping Contingent in the Iran-Iraq War.

Despite being a distinguished graduate of senior military staff colleges and with a wealth of experience as an Infantry Officer, Gary gave up his promising military career to train and be ordained as a Deacon in the Catholic Church. Whilst this is an unusual seguai for an armed forces commander, you will see that the ethics, values and manner in which Gary served in this first career were a smooth transition to the next exciting chapter in his life-a chapter that has allowed his skills and commitment to have a very special personal impact in the world.

In his new vocation, Gary served as Chaplain in both the Australian Army and Federal Police, with multiple deployments to Timor-Leste, The Solomon Islands, Bougainville and the Asian Tsunami of 2004. He also continued to be an active leader in a wide range of communities that he has been a part of, as well as an outspoken advocate for peace, justice and morality.

Gary brought his skills of leadership and management into ministry, leading to the establishment of Friends and Partners with East Timor, which delivered over $1,000,000 in aid and human capacity development to the poorest areas of Timor-Leste.

Through Gary's story we see the power and tangibility of compassion, empathy and communication as skills in dealing with the widest range of people at all levels of society.

A life as a peacemaker has exposed him to considerable danger and personal trauma. Dramatic experiences in the Iran-Iraq war saw him develop Post-Traumatic Stress Disorder. Gary chronicles his own struggle and management of this illness, and his parallel ministry to other veterans similarly affected. His experience and understanding of the comprehensive physical, mental, emotional, and spiritual strategies that he has employed, should help all who read this to understand and deal better with this condition.

Gary's two sons Michael and Paul have followed him in military service, with eldest son Michael receiving worthy recognition on two episodes of the ABC *Australian Story* for his actions in Timor-Leste in separate crises in 2006 and 2008. All three Stone men have served in East Timor in uniform, as well as in a range of humanitarian roles. The whole family have been my guests at my home in Dili, and I have enjoyed their hospitality at the Stone family home in Brisbane. I was grateful to the Australian Government to have seconded Michael to my staff as the President of the Republic of Timor-Leste in 2007, where he served with distinction for over four years. Providentially, both Gary and Michael were on hand when I was shot in 2008, and were instrumental in my survival and the support of my family.

Throughout Gary's life journey we hear of his unshakeable faith in God, numerous miraculous experiences, and his passionate desire to give witness to that faith in action, through healing, peacemaking and advocacy. With the courage of his convictions, Gary publicly protested against US President George Bush's plans to invade Iraq, and relinquished full-time service in the Australian Army in opposition to

Australian participation in the war. Amazingly, Australian Federal Police Commissioner Mick Keelty then personally invited Gary to join his team of Chaplains in the AFP, and Gary was able to continue service in another uniform of his nation.

Gary Stone's journey will take you through a life of adventure around the world. It is a powerful testament of a man who says 'Yes' to God's call of service to humanity; a story of a man who does not back away from a challenge regardless of the risk or magnitude. I know Gary as a man of unwavering vocation and commitment to what he believes in. He is also an inspiring father, friend and teacher. I asked him jokingly some time ago if he would be my full time Chaplain, with the reasoning that with so many sins I would require someone as committed as Gary to pray for me full time. As it has turned out Gary has been there for me, my family and my country.

Thank you Gary for your service to peace and humanity.

Blessed be the peacemakers.

José Ramos-Horta

Preface

Thank you for taking up this story of a life lived to the full. I trust you will enjoy and be uplifted and encouraged by the many experiences I relate in the pages ahead. I hope they will bring a smile to your face and be nourishment to your soul. It has definitely been a journey through mayhem and miracles, traumatic stress and trusting in God.

I have had a most extraordinary life. My life has taken me around the world many times. I have been involved in seven international conflicts, and responded to massive human tragedy. I have undertaken roles as a soldier, commander, husband, parent, instructor, mentor, peacemaker, peacekeeper, minister, celebrant, and humanitarian.

Why have I written this book? Because I want to give witness to the possibilities that anyone can have in contributing to making our world a better place. Despite mayhem, miracles can still occur. Those who experience traumatic stress need not despair, because lights of hope can still guide you through the darkness. I will take you through the many 'body, mind and soul' therapies that I have utilised, but none have been more help than trusting in God's deliverance. For those who struggle with post-traumatic stress disorder (PTSD), reaching out to be grasped by the hand of God can be transformational.

Why should this book be of interest to you? I would like to give awareness of:
- how the people of our Australian Defence Force and Australian Federal Police have contributed to immense good in the world in the last 45 years.
- how ordinary Australian citizens, without any government support, but acting together, can engage in significant humanitarian activity that benefits the lives of the neighbours in our region.
- how you can understand PTSD. I will describe my own experience of this illness; how it can be managed when it is understood properly, and how you can help others with this illness.
- how my experiences and those of many others, have been shaped and supported by being involved in the Missio Dei- the Mission of God-to contribute to restoring humanity to live in the fullness of life, through acts of love and sacrifice, offered to our neighbours.

I hope my stories will be of interest to a very wide audience and not just those with an interest in military, police, religious or charitable activities, but anyone concerned with making the world a better place. Whilst my motivation and supports are underpinned by a Christian worldview, I have collaborated with people of many religions and people with no religious affiliation, in this wonderful mission.

What follows is very much an Australian story, lived out with other Aussies making a positive difference in world affairs. Many of the dramatic experiences of this life have been lived out in far-away places, but all have been underpinned by family life with my wife Lynne, and our children, Catherine, Michael, Christy and Paul, (and not forgetting our granddaughter, Brianna). They have been my consolation and a source of great joy and stability. Both Michael and Paul have followed in my footsteps as soldiers and have deployed on operations overseas, with stories of their own to tell. The whole family has had to carry the extra burden of a husband and father who has been emotionally affected by witnessing numerous crises. When I came home from war, war came home with me. We have hung together well with this challenge.

I began writing this in 2009. Immediately I became aware this was an enormous task, and that as with most things in life, I would need collaborators to make this happen. Many people have helped, but Bob Breen, a Duntroon classmate who had also made a Christian commitment when I had in 1972, has been the primary collaborator. He has written a number of military history books, and assisted a number of other authors. He has been happy to assist me editorially and also to stretch me in reflecting upon, wondering about, and testing the influence of Jesus Christ in our journey. Writing this book is a product of our collaboration. Publishing it has involved the collaboration of one other of our Duntroon classmates, Ian Gordon. Ian has done a fantastic job designing and developing the words into a book of great quality. He, like Bob, has made his own positive contributions to making the world a better place, through service to humanity. Thank you Ian and Bob-friends forever.

None of what I share has been by accident. My life has been guided in a mysterious way by Divine intervention, and my choice to do what I thought was God's will. I am involved in a journey as one of many people engaged in the Mission of God. You will become more aware of what this can entail as you read of my experiences.

Jesus proclaimed, 'Blessed are the Peacemakers', and truly I have been richly blessed. May you be blessed too, as you take this journey with me.

Gary Stone,
Brisbane, 1 July 2014

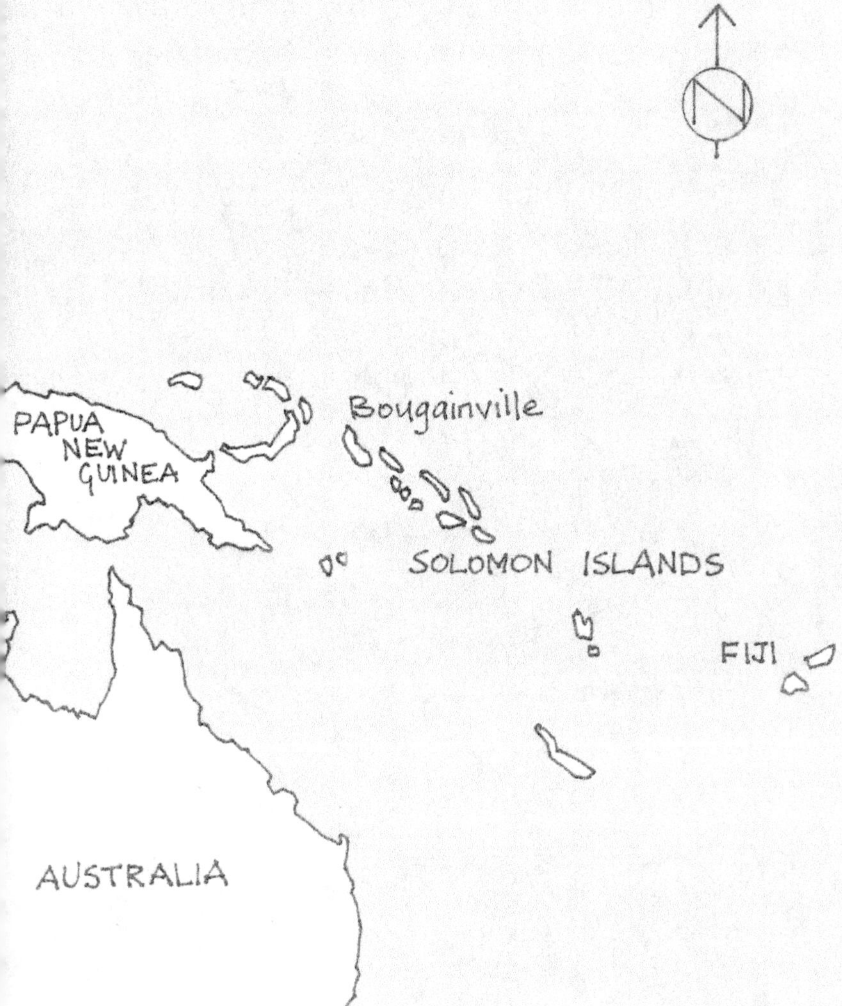
Bougainville
PAPUA NEW GUINEA
SOLOMON ISLANDS
FIJI
AUSTRALIA
Duntroon

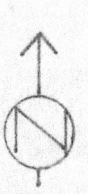

Chapter 1
A Prologue

Two Crises—Miracles or Mayhem?

Two incidents have made me wonder about life in a more profound way. Who or what has determined my destiny? How should I make sense of what happens to me? Did the Christian commitment I made as a young cadet at Duntroon guide my life's amazing twists and turns in the Middle East, Asia and the Pacific—a life of minor and some major miracles, or just one of accidental mayhem.

Holiday by the Sea—Iran 1990

'How far to the Caspian Sea, mate?' I ask my driver, Pavis, a hulky unshaven 40 year old Iranian, on a chilly morning on 24 February 1990. We are driving along a windy mountain track in a borrowed Australian Embassy 4WD. 'See soon', he assures me. I'm taking a break after 40 days working non-stop as a UN military observer patrolling up and down the Iran-Iraq border where the armies of two Islamic empires eye each other off across a 1,200 kilometre long UN ceasefire line.

After turning a corner on the mountainside, Pavis implores, 'Stay calm', as two bearded gunmen dressed in khaki uniforms carrying AK-47 rifles direct us to stop. 'Oh, shit', I mutter, 'Revolutionary Guards.' After four months serving in Iran I have seen the terror that these guys inflict on their own people and the depth of their hatred for Westerners like me. I have spent many, many hours negotiating with these fanatics, sometimes fearing for my life, as well as the lives and safety of my UN colleagues.

'They want know, what—why—we be here,' says Pavis nervously. I tell them slowly using prepared Farsi words, 'I am an Australian Army officer working as a peacekeeper in the United Nations mission trying to bring peace in the long war between Iran and Iraq.' With a friendly smile and open hand gestures, I tell them, 'I am having a day off to see the sights of Iran.' I repeat this all in English. I get no smiles in return.

The two gunmen both begin shouting at Pavis with machine-gun like speed while a third man wearing a pistol appears from a nearby 'porta-cabin', talking into a walkie-talkie. Pavis begins melting down emotionally, pleading with the gunmen to let us go through. He is a family man who has survived the revolution and the war, and has probably witnessed atrocities over the years. He has risked his life driving a detested Westerner around the scenic mountains.

I hand over my travel documentation and UN identification to a short fellow with pock-marked cheeks and a customary thick black beard. He is unimpressed and hands the documents to the man with the walkie-talkie, who then comes close and spits out an angry tirade with fierce eyes, pointing angrily at the front of the car. Unknown to me, Pavis has taken a short cut and used a route that has brought me into a contested area.

Pavis explains, 'Travel papers say we must travel on different route, to east of here. I sorry, I take short cut. They suspicious of us being here. They have rebel attacks here.'

I mentally kick myself for borrowing an Australian Embassy-plated vehicle.

Pointing their rifles at each of us, they wave at us with barrels into a nearby building. I have driven in an Embassy car of a US ally into an area that I have no permission to be in, dressed in civilian clothes. My UN identity papers no longer give me neutrality and safe passage. They implicate me as a spy.

I start thinking quickly about escape options. Running or driving away is out of the question—we would be shot within seconds. Overpowering four armed men is madness. Negotiation, politeness and calmness. Steady, steady.

'Why you on this road?' repeatedly asks a man sitting at a desk in the cabin, flanked by two gunmen, who interject angrily in Farsi something equivalent to 'Get on with it' and 'Damn you, infidel'. They do not believe my patient and polite story that my driver has taken a short cut and that I am very sorry. I am taking a holiday and mean no harm to anyone, but realise my offence and apologise. Pavis talks over me in Farsi emphasising the truth of my answers. Pavis tells me, 'This man say, 'He don't believe you'. No Westerners have been in this area in 10 years, not since revolution start.' I ask Pavis to explain again, but they cut him off. I show them photos of my family, telling them that I long to get back to them.

The questioner goes outside to confer with the others. As each second ticks by, my anxiety level goes up, my heart is racing and my imagination of possible torture by professional interrogators kicks in. I feel my pulse thumping in my brain. Pavis is now sweating profusely on this very cold day. He is terrified. His eyes are twitching crazily. Minutes of anxiety turn into an hour and then another. The gunmen do not appear to be in any hurry to decide our fate. Possibly they are waiting for their headquarters to tell them what to do next. Two hours pass with intermittent questioning.

I fear death. In 1988 Hezbollah gunmen in southern Lebanon kidnapped an American Marine Corps officer, Colonel William Higgins, the senior UN observer, and tortured him in captivity for 18 months before releasing a video showing his blindfolded body hanging by his neck.

So, if there is no quick death, I deeply fear becoming a long-term captive, and being tortured or placed in an underground prison like the poor wretches who are in Evin Prison near the UN Headquarters where I work in Tehran. I experience a flood of absolute powerlessness in the midst of these fearsome bearded extremists. Although I am an infantry officer, trained to lead men in a fight, I am unarmed, defenceless and without communications to anyone outside this miserable 'porta-cabin' in the middle of the mountains near the Caspian Sea.

A wave of fear hits me: anything could happen now and no one would know! Thoughts of my family rush through my mind. If only I could get a message to them. I can't imagine what fear or anxiety they would start to experience once they knew I had been taken captive.

Another intense wave of anxiety hits me: have I initiated an international incident by coming on this trip? I am the senior Australian Army officer in Iran, as well as a senior UN observer. I contemplate the shame of being expelled from the country, or becoming a long-term captive, similar to the American and British captives held by Iranian revolutionaries in Iran and their brutal Hezbollah cousins in Lebanon.

For some reason I look at my watch and an unusual thought pops unexpectedly into my head—time to pray. It is 1pm. I remember that it is 7a.m. in Canberra. Before I had left home, Monsignor John White, an Air Force Chaplain who is also my parish priest, promised to pray daily for my safety during his morning prayers. Risking irritating my captors and disobeying the UN hostage training rule of being accommodating and trying to become a 'grey man', I make the Sign of the Cross, bow my head and quietly pray for Jesus to protect us. 'Dear God, help me now, deliver me from this situation. Please Jesus, my Lord and Saviour; help these men to believe me and to release us.' My closed eyes, bowed head and whispered prayers start a commentary among my captors, as if what I am doing is unexpected and puzzling.

My prayers do not give me any immediate relief, but my actions provoke an argument between the questioner, who speaks some English, and the gunmen. Pavis describes him as the 'Boss man'. He appears to be more on my side than the others; possibly he is an official rather than a Guard.

'What is going on? What are they saying?' I ask Pavis. He just shrugs his shoulders. He's probably safer not talking to me. Each beat of my heart pumps another surge of adrenalin through my veins. Yet for all the physical anxiety I am feeling at this particular point, I maintain a calm demeanour. No one observing would ever know just how much pressure my brain is feeling—it is about to burst.

Without warning the 'Boss-man' shouts, 'Go, Go, Go!' He grabs my arm and we walk quickly in silence to the door. 'Go!' my captor says from behind, shoving me. I dare not look back at the others who are so menacing. They start remonstrating loudly with the 'Boss man', clearly not happy with his decision. 'Go! Go!' he barks.

Pavis jumps into the driver's seat, his eyes staring straight ahead, seemingly in shock or apprehension. The keys are still in the ignition. A gunman standing by the car door yells out his disapproval. I jump into the passenger side and tell Pavis, 'Go! Go! Go!', and we roll forward. Pavis stamps his foot on the accelerator and we barrel back down the road.

'Thanks be to God! Thanks be to God!' I say repeatedly. We return through Pavis' shortcut, get on the approved route and arrive at the Caspian Sea exhausted, but immensely relieved. My heart continues to beat rapidly, however, and does not slow down. I'm conscious of being on edge, and hyper-alert to my surroundings. I didn't realise it then, but this incident has released months of bottled up fear and anxiety that I had absorbed into my psyche as an unarmed peacekeeper negotiating and being threatened and harassed by former combatants on both sides of the ceasefire line. The fear of death or serious injury that had accumulated in my system over four months of daily tension now emerged as hyper-vigilance accompanied by a severe case of chronic insomnia.

As I lie down that night, unable to sleep, I am convinced that God has intervened miraculously to save my life at a time when another Christian was most likely saying a prayer for me. In gratitude, and also believing that my reprieve had created an obligation and a new direction, I commit the rest of my life to exclusively serving Jesus Christ. On my return to Australia some months later I apply to become an Army chaplain.

Was this incident a miracle that prompted an epiphany? Or did it just expose me as a person who chose to misinterpret dumb luck at a remote vehicle check point in a time of extreme stress as a divine intervention that prompted an impetuous life-long promise to a non-existent God?

Christmas Holidays 2012

Waking from a general anaesthetic at 7p.m. on Wednesday 19 December 2012, my mouth feels dry, my head feels thick, my mind is foggy and there is a dull persistent pain in my lower abdomen. Lynne, my wife, looks down at me with concern but is relieved that I am finally awake. Several months before, a doctor diagnosed me with prostate cancer. A surgeon has now removed the diseased gland by robotic laparoscopic surgery, leaving me with the indignity of impotence and incontinence, but saving my life—so I thought as I woke.

I wondered then why this had happened to me. Just over two months before I had been riding a mountain bike in the 600 km Tour de Timor cycling event in the new nation of Timor Leste, involving hundreds of riders. Michael, my older son, and Advisor to President José Ramos Horta, had organised the event that incorporated an unprecedented ride from Timor Leste into West Timor, earning him international recognition as a peacemaker. I had been feeling on top of my game, stronger and fitter than I had ever felt, grateful that in my 60th year I was still making an active contribution to important events, setting an example of practical Christian commitment.

But at Greenslopes Hospital in Brisbane on 20 December, stabbing pains in my lower abdomen wake me up in agony in the 2 a.m. darkness. The nurses tell me, 'You should expect to have such pain after such a major operation'. Panadol tablets they give me have no effect. Bayonets of pain are stabbing me relentlessly.

As dawn breaks through a fog of pain I know that something has gone terribly wrong with the operation. My guts are seething with incredible pain. I had not expected to be pain-free after a major internal operation, but this pain is intense and becoming worse, and my skin is turning noticeably yellow. I can see that Lynne is worried. I am curled into the foetal position trying to find some relief from pain that is greater than anything I have ever endured in my life. I keep telling nurses and the doctors on duty, 'I am in serious pain. Something has gone wrong.' They keep telling me that this is just normal. But I am in agony. Many of Greenslopes Hospital's specialists are already away on Christmas holidays, and no one realises that I am dying.

I am no stranger to death and dying. I have witnessed many people die. I held my mother Daphne's hand as she died from pneumonia in 2003. Most of 2012 has been overshadowed by my father Alfred's steady deterioration, numerous hospital admissions and his own painful death from a final heart attack four weeks before my ordeal. I had watched his life steadily slip from his body over several weeks. I am still angry that hospital staff had been unable or unwilling to provide him sufficient pain relief. I vividly remember his body shaking, and his eyes bulging as Lynne and I, assisted by our daughter, Christy, tried to lovingly hold his body as it went through its death throes and finally died.

At 3 p.m. a day after the surgery a nurse asks me, 'On a scale of one to 10, how bad is your pain?' I reply, 'It is ten out of 10.' I am a wreck, curled up in the foetal position holding a heat pack on my stomach. I plead with her, 'Please can you give me morphine?' At 3.30p.m. she shoots a needle into my thigh. She tells me, 'You should have relief within ten minutes.' She returns thirty minutes later. 'How is your pain now?' she asks. I reply, 'It is still ten out of ten; please can you give me more.'

Fifteen minutes later she returns with a resident doctor and she gives me what she calls a double shot of morphine. They leave and return again at 4.30p.m.

'How do you feel now?', she asks.

I tell them once again, 'The pain is ten out of ten. There is something seriously wrong with me.'

By now my breathing has become short. I look at Lynne. No words are necessary. We both realise that I am very close to dying.

Lynne and I implore the nurses to ask a specialist to come in and diagnose these alarming symptoms. After 15 hours of enduring this ordeal and being told that my pain would pass, at 5p.m. on day two, Dr Peter, the surgeon that supervised the operation the previous day, arrives. I know he is a good man. He listens to my abdomen through the stethoscope. After several minutes of silent contemplation, he finally takes out his mobile phone, rings another specialist and describes my symptoms, including Lynne's assessment that I was suffering from peritonitis.

Peritonitis is a killer bacterial infection of the peritoneum, a silk-like membrane that lines the inner abdominal wall and covers the organs within the abdominal cavity. Any rupture or perforation of the abdomen or bowel can result in peritonitis. Maybe the surgeon has accidentally nicked an organ or my bowel, and it is bleeding or possibly worse, releasing excrement everywhere. This is a particularly alarming thought because only twelve months before a fellow Army chaplain, Mick Lappin, who was one of my closest personal and spiritual friends, had died unexpectedly from peritonitis. Lynne, remembering some of Mick's dramatic and distressing symptoms and seeing me, concludes that I have peritonitis and will die if I remain untreated.

I have been praying that someone will come in to identify what is going wrong. I have been praying every prayer I know to try to relieve the pain. But there is no relief yet. Though I have been praying for God to help end my ordeal, I have also considered that for some inexplicable reason I am possibly going to die. My usefulness to God on earth may be coming to an agonising end.

Is the God that I believed to have saved my life near the Caspian Sea 23 years before, now allowing me to die with a gutful of blood, faeces and pus? I am full of anguish about leaving my family. Why is my life being cut short in this agonising way?

Finally, at 6p.m. Doctor Nick, a bowel specialist, appears at my bedside, examines me, concluding immediately to a gathering of perplexed staff, 'We must prepare a theatre, and operate immediately.'

He pulls out his mobile phone and begins organising his surgical team.

Lynne and Christy hold my hands. Christy tells me that she has put a post on Facebook asking for many people to pray for me. I am beyond talking or even praying. I am totally exhausted and spent, lying on the bed, unable to do anything to help myself. I recall José Ramos Horta being in a similar way after being shot four years before. I had held his hand, trying to give my energy to him. He survived. I wonder if I will survive or die three days before Christmas.

Shortly after Doctor Nick began his call, orderlies come and collect me, wheeling my bed and its associated drips through the corridors, down the lift, and finally into the coolness of the theatre. I look up at the lights. Someone in surgical garb bends over me, telling me that I need to give written permission for them to operate. I squiggle a couple of lines on the sheet. All energy has drained from me. Someone places yet another cannula in my arm and I drift off to sleep.

At 10 p.m. on the day after the first operation I come around in the recovery room. Dr Nick tells me that my intestine had been punctured during the operation to remove my prostate gland, and that faeces had leaked out into my abdominal cavity causing a massive infection. He said that once he got inside my abdomen it was already full of pus and excrement. He eventually found a tear in my bowel about the size of a five cent piece that he sewed up.

Dr Nick goes on to inform me that I was a few hours from death when he and his team intervened. Hours from death? How can this have happened? Isn't my father's death, coupled with a diagnosis of prostate cancer enough of an ordeal? He then tells me that I have quite a journey ahead of me in recovery. The infection has to be dealt with and there are serious risks of further complications. Thank you, doctor, and a Merry Christmas to you too!

For the next ten days my body closes down in response to the trauma. I have two drips going into me and two tubes coming out of me. I cannot eat. I cannot defecate. I just cannot function except to try to cope with incredible discomfort and pain. Massive doses of antibiotics do their work, but my digestive system is totally blocked. The pain of acute constipation adds to my misery. I blow up with fluid that is just not passing through me. The staff hold me down and push an evacuation tube up into my nostril and on through my nose and down into my abdomen . It is extremely uncomfortable and my body reacts violently. A nurse sucks up the material in my stomach with a big syringe and drains it hourly.

After five days without food, the orderlies wheel me back into theatre to get another drip line inserted into my heart to give me protein and some nourishment. Christmas Day and New Years day come and go with me a prisoner bound up in tubes and confined to a bed. Finally on day 12 in hospital, my bowels start moving again. What a relief!

I get better slowly over the next six months. I wonder again about my life's journey. I have been delivered once again from a perilous situation, but I wonder why a good person like me—a dedicated servant of Jesus—should be smashed by two simultaneous health crises. Yes, worse has happened to others. Children, babies and innocent people die in agony every day. I not only wonder 'why', but also 'where' this experience will lead? Another miracle, another divinely inspired change of direction or just mayhem? I can but hope that this will be used by God for his purposes.

While still in hospital I write this poem and post it on Facebook for my friends who have been praying and thinking of me:

Life is a journey thru darkness and light, thru good times and bad and sometimes a fight.

If we lived without sorrow, nor struggle nor stress, we'd scarce have resources to help those in distress.

If our lives were untroubled, and our faces always bright, we might never call those who can help us with light.

So when darkness befell me, and the sky seemed to fall, I called God thru you, and He answered the call.

God sometimes does miracles, but normally just needs, that we stretch hands out in prayer, and love those in need.

My pain was unbearable, I knew death hovered near, but minute by minute, I knew you held me in prayer.

As I've taken this journey thru suffering and scare, I've seen God at work, thru you who've showed care.

I've survived this last challenge, it's been a tough fight, but only got thru with your prayers and Gods might.

Your love and concern gave me strength to endure, you are God's gift to me, and He helped me thru you.

Thank you and may God bless you.

Gary Stone, Greenslopes, 1 January 2013

The recovery from the peritonitis and prostate surgery took months, but gave me more time for focussed reflection on the many events in my life. My ordeals in Iran in 1989/90 and before Christmas 2012 were not picnics or thrilling adventures. I would not wish on anyone, the pain and discomfort of my time in hospital nor the terror of having to deal with Iranian revolutionaries, nor the debilitation of Post Traumatic Stress Disorder. I am still developing my understanding of 'Why?' and 'How?' I am confident that goodness has and will continue to emerge from them.

Chapter 2
Foundations

Every life is built on foundations. The behaviour, character, and future destiny of every individual are inextricably linked to the story of their formative years.

I am no different. A range of experiences, adult mentors, and interaction with contemporaries are to shape my life in ways I cannot comprehend. I am who I am today because of these foundations.

Getting Started

World War II is still fresh in the minds of all Australians when, on 17 September 1952, in the leafy riverside suburb of East Brisbane, I am born as the first child of Daphne and Alf Stone. My deeply sun-tanned dad is a clerk who works at the local abattoir and at the horse races. In his youth he was a lifesaver at Palm Beach on the Gold Coast. My bright blonde mum is a homemaker and seamstress, who voluntarily makes clothes for a local orphanage. Dad and his brothers build our family a house at 719 Wynnum Road, in the inner city suburb of Morningside. We spend our Christmas holiday each year at the Gold Coast, where Dad takes me on early morning runs and swims. I enjoy hard physical exercise from an early age. At the age of ten, I learn to shoot a .22 calibre rifle and go off on regular rabbit-hunting trips with my dad and his brothers, Vic and George, to properties along the Mt Lindsay highway, southwest of Brisbane.

The early post war years are a transition time for a society that has endured and not forgotten the Great Depression, and then the privations of a World War and fear of invasion. I'm sure many parents would have been like mine in teaching us frugality and moderation in all we do, as we might never quite know what pressures may lie ahead. Men and women dress modestly and conservatively with hats and coats the norm. Strict teachers enforce discipline in schools with corporal punishment the norm (having your body whacked with a cane) for even the slightest of infringements. A Cold War has begun with the threat of Russian and Chinese Communism spreading into our region and Australia has participated in a fighting war against Communists in Korea. Every city and town has a prominent war memorial for all to see. Concrete air raid shelters in our suburbs may have been converted to bus shelters but the signs and symbols of war remind my 'Baby Boomer' generation that national security is of highest priority.

Every Saturday for all of my first 17 years, while Dad is working at the races, we go around to my Uncle Jack's house, a few streets away. Jack is Mum's younger brother. Their Dad had died when they were young, and Mum seems to have taken some responsibility for caring for Jack, who Mum says is still getting over his experiences in World War II. Jack had served as a machine gunner in 61st Battalion of Brisbane's own 7th Brigade, in New Guinea. Week after week I hear Jack's stories of service in the War. I sit at his feet on the wooden floor of his War Service home, while he sits in his favourite lounge chair and stares into space recounting some experience. While he's been home from the war for a few years, it seems to be still at the forefront of his mind. He's tall, handsome and solid, but he never marries. He's quite 'matter-of-fact' about things and seems to get regularly sick from what Mum calls 'malaria'. I'm fascinated by his stories. I also read through an anthology of stories he has from the war, in an Army public relations book called 'Soldiering On'. The book reflects the human stories of soldiers—their humour, their mateship and camaraderie. I am drawn to the life of adventure that they have experienced.

One day I ask Jack, 'What was the scariest time for you?'

He replies, 'One night of the battle for Milne Bay we thought we were gone for sure. I was manning our Vickers gun at the western end of number 3 airstrip. We had orders to fire the gun on a fixed line along and across the air strip, down to the eastern end. Our battalion was in defence all along the southern side of the strip. But it meant that in our Gun position we had to be side on to the Japs who had massed all along the other side of the strip. The riflemen either side of us were meant to protect me and my mates in the Gun crew. After last light the Japs had started to taunt us with the sounds of their torturing prisoners from our B Company that they captured at K B Mission, (He falls silent and tears start running from his eyes). It is pitch black in the jungle fringes of the strip and we can hardly see our own men beside us, let alone the Japs who are no more than 150 yards away .

He grips the arms of the chair as his voice slows and his eyes bulge wide in an eerie stare. I can tell he is reliving the event. I suddenly feel a bit uncomfortable that I have asked him about this. I say, 'It s OK Uncle Jack, you don't have to talk about this.'

He looks at me then replies, 'I want to talk about it. Nobody has ever asked me about this. I need to tell you what it was like.'

He pauses, resumes his stare into past nightmares, then continues talking as if he was reliving it:

'We are cold and wet from the frequent rain squalls. We are waist deep in water in our trench. Shots ring out every few minutes. We've been like this for over a month as the battles forward of the strip have been fought. None of my team has even seen a Jap yet but we are mighty scared of them because we have heard the stories of their barbarity. I am only 19 and I have spent too many long nights on sentry staring into the darkness wondering if I will ever see home again.

'We are exhausted and tired but we dare not sleep. At about 2am, a bugle sounds, whistles fill the air and we hear *banzai* being yelled' He gasps and goes silent. 'The order comes to fire. I squeeze the trigger and don't let go. Some flares go up and I can see a line of Japs running into my tracer down the eastern end of the strip. They go down like nine pins. The noise is deafening. Mortars are exploding all around, artillery is whistling overhead, and the infantry close alongside us are firing rapid on their 303's and Bren guns. Wave after wave of Japs keep coming, and all of sudden I get a stoppage on my gun. It is smoking red hot and I burn my hand (his hand jumps) trying to clear mud from the feed plate. My section commander is yelling at me to get it back in action, but it's dark, it's raining ,everything including the ammo belts is now covered in mud, and I' m shaking like a leaf.' His hands shake in front of me.

'Somehow I get the gun going again, but I'm worried about the Japs to our front. Their bullets keep cracking over our heads. That battle goes on all night with sporadic shooting but thankfully no more attacks. At dawn we see hundreds of Jap bodies all along the strip. Some got to within 30 yards of our gun position.' He goes quiet once again. 'I've never been the same since that night.' He starts sobbing.

'Wow', I say. 'That is just so amazing. Thanks for telling me that'.

As he has been speaking I have been creating a movie of this happening in my mind. It's easy to imagine for me actually, as there are lots of movies out at this time both in the picture theatres and in the newly introduced television, about our victories against the Japs and Germans, and I've seen them all. Audie Murphy and John Wayne play inspirational parts leading their men into battle. Of course we are in victory mode and in the movies we always win and our troops are hailed as heroes. Perhaps naively, I am fascinated by the rough tough life of a soldier and imagine myself as a military man.

For a dress-up birthday party one day, my mum sews me a cut-down version of my uncle Jack's jungle greens from the war. To my mum's horror, I tell her I would like to be a soldier one day. She says, 'I don't mind you playing soldiers, but I don't want you going off to war. Your uncle Jack has never recovered. When he came home from New Guinea, he just sat and stared for months on end. I had to get him into a job.'

I don't comprehend what she is saying. I can't imagine that happening to me.

On Sundays, my brother Craig and I play soldiers together against imaginary enemies in the forest park near my grandparent's home at Norman Park. The park was the site of a US Army Anti Aircraft battery during the war. Cement bunkers and trench lines are still present on the hill that has a commanding view in all directions of this eastern part of Brisbane.

Craig looks a lot like Jack, with sandy wavy hair. Craig is five years my younger. 'Pop' Stone, a tall, strong man, who grew up in Victoria, shares with us his stories of the First World War in the 18th Battalion of the first AIF—a legendary volunteer force. He doesn't talk at all about battle; indeed he avoids it, but talks about all his happy memories of singing along with his mates around a camp fire at night, of shooting competitions, of boxing, and going on long marches. Pop tells me, 'Join the Army and it will make a man out of you.'

I am intrigued and captivated by the adventurous life of the soldier. Pop has clearly had an adventurous life. After the war Pop had returned to rural Victoria and worked in gold mines, shot rabbits for a living, worked in a circus, and then moved to Queensland where he opened a fruit shop. Dad reminds me often, 'Your Granddad fears no one or nothing-and his devil-may-care attitude has landed in him in lots of trouble at times. Nobody bosses him around.' At an early age I feel that's how I want to live, and want to have a go at anything. And I don't imagine that this enthusiastic attitude will come with serious consequences at times.

Craig and I are happy lads in a happy family living in a working class suburb of Brisbane. We only have one family income but we don't seem to be as poor as some of the other kids at school. Our family home is on the busy Wynnum Road. We grow up with noise and action, and people popping in. I enjoy school and get better than average marks. I also enjoy sports, playing cricket, tennis, hockey and volleyball. I enjoy doing things with people, whereas many of my classmates are more interested in science, or trade skills, or technology.

At the age of 13, I join the Balmoral State High School Army Cadet Unit and don the 'jungle green' emulating Pop and Jack. I also join the Cannon Hill Rifle Club and shoot well at an early age. I thoroughly enjoy the Cadet experience, especially the mentoring we receive from our veteran instructors who are coming from or going to the Vietnam War. We go on camps at Greenbank training area, on the outskirts just south of Brisbane, where we learn to live in the bush, navigate cross country, fire a range of guns, and work as a team on military-type missions. I just love being out in the bush, sleeping under the stars, waking each morning to the fresh smells of the bush and the sights and sounds of wallabies, rabbits, birds and insects.

At age 13 I join the Australian Army Cadet Corps.

I advance through the ranks from Corporal, to Sergeant to Under Officer after attending 10 day courses at the end of each year. I enjoy leading, and organizing activities. I learn to 'lead from the front' giving example in whatever my team are doing. I volunteer for any opportunities to do something when so many others seem to hang back. This seals my desire to join the Regular Army when I am old enough. Having successfully performed as a Cadet Under Officer, our unit's Regular Army supervising staff recommend me for admission to the Royal Military College, Duntroon.

One of my contemporaries, Jim Wallace, rises through the ranks in parallel with me. Jim is tall, dark and wiry, and excels at sports, especially the endurance events. He is a courageous young man. He wins a Duke of Edinborough Award, after completing a range of adventurous activities and in due course he becomes school captain. We are great mates, but cannot yet imagine that our lives will be linked for years to come. Upon graduation from high school in 1969, having passed the Duntroon selection board and met the academic prerequisites, we set off to train to be Army officers.

It is unusual for Morningside boys from working-class Brisbane to want to be Army officers. Most of my mates from school are heading off into trades or retail jobs. Some bright ones aspire with parental encouragement to become teachers. Most will stay living in the same area—some are still there today.

The choice to join the Regular Army is also controversial because the war in Vietnam has become very unpopular by 1969. The majority of people in Morningside are Labor voters and would follow that party's opposition to Australia's participation, and the conscription that fed young men into Australia's military forces to fight in Vietnam. American and Australian soldiers are dying at an increased rate, and there seems no prospect of victory.

Jim and I aren't like many of our mates. From the beginning I don't see soldiering as a job, as even at this young age, I see it as a profession, and in some way a noble calling to defend the Australian homeland and fellow Australians. There is nothing else—no other career stream—that has any interest for me. I have somehow received a quest for adventure and the extraordinary. Duntroon is about to receive two very enthusiastic, patriotic teenagers keen to take on everything at full throttle.

My Mum and Dad are very reluctant to see me go. Mum counsels me relentlessly about the trauma that Uncle Jack had experienced, both during and after his war. She frequently repeats: 'Jack spent the first year back from the war just staring into space. I don't want you to have to go through what he went through in Milne Bay and Bougainville.' She is right of course—military service takes its toll. But I cannot see that in January 1970 at 17 years of age—for this is what I am called to do.

Duntroon

Jim and I depart Brisbane by train on 19 January 1970 for the Royal Military College, Duntroon, in Canberra. Some 17 other cadets board the old wooden carriages at South Brisbane station. Mum and my aunties are in tears. I can't imagine what they are worried about, for I am exuberant. I'm going off to become a real soldier at the nation's premier military academy. I imagine the action and adventure and friendships I'd developed on 10 day cadet camps becoming a way of life. The train goes 'clikety clack' all night, arriving in Sydney at dawn where 30 or more New South Welshmen get on board. We are met at Canberra station by barking drill sergeants, and the Regimental Sergeant Major, Warrant Officer Norm Goldspink.

'Look lively gentlemen, you have a lot to learn and some bad civilian habits to get rid of.'

The RSM and what we would come to know as 'Drillies' don't scare me. I treat this as a tough survival game. I want to become strong and tough as these seasoned soldiers.

Buses deliver us to the picturesque grounds and barracks at Duntroon, nestled on the slopes of Mount Pleasant—oddly named considering the physical pain that was ahead on both the obstacle course located on its slopes and its steep climb to the top . Later in the day the Adjutant, Captain Ivan Cahill, recently returned from combat in Vietnam with the US Marines, leads us in making a solemn commitment, with our hands on a Bible.

'I swear by Almighty God that I will serve our nation Australia, as a soldier of Her Majesty's Australian Military Forces, defending this nation against all aggressors, upholding this nations' Laws, and submitting myself to those Regulations and Orders prescribed by the *Defence Act 1901*, so help me God.'

A photo of my attestation, alongside fellow Brisbane entrants Peter Keane, and Richard Greville appears in the *The Courier Mail* on 22 January.

We are immediately immersed in a process of training, learning and development that is to have a life-long impact upon us. The College motto, *Doctrina vim Promovet*—Learning promotes Strength—is our starting point for understanding the Profession of Arms. I am proud to be a cadet at Duntroon. I am blessed to be part of a brotherhood of professionals many of whom become lifelong mates. Little did I know then that as I follow my grandfather and uncle into military service, my sons would follow me as well.

The course at Duntroon is four years long, in an environment of disciplined activity, academic learning, military skills development, field exercises, plenty of sport and physical training. But I remember best the shared experiences, through which we develop our attitudes and world views, and more significantly, relationships with our army mates. I keep a daily diary.

> 21 January 1970. In barracks I have been allocated to 7 section, of 3 Platoon, Alamein Company. My cadet platoon sergeant is Paul Stratton, a former Villanova College man from Brisbane who seems quite firm but fair. My cadet section commander is Ian Flawith who is very strict and has warned us that he wants us to have the highest standards in the company. I think I am very lucky so far because further down the corridor, the corporals and sergeant of 2 platoon haven't stopped screaming at their new arrivals.

As I reflect 44 years later, it is amazing to consider that I feel a special relationship with every one of those 120 men I entered the college with; especially the 58 that would graduate 4 years later, and numerous others that touched our lives from other classes during this experience. We came from every state in Australia, from private and public schools, from wealthy and poor families, from good homes and from broken homes and there were even a bunch of New Zealanders who joined in this mixed bag of young men to become a close military clan. We were lean, fit and keen.

Duntroon is a foundational experience. We are to be matured in a time-tested process of development to be ready to take on the challenges that are presenting themselves on the modern battlefield. We are at war in Vietnam and marble headstones in front of the College flagpole bear the names of graduates who have been killed in action, some only recently. Some of the current senior class will graduate and deploy overseas soon after graduating. Knowledge and skills will be important, but it is the development of our attitudes and approach to leadership for the battlefield that will see us undergo plenty of tough physical training in the years ahead.

I note in my diary some comments from an introductory address by the college Commandant, Major General Sandy Pearson:

> The staff will present you cadets with repeated and demanding experiences—some 1460 days duration in your case—and provide you with the best mentoring as your instructors. You are to learn from the successes and failures of your experiences, and be inspired by the example of the staff. In addition to a solid military training you also have to complete a Bachelors degree in Arts, Science or Engineering from the University of NSW.

General Pearson has a chest full of medals from the Second World War, Korea and Vietnam. We are inspired by this tough nuggetty former Rugby Union international with laughing eyes and an exceptional ability to speak with cadets, rather than down to them, as some other Duntroon staff tend to do.

I experience many happy times at Duntroon. Our first five weeks are spent camped under tents at Point Hut on the Murrumbidgee River.

Our days are absorbed in weapon training, drill and physical training, and we all go for a swim each afternoon in the river, with a good amount of wrestling and acrobatics. At night we are shown movies on the conflicts in Vietnam and Korea, and training films on the evils of venereal disease that unwise soldiers contract while serving in Asia! Warrant Officer Keith Payne VC, is in charge of my group and fires us up with aggressive passion, putting us through bayonet drills and encouraging us to swear and scream angrily at dummies. He also shows the importance of compassionate leadership by listening to and helping us when we feel homesick.

With no phones out in the bush, and after two weeks without any mail I ask Warrant Officer Payne, 'Sir, I thought I might have got a letter from home by now. Do you have any idea of how the mail system works.'

He replies, 'Son, don't get worried about that, I'm sure your parents still love you. But I will check.'

At the end of training that day he turns up at our tent with a great bundle of letters. 'Thanks to Staff Cadet Stone for prompting me on this, I've discovered your mail has arrived and been sitting in a pigeon hole in the orderly room that I didn't know about. Sorry about that. I should have been on to this before now. It's a very important responsibility that you will have later as leaders to ensure the mail system works.'

We are immediately impressed by his honesty, and I am grateful for his immediate attention to my request. I note these as signs of good leadership. Like Sandy Pearson, Keith Payne talks to you, rather than down at you. This is most impressive for a bunch of 17 year olds who know that he has won the Victoria Cross in combat in Vietnam.

Few of us have been away from our families for more than two weeks, let alone months on end. My diary entry on 20 February records:

One of the guys in 2 Platoon has gone AWOL (Absent without Leave). Can't understand why. Meeting and making some good friends. Training is hard and tiring, but this is real soldiering. Looking forward to getting back to Duntroon and a hot shower. I realise that soldiering is not for everyone.

I just can't imagine going AWOL. I love it here. I've made some very good friends and we are all in this together. We are training to be combat leaders, which starts with understanding that we are members of the Australian Army. Our company commander, a tall lanky Major Jake O' Donnell tells us,

'We are part of something bigger than ourselves. We are custodians of a tradition of service to our nation. Ultimately we may have to fight our country's wars but we also will help out in responding to natural disasters, and in aid to the civil power, and in our very presence in Australian society give witness to the values of integrity, honour, duty and service'.

Great stuff! I feel so proud to be part of this great national institution.

As with any institution there are many rules and regulations, and it is clear that the senior classes pick and choose which they will enforce. But there is one inviolable quality that there is to be no compromise on, and that is 'integrity'.

It is clearly expected that we will 'test the system', take short cuts, and make mistakes, and if caught we will get minor punishments like an extra drill, that involves rising early in the morning, putting on uniform, pack and webbing, shouldering one's rifle, and spending 30 minutes following the commands of the Duty Officer on the Parade Ground with a bunch of other 'defaulters'. But integrity is absolute—Duntroon cadets are expected to tell the truth, and not to cheat or steal. We are told right from Day One, that offences against integrity will attract automatic dismissal from the College. In a broader Australian society where the truth and honesty is interpreted more flexibly, there is no room to move or compromise on these matters here.

An ABC film crew comes to the college in mid 1970 and interviews a number of cadets. One of the interviews that go to air on *Four Corners* is with classmate Merv Jenkins, a blue eyed stocky surf club fanatic from Perth.

The interviewer asks him, 'What character traits does Duntroon instil in you?' He says, 'At Duntroon we embrace and cultivate integrity in all we do. We are encouraged to follow our conscience and tell the truth no matter what consequences we may fear. It's foundational in the establishment of trust between us.' Merv's uncompromising stance on integrity will later cost him his life.

The training regime at Duntroon is deliberately tough and demanding so that all of us are bonded together in adversity. I learn to depend on my class mates and they know that they can depend on me. To facilitate bonding and team work, we are not permitted leave in the first 20 weeks. Our first break is to spend Easter camping in the bush on the NSW south coast near Narooma. At the Easter Recreation Camp, we are given fresh food to cook ourselves and have a free programme to go swimming and fishing, and to participate in beach sports, or just sleep anywhere at anytime, after several months of high-pressure training. The free time enables us to really get to know each other, sit around a fire at night and share stories. In addition to ongoing friendship with Jim Wallace, I develop close friendships with Terry Oldfield from Perth, Bob Breen from Melbourne, Geoff Kaslar from Sydney and Peter de Haas from Brisbane. This first hand experience

In 1972 the family joins us for a Duntroon parade—Crown Prince of Thailand, Vagiralongkorn Mahidol is one of my section members.

of leisure in good company teaches us the need to balance hard work with recreation.

By the end of the first year, life at Duntroon has developed a rhythm of drill and ceremonial activities, academic studies, physical training, team sport and military field exercises. We are indoctrinated into a work-life balance that will continue for many years to come.

Turning to God

In my third year at Duntroon, my best mate, Jim Wallace, invites me to a Christian Fellowship meeting at a staff member's home. Over a meal, a young Army officer, Lieutenant John Ridgeway shares with us his testimony of entering into a personal relationship with Jesus Christ.

He tells us, 'the Scriptures show that God loves us so much that he sent his son Jesus, to show us God's love in action, (*John* 3:16)'.

What he offers us is a new angle on a familiar historical story. The new angle is that we can make a serious commitment to a Christian life, and experience the power of God in our daily living. Moreover he puts this in the context of being an Army officer. John reminds us,

'The first miracle of Jesus was with the Roman Centurion, who asked him to heal his servant (*Luke* 8:28). Jesus says of this man: "No greater faith have I seen in all of Israel". He relates the particular responsibility Christians have to be peacemakers in the world (Blessed are the peacemakers–*Matthew* 5:9).

Of course the Christian worldview and its recommended behaviours are not the prevailing influence in the hedonistic Seventies. Many young Australians are copying overseas cultural trends, embracing 'Sex, drugs and rock-and-roll' and in rebellion against the Establishment.

While I am proud to be a cadet at Duntroon, John's Christian message is in sharp contrast to the lifestyles of some cadets that reflect those of many of our civilian contemporaries. In particular there is bullying behaviour, drunkenness and promiscuity that are common in boarding schools and residential colleges of universities at the time.

The meeting and testimony from John Ridgeway is a major life crossroad for me. Which direction would I choose next? The Christian life of service is a challenging revelation for me. A voice inside me affirms that this is the path I will travel. Jim Wallace, my best mate, is utterly and passionately convinced of the importance of following Jesus Christ. He and I, as well as a number of other cadets, commit our lives publicly to following Jesus. I start a journey of faith and begin to get to know Him personally, through weekly Bible studies.

Making this Christian commitment has an immediate impact on my life. I have a new spring in my step, and a new confidence knowing God is with me—on my side! I have a new text book for daily living—the Bible. I have a new worldwide community of friends. I get involved in daily prayer, and start to see God's answer to these prayers in small ways. My behaviour has some changes as I try to stop swearing, and not participate in some of the ribald banter that can come out in a group of testosterone charged young men who are training for combat—and we are at war in Vietnam. This is brought home to each of us when the big ceremonial parades in December and June are dedicated to the last Duntroon graduate killed in Vietnam. We are a tough school for warriors, constantly tested by staff and senior cadets.

Some classmates and senior cadets who observe changes in my behaviour and the behaviour of others who have committed to the Christian life mock us as 'Holy Rollers' or as the 'God Squad'. I realize I have taken a controversial stance on what is important in life. Perhaps naively I count this as part of the Christian life, but silently hope my persecution won't be too difficult to endure. Jesus assures Christians that they will be criticised and persecuted, but promises that no trial will overcome a Christian who seeks His help through prayer.

My relationships with other Christian cadets, find new depth and substance. But I don't seek to separate myself from the wider group of class mates. Though some are afraid of public commitment, quite a few of them are contemplating what Christian life might be all about as well. Perhaps some are waiting to see how we 'converts' survive. I have created a new public identity as a church-going Christian. Many will challenge my way of life and question whether combat leaders can be Christians and vice versa. The teachings of Jesus that emphasise love and surrender to God's will may appear to contradict the need to defeat enemy forces in battle. Ironically, Australia's military ethos encourages mateship that epitomizes Christian love, and standing up for what is right, that echoes Christ's message to oppose what is evil in the world.

A few cynical senior cadets mentored me in my early days at Duntroon by saying that the way to get through Duntroon (and life) was to become the 'grey man' and not stick your head out above the parapet or identify yourself as different. I ignore that advice by declaring myself as a committed Christian. I will have to swim against the tide and make choices on an almost daily basis that will oppose the prevailing culture. But identity is part of this package.

Christianity was not a totally new revelation to me. Like most people of that era, I had been baptised and confirmed in our local church. Dad's family were Irish Catholics and Mum's were Scottish Presbyterians. But Grandad Stone had a serious falling-out with the local Catholic priest over his overbearing and authoritarian nature, and told the family they were not to enter a Catholic church ever again! So I was baptised in the local Anglican church! None of my family has ever tolerated abuse of authority. This attitude is clearly in my genes as well. We rarely went to church as a family, but I had an awareness of God from an early age, through regular religious instruction at school.

I don't fully realise it at this time but this decision to follow Jesus is to have the most significant impact on the rest of my life. I have a lot to learn, and I want to be open to many teachers and guides along the way. Two of my guides and mentors are to be the college chaplains.

The chaplains provide religious services and pastoral care of us. While the Army does not expect them to overtly proselytise the merits of a Christian life in an evangelistic manner, they are encouraged to reinforce Christian principles that also cover soldiering values of service, integrity, honour, courage and sacrifice to a common cause.

During my time at Duntroon, the College Chaplains are Padres Les Thompson (Anglican) and John Hoare (Catholic). Padre John has been at Duntroon for more than 20 years and has been instrumental in building the beautiful Anzac Memorial Chapel of St Paul. I can't imagine then that 28 years hence I will be conducting ceremonies and preaching at this chapel. The Padres come out bush with us on exercise, and offer

Sunday services at the Chapel. The Chaplains seem to be accepted players in the military system, and that is very reassuring for me.

Padre Les was an infantryman in the Second World War, and he and Father John take us through the theological underpinning of military service in lessons called Character Training. Notes in my diary record Padre Les stating one day,

> I want to affirm to you that, as soldiers, we are to be special ministers of peace and defenders of the innocent and afflicted. We will only use our weapons under strict rules of engagement as a last resort, and we must always discriminately avoid civilian casualties. Not everyone in society agrees with what we do, and some soldiers have not acted appropriately at times, but you are the ones, as platoon commanders on the ground, that can influence the behaviour of our troops and uphold our good name .

I have to ask myself, 'How can a Christian in conscience serve in the military and in war?' The Padres talk to us about the right and obligation we have to protect the innocent, and to resist evil. But I don't underestimate the complexity of the issue. The US military and its allies in Vietnam have killed many innocent civilians. I know that modern war does involve collateral damage and the tragic Mai Lai Massacre demonstrated that there can be callous indifference to innocent lives.

The conundrum of living the Christian life in the military does not go away and remains a constant challenge to me, with daily reminders of my own shortcomings and compromises to 'keep a foot in both camps' —to be in the world, but not of it. I am young and new to Christianity in 1972. And really, at this time I do not think too deeply about broader moral dilemmas and social issues, as I have plenty of other things at Duntroon, like study, sport and recreation with mates, which attract my attention more. In coming years this conundrum will test me time and time again.

In my first two years at the college I do not go to church regularly, although I always go to the Padres' services 'out bush' on exercise. Weekends were a chance to escape from the cloistered life of Duntroon. After my conversion, and with the support of great Christian mentors like staff member, Robyn Dennis, I now start attending chapel, alternating between the Anglican and Catholic services. Most of my close friends are Catholics and are better church attenders than the Anglicans or other Protestants, but one thing the Duntroon chapel can't provide is girls to meet. I definitely would like to meet some nice Christian girls!

Pairing

Members of my RMC Christian Fellowship group encourage me to experience the wider Christian community. Over several months I visit many different churches in Canberra. All the churches have good music and scripture and teaching, but I am intrigued by the Catholic belief in Christ's real presence in the Eucharistic meal and the reception of Holy Communion. Our Duntroon Chaplain Father John Hoare also presides over St Thomas More's Catholic Church at Campbell, the next suburb to Duntroon, and I find it convenient to go there.

One day I am discussing Catholic beliefs with one of my mates who is a practising Catholic—Bob Losik—a rugged and nuggetty rugby player from Sydney. He suggests I should go to the massive St Christopher's Catholic Cathedral for Mass on a Sunday night. He also says with a smile, 'The place is loaded with chicks'. I must confess to being drawn by mixed motives at this revelation. I want to grow in faith, but I would also love to be in love, and be loved, in a committed relationship.

I had a number of 'dates' with girls over the years at Duntroon, but in my pre-Christian lifestyle I was hardly seeking a marriage partner, and my motives and desires were definitely self-centred. The prospect of meeting a Christian girl now really has me thinking that I need to have a big clean up of my motivations and behaviour. It is in this area of sexuality and intimate relationships that the male chauvinistic culture at Duntroon, has not prepared me well, but rather led me astray. The consequences of my faith commitment are becoming starkly challenging now. I must really practice what I preach in the days ahead in my interaction with women.

On the very first night I go to St Christopher's, the church is packed and the music is lively. I spot a beautiful girl, one of the singers in the music group. After Mass, everyone goes for fellowship in the church hall. Several other Duntroon cadets have been coming here and I ask one of them, Tim McKenna, if he can introduce me to this petite young lass with long brunette hair. He obliges. Lynne and her sister, Christine, come over and make me feel very welcome.

Lynne says, 'It's wonderful to have you Duntroon boys here. Hope you can enjoy our fellowship.' But then she moves on to greet others. Lynne has an ever-present smile and is wearing a body-hugging bulky knit jumper that shows off her very sexy figure. My quandary over why I am seeking to meet girls emerges. I don't delve too deeply into the morality of my 'looks of lust'. Everything about Lynne is great. This is a 'love at first sight' experience. I thank God that my prayers have been answered. Both Lynne and Christine exude warm hospitality, but my ambitions are more far-reaching than what they are imagining. I am absolutely smitten by Lynne's good looks and friendliness. I am infatuated at this point, but I also have an intuition that my life is to be changed forever.

As the night is about to finish I ask her, 'Would you come out to the movies with me?'

In 1973 I fall in love with Lynne Smith.

I am clearly overstepping the mark, as she tells me, 'My dad has to meet any man I am to go out with first!' I back off telling myself to be more patient. Be still my beating heart!

Going back the following week I am shocked to find that Lynne is not there. I ask Tim to help me get in contact with her, and he tells me that she will be back next week. My prayer life goes into over-drive. 'Please, God' I plead 'Make this work out.'

Lynne is there the following week. I am delighted, but she must be detecting my enthusiasm and plays a little hard to get. She wants to circulate around the 100 or so young adults present. She is one of the leaders and sees her role as encouraging everyone—not just an infatuated 'Cordie', a nickname given by Canberra girls to Duntroon cadets. After succumbing to my persistence, she says,

'You can come out to a family dinner next Friday night, and if Dad agrees, perhaps we could go to a Saturday movie.'

Another week of frantic prayer ensues as I await the 'family meal test'.

Meeting her father Ray and mother Marie is easy enough for me. I am a likeable looking lad—well groomed, well-mannered and respectful. I assure them of my best intentions, guaranteeing that I will have Lynne home by 11p.m. after the movies. The following night we go to see *Dr Zhivago*. In the course of the evening I learn more about Lynne's hairdressing apprenticeship with her mother, and her own extensive travels as the family moved around Australia and to the UK, with her father's work with the Immigration Service. Back in the car after the movie, I place my hand on her leg. She quickly slaps it and says: 'Take your hand off me. I'm keeping my body for the man I will marry'. Phew! I quickly withdraw it, respecting her wishes, apologising profusely, and hoping I have not overstepped the mark on the first date. As I drop her at home, at 10:45pm, she suggests that maybe we could go out again the following week. I am 'over the moon' but manage a modest, 'Yes please' reply.

The following week's outing goes reasonably well, although my selection of the opening screening of *The Exorcist* is hardly the foundation for further romantic overtures. Twisting heads, girl's vomiting green bile, spooky scenes of extraordinary happenings and the priest taking the evil sprit into him and jumping to his death have us gripping our seats and feeling nauseous. Nevertheless on returning her home, Lynne permits me to give her a little kiss on the cheek. I am stoked. She invites me along to a number of youth group activities, as well as prayer meetings, and my faith life and personal romantic life grow together as one.

As I continue to get to know her, the positive faith witness of Lynne is inspiring to me. She has not just a personal faith but also a comfortable belonging to the Catholic Church. I also find in the Catholic community, strength of conviction, commitment and a practical Christianity that blends well with my life in the military. I decide to start a journey to be received into the Catholic Church.

In due course, a number of other Duntroon mates—Bob Breen, Ian Steel, and Peter de Haas, to name a few, are to also make their own adult Christian commitments, and keep them for life. After successful military careers, Peter de Haas is ordained a Catholic Deacon in Cairns in July 2010. Two years later Bob is elected to be a Deacon in the Baptist Church. A practical result of their faith commitment leads these men to establish the Podmore Foundation, which has provided more than $800,000 of aid to orphans and the disabled in Timor, and education to disadvantaged Aboriginal children from remote communities in Australia. Jim Wallace will go on to be the leader of the Australian Christian Lobby. God is very much at work at Duntroon in the Seventies, and He will be bearing fruit from that many years later!

Launching out

We await graduation at Duntroon with great expectancy. A band at the time, The Animals, has a theme song *We want to get out of this place*. We embrace it and its lyrics are heard regularly in our barracks.

Every year concludes with a month-long field exercise in the mountains of the South coast of NSW. We practice the tactics of advance, attack, defence and withdrawal in the manner of our Second World War forebears, and then conclude with a Vietnam-style counter-insurgency exercise. The last month of our time at Duntroon is spent in the mountains near Moruya. Having been allocated to Infantry, I enjoy the opportunity of a month in field command of the cadets of my platoon prior to our graduation parade on 11 December 1973.

On a brilliant, clear Canberra day, to the tune of *Auld Lang Syne* we march off the parade ground for the last time, having been given our Graduation Certificates and University of NSW Batchelor Degrees. That night at the Graduation Ball, I stroll down the aisle with my mother and girlfriend Lynne Smith on my arms. At midnight, the 'Days-to-go' board clicks over to zero and stars are pinned on our shoulders, to the applause of all present. I am to leave my home of four years, and march in to my new unit—the 8th/9th Battalion of the Royal Australian Regiment, in Brisbane, as a rifle platoon commander.

Lynne has to complete her hairdressing apprenticeship in Canberra, so I must leave her behind as I move to Brisbane. We get engaged in March of 1974, and Lynne and I plan to marry in the Cathedral where we first met, on 23 November 1974. The time apart during this year is very difficult for both of us. It's clear that her mum would like her to stay in Canberra, and work in her business, but her dad seems quite keen that we marry. I do not like the times we are apart, and am embarrassed to admit that I pressure her too much into joining me in Brisbane.

Our wedding is wonderful, despite it being a rainy day in Canberra. Indeed it is a double wedding, where her sister Christine marries Terry O'Callaghan in the same service. We notice a heavy storm beating on the roof of the Cathedral during our service, but as we depart through a uniformed Guard of Honour, sunshine breaks out upon us. Jim Wallace is my best man, and he delivers a wonderful speech at our wedding reception. He says, 'During the wedding today, a huge storm lashed through Canberra. None of us were injured or even got wet. We were in God's house. It will be the same for this marriage—it is under God's protection.'

On 23 November 1974 we marry at St Christopher's Cathedral, Canberra

We just get a couple of days to honeymoon at Binna Burra Lodge in the Green Mountains south of Brisbane, before I have to be back at work and deploy to Air Base Butterworth in Malaysia for three months of Airfield Defence duties. Fortunately, Lynne is able to come along with me, and we start our marriage in a delightful, tropical Asian setting.

During this first year of my commissioned service, very much I am also laying the foundations for a marriage. Over time I have come to see how deeply caring Lynne is. She has a quality of compassion and concern to help others like no other. She is energetic, vibrant and athletic. She is a great listener and attentive companion. She is so pretty. I am just so much in love with her.

We are to launch out into the unknown, uncertain of the future, but trusting in God, and confident that I have had a solid foundation in both faith and military service.

Chapter 3
Towards Higher Command as a Soldier of Australia

The Australian Army Hymn is titled, *Soldiers of Australia*. The full text (to the tune of *Walzing Matilda*) is at Appendix 2. An extract is:

Soldiers of Australia, ready to be called to serve,
Training together we strive for peace;
Whether home or away, through the darkest night or longest day,
We trust God's guidance will never cease

I am proud to be now serving as such, under God's guidance.

What follows for me would be seen by some as an interesting, diverse and at times extraordinary military career at home and abroad. It certainly is all of this. But it is more. Over time I have come to realise this journey has been fundamentally guided by God's destiny for me. What follows is an interwoven cord with strands of faith, family and soldiering, binding as one. The journey appears as a diversity of experiences, but nothing is random. Though I have no foresight in how my life is to unfold, the pathway that I follow is very much—'The Way', El Camino (in Spanish)—the way of Jesus, that God reveals and invites me to take, day by day. I still get to choose or not to follow this Way, but I do my best to follow the destiny set before me.

Training for war, and securing the peace

On 15 January 1974 at 0730 hours, perspiring and perhaps a little apprehensive, in a starched jungle green uniform, I march into the massive Enoggera military barracks in the near north west of Brisbane which has been Queensland's major military training base since the establishment of a Queensland Defence Force in the 1880's. I report to the Second World War creme coloured two storey wooden house that contains the Battalion Headquarters of the recently amalgamated 8th and 9th Battalions of the Royal Australian Regiment, now dubbed 8/9 RAR.

Upon entering the office of the Adjutant, Captain John Langler, I receive a smile and a warm handshake, 'Welcome aboard' he says; to my surprise he is dressed in a maroon football jersey and black shorts, and tells me;

'Relax for now, and go up to the Officers' Mess where the staff will allocate you a room. We do PT every morning at this time, and then all the officers gather in the Officers Mess for morning tea at 0900. There you will meet the Commanding Officer, Lieutenant Colonel Clunies-Ross, and your new Company Commander Captain Dave Procopis. You have been allocated to Bravo Company and Dave will tell you what he expects of you there. You should enjoy working for Dave. He has just come to us from the Special Air Service Regiment where they encourage people to use their initiative and take plenty of risks to get the best outcome. Enjoy!'

He says all of this as he dashes out the office and runs to catch a group of soldiers jogging up the road.

'Wow!' I think. What a great start. Nothing like the 'barking' of the Drillies and unsettling 'carry-on' of my arrival at Duntroon. The staff at Duntroon had warned us that some of us might get the 'new boy' run around by old timers wanting to test us out, but the atmosphere here in Enoggera seems good so far. After finding my room in the Mess, I join in the morning tea, and get a friendly welcome from everyone there. My company commander, a short, dark, soft spoken West Australian, then takes me to his office, telling me how he wants me to organise interesting training for my troops, but also encourages me to slow down from the pace of life at Duntroon, and ensure I have a good balance of work, rest and play. He seems so friendly and almost casual, compared to the seriousness of staff at Duntroon.

My first command—6 Platoon, B Coy, 8/9 RAR at Enoggera after winning a cross country run competition.

Captain Dave tells me I am to be the commander of 6 Platoon, a rifle platoon of 34 men. My platoon sergeant is a 'crusty' 30 year old, 'Barney' Barnes, a veteran of the Malayan and Vietnam campaigns. My Section commanders, Bill Parry, John Jeffers and Bruce de Jersey, all in their mid-twenties, are also Vietnam veterans, and have an air of confidence about them that I am yet to attain. No doubt their overseas service matured them and developed them much faster than civilians of their age. I feel quite humbled and a little in awe at the experience gap between us as I start by having them each share something of their life stories before laying out my own command philosophy.

I start by saying,

'I want to acknowledge that all of you have had significant operational service, and while I have had 4 years training at Duntroon, I'm keen to learn all I can from you. I will be fair, firm and friendly and I ask you to be frank and honest with me. I want to emphasise three Cs—Communication, Common sense, and Care for our diggers. There's another C too—Collaboration—I won't be making any decisions without getting your advice—I see us as a command team'.

Bill Parry, a solid, quiet spoken, country-reared man, is first to respond.

'Boss, we've had lots of young platoon commanders, and we appreciate that it is probably a bit scary for you starting out, but if you have confidence in the training you got at Duntroon and keep to those principles you've just laid out, we are going to get on just great.' I feel relieved and received.

Day two in Bravo Company is scheduled on the training programme as Roping and Rappelling. Our SAS trained company commander is to take us out to the cliffs at Kangaroo Point along the Brisbane River, and show us how to rappel down the rock escarpment. This is something we didn't cover at Duntroon! As we get to the spot, I look over the cliff, my stomach churns and fear engulfs me. I can see most of the soldiers are feeling the same. The brown basalt rock face is a striking landmark on the inner city horizon, and has been the scene of many people falling to their deaths either intentionally or accidentally.

Towards Higher Command as a Soldier of Australia

Captain Procopis tells us,

'Fellas, you might never have to go down cliffs on operations, but you will need to confront fear. I am going to show you today that you can confront fear, by having confidence in your training and by following your leaders. I am going to explain how you do this, then demonstrate it, and then in turn have your officers, NCOs and then yourselves, do it.'

My heart is pumping! I must have a fear of heights for I cannot imagine how I am going to do this. The cliff is a sharp 70 metre drop to rocks below. Captain Dave then shows us how to make a rope harness around our waist, connect a carabiner, feed the rope into it to slow our descent, then with gloved hands gripping the rope above and below the carabiner, lowers himself down the cliff. He does this all effortlessly. On returning to the top of the cliff via some stairs, he then says, 'Any questions?' Silence reigns.

Sgt Barney Barnes whispers to me, 'If it's any consolation Boss, I can tell you that all of us including me are scared shitless about doing this!'

'Platoon commanders, front and centre!' the Captain orders. Cheers and clapping erupt from the troops to break the icy nervousness. 'Don't worry boss, we'll come to your funeral.' some wag calls out.

Three ropes are tied off to the safety fencing along the cliffs and along with fellow platoon commanders Lex Shuttlewood and Peter Klekner we step forward and hook on. My heart is pumping and I am shaking inside whilst trying to look composed. Captain Dave says to us,

'I know you are scared, but I want you to overcome those fears by trusting me, trusting your training, and trusting this equipment, and if you are still scared, say a prayer. Don't think about the height, just focus on the drill I've taught you and follow my instructions'. I say a quick prayer!

I cautiously edge out backwards towards the cliff with a vice like grip ready to lock the rope around me. 'Loosen your grip Mr Stone, let the rope through your carabiner, and push yourself off.' I am loathing letting the rope loose in my hands lest I lose grip of it. 'Loosen it, Mr Stone, trust me, and start walking down.' I say another quick prayer, 'God help me!' I do loosen it a little and I start to descend. A few more steps and I get to feel in control of the descent.

Captain Dave says, 'That's good, that's really good, now start pushing off and bounce down in small bounds '. I follow his instructions and gain confidence that I am in control. Within a few seconds I am at the base and there is whooping and hollering from the troops above and below. Captain Dave yells out. 'Well done. Now race back up here and do it again, and show your diggers that you can overcome the fear of doing this.' With the adrenalin pumping in me I bound up the steps, and connect to the rope again and push my self off now oblivious to the height, but with my mind locked on to the task at hand, confident that my leader has my best interests at heart and I can trust him . The whole company goes through this process and by afternoon we are virtually running down the cliff with total confidence.

At the end of just my second day in the infantry, I have learned by the example of my leader, and by his coaching though a practical experience, that we can manage our fears. At least in my case, the prayer helped as well. I store this all away as a fundamental foundation of leadership. Explain, demonstrate and then mentor others in imitating your behaviour. And always say a prayer (ASAP)!

The next challenging event for my platoon is the Brisbane floods of 1974. Within two weeks Brisbane is devastated by its biggest flood in 100 years and we are to spend several weeks shovelling mud and clearing debris from houses all along the river. We are proud to be helping our community, and the local people welcome our support.

On 28 January 1974, all available military people deploy onto the streets of Brisbane, not with weapons but with shovels, wheelbarrows and trucks. In a classic military operation, we receive orders, tasks are assigned, and we move out to designated areas of operations. My platoon deploys to the once beautiful leafy green area of St Lucia. We are shocked to see the devastation. Homes along the waterfront have been flooded with water up to their ceilings. Mud and debris is everywhere. The faces on the residents are glum, but when they look up to see us we get some arms, beckoning us to come to their assistance.

I allocate my sections to various areas of the suburb, and then start going from house to house trying to get a deeper understanding of how we can best be of assistance. At the first house I come to, a lady greets me at the door in tears. She invites me to come and look through her house. Stinking mud sits 6 inches deep above the floorboards, all the windows are smashed, and all of her property is damaged by water that has flowed through the house in a raging torrent. 'Oh my gosh'. I say to her. 'I am so sorry for what has happened to you. What can we do to help?' She just stands there sobbing, unable to speak. I say to her, 'I will get some soldiers to come here and help to get the mud out of the house. In the meantime can I make you a cup to of tea'?

She looks up somewhat startled. 'How can you do that?' she says. 'There is no electricity'. I say to her, 'Madam, we are the army, and we can do lots of things including making you a cup of tea without electricity!' I get my signaller to get out his ration pack and hexamine stove and we are able to give her a brew and some biscuits. She starts smiling. 'Thank you so much,' she says. 'It's just so nice that you are here with me. I don't have any other family to help me. I am all alone.' I say to her, 'We are your soldiers. We are proud to serve you. I didn't quite imagine doing this when I graduated from Duntroon last month, but we are very happy to be of assistance'. I reflect that in essence this is what being a soldier is about—being ready and adaptable to meet any need that the nation might ask of us. I feel proud to be an Australian soldier. I can see that helping others and showing compassion in real practical ways, is going to be a part of this vocation.

We train for a year in the forests of south east Queensland, until my company deploys to protect Malaysia's Butterworth Airbase, and two squadrons of RAAF Mirage fighters that are based there. We are protecting the base from Communist saboteurs who have been waging an insurgency against the Malaysian Government for almost twenty years. We patrol the environs of the massive base by day and night, with loaded rifles and machine guns, although we do not fire a shot in anger during our three month tour of duty. Intelligence confirms that there is at least a company of 100 terrorists operating within 30 km of the base, but perhaps because of our vigilance, they strike at targets of opportunity on roads and railways away from us, killing some Malaysian soldiers and police, and creating fear amongst the people. Still, we gain valuable experience in jungle operations, and working with the Royal Australian Air Force and Malaysian armed forces. From going to weekly Operations and Intelligence briefings at the Base HQ, I gain awareness and a practical insight into the Counterinsurgency warfare we studied at Duntroon, that the British had developed many years before, and the Malaysians have employed successfully.

On patrol in the Malaysian jungle in defence of Air Base Butterworth 1974.

The deployment poses a few moral challenges as well. Brothels and booze are great drawcards for the soldiers when off duty. I don't quite know how to discourage involvement in this, apart from staying sober and giving a good personal example myself. I am definitely open about my faith and worship weekly at the chapel service conducted by the RAAF Chaplains. My men are aware of my moral stance but I can't impose it on them. I am proud that fewer of my men get into trouble with venereal disease and arrests for drunkenness than in the other platoons. I just hope that my example has moderated their behaviour. As a young platoon commander it is difficult to dictate personal off duty behaviour to soldiers. Over time I will learn that the personal values and behaviour of commanders will strongly influence the behaviour of soldiers. On reflection I wish I had been more direct, as one of my Corporals gets arrested for drunken behaviour by the Malaysian police, and is kept in Malaysia for three extra months pending trial.

Something about this man's behaviour puzzles me for years to come. Corporal John is just a fantastic soldier most of the time, but he seems hyper aroused and occasionally 'flies off' in real anger. Off duty he gets drunk easily and into fights. I counsel him and he tells me that he was a forward scout in Vietnam and has a 'sharp edge' now. In Malaysia one night, he is travelling in a taxi and hears some noise he thinks is gunfire and grabs the wheel of the taxi and pulls it off the road and into a ditch. There was no gunfire, perhaps just a car backfiring, but he writes off the car, injuring the driver and is arrested and locked up. Like so many of the veterans, he gets drunk most nights. I wonder what is going on here. I try to support him, but even when back in Australia, his extreme reactions continue until a man dies in another drunken incident, and John is discharged from the Army. Many veterans seem to be alcoholics. My sergeant tells me that is the way they deal with stress. The Army seems to accept this is normal. I ponder what is going on. We have so many veterans with dysfunctional lives and nothing is being done about it. In years to come I will find out about Post Traumatic Stress Disorder from personal experience, but even then I will have to struggle to know how to deal with it.

We return home to train for operations that might be needed in Defence of Australia, which admittedly seems a most unlikely possibility. But four years at Duntroon has taught me patience, and I know we must serve faithfully as required. The years of peace are to give us the opportunity to perfect our training, and train hard we do.

Diverse faith filled experiences along the way

Lynne and I commence an exciting journey of postings around Australia and overseas in the 1980s. Every place we go, we get involved in the life of the local church. Each community seems to offer something special. We are able to experience fellowship and growth in faith, life and love through various prayer, bible study and renewal groups in the parish. At the same time we maintain ecumenical fellowship with other Christians through weekly meetings of the Military Christian Fellowship, which is a group of like minded Christians in the military. We gather weekly on base during lunchtimes or at homes of an evening, and spend some time reflecting on a scripture passage relevant to our service life and also singing and praying together. Significantly we grow in deeper friendship with other Christian families, especially including our Duntroon classmates—the Breens, the de Haass, the Wallaces, the Steels, and the Swans. Practical Christianity is very much about community, and we enjoy a very wide one.

God blesses our marriage through the birth of 4 wonderful children: Catherine in 1975, Michael in 1977, Christy in 1982 and Paul in 1984. These are definite spiritual moments, where we marvel at the gift of life. We celebrate these births with baptismal ceremonies soon after, and select fellow Military Christians to be the children's Godparents,

We enjoy many holidays together at the Gold Coast, and the social life of the Army messes and local parishes. Lynne plays netball, and I play hockey and tennis. We spend lots of time with extended family, alternating our Christmas holidays in Canberra and Brisbane. Time with our extended family is very important to us and will continue to be so. We see the family as the 'small church' that clusters together with others to form the Universal church.

Off to Europe and other interesting places

After serving as a staff officer in Canberra for two years, Lynne and I pack our things, and on our son Michael's first birthday, 2 September 1978, fly to the United Kingdom for me to take up an appointment as exchange instructor at the Royal Military Academy, Sandhurst. This is a prestigious military academy, with hundreds of years of history, that includes offering places to many international students who go on to be defence chiefs, kings, presidents and prime ministers—astute British diplomacy. I am honoured that the Infantry Corps has selected me. I begin as a platoon commander to a series of officer trainee courses. After a year I become Assistant to the Chief Instructor—another honour.

We move into military quarters in the beautiful village of Camberley, just as the brown autumn leaves start falling. Hundreds of military families live together in identical but quaint cottages, and we get to meet many international students who are attending the co-located British Army Staff College. We get our first snow fall in December, and pretty though it is to look at from indoors, mine is an outdoors job where being cold, wet and shivering is to become the norm.

The British Army is heavily involved in operations in Northern Ireland, and cadets will graduate to join their Regiments on counter-terrorism operations. My Company Commander, Major Charles Dawnay, Welsh Guards, has already had 9 tours of duty in Londonderry (or 'Derry' as the Irish would prefer it known). I gain important insights into the training of officers. Many of my predecessors have gone on to very high rank, and all subsequently trained future officers in Australia.

From my very first exercise in the wet misty mountains of Wales, I experience how the training is physically tougher than we have in Australia. It is conducted in arduous weather conditions where some cadets succumb to exposure, and I learn how to 'tough it out' with them. I have a platoon of cadets to mentor with my Platoon Sergeant, 'Tug' Wilson from the Royal Artillery. We demonstrate and then get the cadets to copy us in a range of leadership tasks like conducting an attack, setting an ambush, or preparing a defensive position. This was easy in Australia, but when cold, wet and windblown, without seeing the sun for days, the skills of leadership and motivation are particularly needed.

Cadets at Sandhurst learn the importance of understanding other cultures through a trip to the multi racial environment of Cyprus for their final exercise. In accompanying them I learn the importance of studying and understanding the history and ethnic issues that lie at the root of conflicts. The 'Brits' have a worldly wisdom of gentle personable engagement with cultural leaders that helps them get entree into societies closed off to other westerners. I take particular note of their cultural awareness and try to develop this myself by being inquisitive with people of other nationalities that I come across, and getting to know some words of greeting in the various languages of Europe as we travel on leave.

Adventures in the Holy Land

A bonus opportunity arises when we are on training in Cyprus in 1980, when the Sandhurst Catholic Chaplain asks me, 'Will you come with me for a few days in the Holy Land at the end of the exercise. It's a chance in a lifetime.' (Father Austin Griffin is a short wiry priest from Liverpool who we have become good friends with, despite him beating me regularly at tennis). He tells me, 'This will be a great insight for you in understanding the scriptures. We will walk where Jesus walked'. I am fascinated by the potential religious significance of this.

I reply, 'Austin I'd love to, but how are we going to swing this with the authorities?' Israel and Palestine have been unstable with wars being fought there in 1967 and 1973. The Israeli Army occupies the West Bank of the Jordan, and continues to be resisted by Palestinian militias with occasional bombings and ambushes of military elements. However both sides are sensitive to the need for tourist dollars and people on pilgrimage have rarely been troubled.

He replies, 'It's easier to ask for forgiveness than permission. We can be there and back before anyone in the UK knows!' The local commander doesn't have any objections to us going 'on leave' and we can get a civilian flight to Tel-a-Viv which is only 45 minutes away. Had I requested permission to go, through the Defence Staff at the Australian High Commission, it would have been unlikely to have been approved for fear that something might happen to me!

In landing at Tel-a-Viv I am immediately struck by the preponderance of machine gun carrying Israeli police and military, in the arrivals hall. We are subjected to a thorough search and detailed questioning by a series of officials and then get outside and hail a taxi. We must have engaged the fastest and most dangerous taxi driver in the world and as we swerve in and out of traffic, I contemplate the prospect of dying or being seriously injured in a car accident in Israel while undertaking an unauthorised trip. This could be an ignominious end to my military career, but Austin assures me that they all drive like this here, they are very skilled at it, and I should join him in praying the Rosary! I join immediately as we pray aloud 'Hail Mary full of Grace ...

We survive the hair-raising taxi ride up through the dry rocky Judean foothills, and we arrive at the Jaffa Gate of the Old City of Jerusalem about 10.00 p.m. on the Monday of what is the Holy Week of Easter—a fortunate coincidence in timing, for two pilgrims seeking spiritual insights. I am awestruck at the floodlit walled embattlements that are pockmarked with bullet holes from various campaigns. There is an eerie stillness in the star filled Judean night sky as we walk the cobbled stone streets in search of accommodation. The Inns are all full—it's Holy week after all! About midnight, with the streets empty, Austin sees someone looking out the window of a small hotel at us and he pleads with them to let us in. It turns out to be the owner and once he realises that Austin is a priest, he opens the rustic wooden door and lets us in.

A dark skinned anxious looking man apologetically says, 'I've no beds to offer you now, but you can sleep on the couches tonight, and tomorrow I'll get you a room.' He offers and we accept. He then breaks open a bottle of port and spends an hour telling us of the harassment and restrictions that his people, Palestinian Christians, suffer under the occupying Israeli military. We get a few hours of sleep and rise to go to attend Mass at The Holy Sepulchre—built over the tomb of Christ. I can scarcely take in the myriad symbols and sounds of this vast Cathedral packed with numerous chapels and pilgrim groups worshipping in many tongues.

In 1978, during a British Army deployment in Cyprus I get to visit the Holy Land.

The next two days we scamper around the most famous biblical places of Judaism, Christianity and Islam—the Wailing Wall, the Mount of Olives, The Dome of the Rock, and the Grotto in Bethlehem where Jesus was born. We walk in prayer the Via Dolorosa where Jesus dragged his cross. Austin explains to me the significance of so many biblical stories and I grasp the historical background to the gospel stories. I fully imagine Jesus walking these streets, preaching and teaching, and finally dragging a cross to the hill of Calvary, where I place my hand in the hole in the stone where his cross is thought to have been placed. It is a breathtaking moment, and I wonder how and if, I will suffer for my faith.

In a parody of the Roman occupiers of this land 2000 years before, young Israeli soldiers are everywhere throughout Jerusalem controlling movement and liberally wielding truncheons into the legs and backs of Palestinians who they find some issue with. The sharp crack of their M16 rifles occasionally gets our attention. They seem to be used as warning shots, as we don't see people killed, but people still scurry off the streets in fear. We board a bus to Bethlehem, only to have it stopped at a military checkpoint where young soldiers come on board, and pointing their guns at each of us in turn demand to see identity documents. The Palestinians are angrily ordered off the bus and told to walk. An old lady is ordered off and Austin speaks up to appeal that she be allowed to travel on. 'Shut up' barks the soldier, menacingly pointing his weapon straight at Austin. My heart races and I say a silent prayer. I notice the soldier's finger is on the trigger. Austin quietly says to me that we should sit still. Afterwards Austin reflects to me, 'Jesus came with a message to the people of his day that they should love their neighbour. They wouldn't accept it then and they still haven't got it here and now. Their tribalism has prevailed over their faith in God. Jesus was killed because he sought to unite all humankind, but his message of peace and reconciliation has been passed on, and we must try to live it out.'

It's as if a light goes on in my brain. Yes I get it. Loving your neighbour is the most fundamental teaching of Jesus. He wants us to love our neighbours, meaning the other races and cultures that we live alongside. But there will not be peace without justice and liberty.

Oppression will just keep begetting violence in response. No doubt there have been acts of violence by Palestinians against Israelis, but I don't witness or hear of any during this trip. (In coming years, violence and acts of 'terrorism' will increase by both sides).

In my stark witnessing of the brutality of the occupying Israeli forces and the ongoing persecution of the Palestinian people—both Christian and Muslim, I realise my heart must embrace the need for justice in the world, and the need for courageous people to campaign for it. The trip is something of any eye opener for me as I contemplate a higher dimension to the Christian life. Faith is not just a personal relationship with God, it has a communitarian dimension. We must have concern for the wellbeing of all people. I'm not sure how this can be realised in my life at this time, but I return to the UK emboldened to live out my faith as a peacemaker and man of God. This ever so brief pilgrimage with Austin deepens my faith and gives me an inspiring insight into the life and thinking of a military chaplain. A seed of humanitarian concern is sown in me that will grow and hopefully bear fruit in years to come.

Significantly for us also, Lynne and I participate in the life of the Sandhurst chapel community, and meet up with members of the Officers Christian Union, who organise scripture studies and retreat programmes for the cadets. One Christmas, we go on one of their two-week retreats in Switzerland—ski-ing by day, sharing in fellowship by night. We have as a guest speaker, former Second World War US Army Captain Leo Buxton, who shares his vision of supporting Christians in the military though the worldwide Association of Military Christian Fellowships (AMCF) which he founded.

Leo tells us, 'During the campaign in Italy, I went from being a platoon commander to acting battalion commander in the course of 18 months. I wasn't that clever; it's just that every one up the chain of command got killed or wounded! Many days I thought I would die but I kept having these re-assuring thoughts that God was with me and had a purpose for me to share my faith with others after the war. When I came home I got some friends together and we started a Christian Fellowship for military people. It has been my life's work.'

I am enthralled by Leo's life witness and concern for the spiritual needs of military people. The following year, near London, we attend a world conference of the AMCF, meeting 500 military Christians from around the world. High school friend and RMC classmate Jim Wallace and his new wife Poppy also attend. Jim and I are inspired to get involved in ministry to soldiers in our own country, which we foster on our return through taking over the running of a new all-ranks fellowship (which today has developed into the Military Christian Fellowship of Australia-MCF). By the age of 29, I am immersed in organising lay ministry as a Christian Soldier. It is a sign of things to come.

As a family we are able to travel on holidays through Europe twice—through France, Switzerland, Austria, Italy, Germany and the Low countries, staying in 'Bed and Breakfast' houses and getting to meet the locals. We just love it . We are people who love meeting people . We share meals with people of a dozen different languages and feel at home with our brothers and sisters in humanity no matter what country we are in.

We are certainly more worldly wise by the time we return. We have experienced many different cultures at Sandhurst and while travelling, and come to see ourselves as world citizens, not just Aussies. I start to realise how important it is to be able to understand other cultures to effectively undertake military operations. It seems that many crises around the world are the result of, and are sustained by a lack of cultural understanding.

We have also come to see, and be proud to be part of the Universal Church, from the Vatican down to small chapel communities in remote country areas. It's wonderful to be able to go to Mass in any number of languages and be able to participate fully in a universal liturgy that recalls the life, death and resurrection of Jesus, and nourishes us for mission. We see also how Christianity certainly has made a defining mark in architecture, the arts, education, health care and social structures across the world.

Our children, Catherine aged six, and Michael aged four, have benefited from this overseas experience as well, growing up with the diverse group of children from around the world that lived in our military precinct at Sandhurst. Over one quarter of the staff and students at Sandhurst and the co-located Army Staff College are foreign nationals. One day these children will be able to make their marks on a world stage, at ease in engaging with diverse cultures.

Soldiering in Australia

Upon returning to Australia, I command in succession Administration Company and Alpha (rifle) Company of 6 RAR, an infantry battalion in Brisbane. There are many valuable components of any army but the tip of the spear, the men who eventually have to kick in a door, or fight a violent opponent are the infantry. The 'tip of the tip' is the rifle section of eight men commanded by a corporal. When I take command of Alpha Company I decide to empower my corporals.

I tell them, 'I want you to use your initiative, to not be always asking for permission, but to make judgements based on my broader guidance, and to do what you think is right. I expect you to make mistakes, but

I will not punish anyone for acting in good faith.' It is common practice in the army at this time to charge soldiers for seemingly small breaches of discipline or misconduct. This bred a 'no fault' mentality. At its worst it crushed initiative and meant that people would do nothing, rather than take the risk of doing something, and get into trouble for it. I receive a marvellous response. Throughout the year there are a number of competitions between platoons and companies in the areas of sports and military skills. With the energy that my empowering the junior leaders releases, we win most competitions in the battalion. We get the title of 'Champion Company'.

In 1982 my Company wins the Champion Company competition in 6 RAR.

I thrive in the role of leadership. Communication is key. First thing every morning and last thing every afternoon I speak to the troops, keeping them informed of what is happening, and affirming the good things that people have done. Nothing breeds success like success. I discern that one particular sign of achievement for an infantryman is to become qualified as a marksman and be able to wear the coveted 'crossed rifles' symbol on their uniform. I note that only a handful of soldiers have ever qualified as a marksman in the Battalion. In a targeted effort to enhance self-esteem of the soldiers, I make marksmanship training a priority and allocate additional time and resources to it. Within the first six months, approximately 80% of the company qualify for their Marksman badge. The morale of the soldiers grows higher because they are proud of the standard of excellence that they have achieved.

Lynne gives birth to Christy, our third child, in May 1982 in Brisbane. Life is good for the Stone family. We also enjoy parenthood and being close to extended family. Lynne and I play tennis together, go riding bikes with the kids on the back, and enjoy the social life of the Army Officer's messes.

I then attend the Command and Staff College in Queenscliffe in Victoria in 1983. I am the first and only RMC graduate of 1973 to attend this course. We will make many friends a little older than us and I will have the opportunity to become known to officers more senior to me, as well as the staff. This is a most important year for all Australian Army officers who aspire to senior rank. It is a twelve month sabbatical study program, where the Army compares 60 majors to each other. We study leadership, tactics and administration to prepare us for command at the next level. We travel the length and breadth of Australia, contemplating the defence of the continent against a range of threats. A contingent of foreign officers and staff add to the learning and social experience. The study program is busy and competitive and the tempo of social functions adds to the pressure as well as to the pleasure of this important year. Though I am in no way driven by ambition, those senior to me at the College, comment that I am clearly 'ahead of the pack' as it were, in the promotion stakes.

Truthfully I am not engaged or concerned about promotion, nor see myself in competition with my peers. I am just happy to be serving my God wherever he leads me. We participate in a weekly Bible study with other Christian couples on the course, and Mike Swan and I meet for prayer every morning just before studies start. The majority of students are from the two RMC classes head of me and most others know me from around the Army. I participate in a wide range of sporting and social activities and am well accepted by these peers, even with my Christian worldview. Some of the supervising staff are not quite as gracious.

At the end of the course, the College Commandant gives me my end of course report. He says to me, 'Your results on the course have been very good Gary. You are clearly a very competent officer. I note though that you are somewhat of a 'God botherer'. If you want to get anywhere in this Army I suggest you tone this down. People might write you off, as a bit of a softie and a pushover. To be a good commander you need to be tough.'

I respond, 'Thank you Sir, I note your comments, and where toughness is needed I'm sure I can provide it. But I feel as if I am living life the best way I can. My faith is an integral part of the way I live out my life as an army officer. It hasn't been a deterrent or an obstacle so far and I cannot imagine it will be in the future. I have to be true to myself—to do so for me is a matter of integrity.'

He moves uncomfortably in his chair. I can see he is not happy with my response. He moves his lips and mulls over a response for quite some time and then says, 'We have in this country, a separation of church and state you know. I suggest you keep your faith to yourself. That is all.'

He has the last word and I am dismissed. I am happy to have said what I did, but I clearly recognise that there will be others like him who are dismissive of the concept of a 'Christian Soldier'. I see that as their problem, but I also am conscious that there is going to be testing of my resolve.

My next assignment is to be Senior Instructor at the Officer Cadet School in Portsea in 1984. Professionally this is an outstanding experience. I am responsible for a team of ten Captains and ten Sergeants, teaching and developing young officer cadets in a pressure cooker environment to be platoon commanders in battle. I am inspired at Portsea by the leadership of our Commandant, Colonel Phil Davies, who has arrived in this posting at the same time as us.

In his opening address to assembled staff in 1984, he declares,

'We are here to bring out the best in these young people. We are here to build them up, not break them down. Let's be honest with ourselves, we've all made mistakes, and these cadets will make them too. They will probably learn as much from their mistakes as they will from formal lectures, so let's not have them developing an aversion to risk taking, that seems to be creeping into our society. Be mindful too of the foreign students here from Papua New Guinea, New Zealand, Brunei and the Philippines. They will struggle to understand us, so don't presume they get it, and keep checking that they are keeping up. One day some of them may be the leaders of their Defence Forces. They will remember how they were treated by us. Treat everyone how you would want to be treated yourself.' I am intrigued that he starts out with this emphasis. I wonder what has prompted this.

I discover Colonel Phil is a committed Christian in the Catholic tradition. We see him at Mass on Sundays. He lives out his faith in practical ways, but he warns me one day, 'Gary, it's great to see you are a man of faith, but don't get discouraged when you get opposition, because surely you will. Give me a ring if you ever need advice.' I greatly appreciate his counsel.

The Officer Cadet School at Portsea has developed as a very tough training ground for potential officers. There is a 'work hard and play hard' mentality among the staff. As I arrive I observe a culture among the staff and among senior cadets of wanting to place extreme pressure on any new entrants to the school. From the minute that new entrants get off the bus and throughout their first six months they are continually yelled at, berated, and kept under high pressure. I reel at the oppressive atmosphere of the place. The physical training standards for cadets are the highest I have seen and certainly much higher what is expected of a soldier in an infantry battalion. There are 21 physical training tests in all, most of which involve running through the sand hills on the base loaded down with heavy equipment. At least half of each year intake fail or will voluntarily resign within the first nine months.

At my first Board of Studies, where the progress of each of the cadets is discussed I am amazed at the critical and negative disposition that so many of the staff have towards the cadets. It seems that only a handful of the 200 cadets we have are performing at satisfactory levels. Most of the evidence relates to their performance in physical training. I am aghast at the criticism that some of the Captains have of the cadets. So many are recommended to be placed on warnings for discharge, that I make the comment that the expectations the staff have of these young people are surely unrealistic for the levels of training and development that they have received. Another major on the staff responds to me, 'Gary we have to weed out those that are not likely to be good army officers.' I respond, 'The selection board that recommended these cadets for training clearly thought all of them have the potential to be future army officers. If we are saying that most of these people have significant deficiencies, then either our selection process is inadequate, or our training and development is deficient.' The discussion ends there as the Chief Instructor wishes to move on and by the end of the Board of Studies more than half of the cadets are placed on warnings.

After the Board, back with my staff at my training wing building, I bring my Sandhurst experience to the fore, telling them how we could approach training and development differently. I put it to the staff that they need to be role models for the cadets and indeed should be able to complete the physical training tests with them. Some don't like this and protest, but I say that we either lead by example or we are not leading at all. From my arrival I have been getting out there and doing all the physical work with the cadets, something my predecessors apparently hadn't done.

I then invite them to come and do some of the tests with me. Over the coming weeks we discover that quite a few of the staff cannot pass some of the tests and all struggle as much as the cadets. A new empathy for the cadets' experience emerges.

I also have discussions with a wide range of cadets about their experience. Almost all speak of it being a fearsome experience where they are scared to take a risk for fear of failure. I put this back to the staff that we have had the emphasis of training weighted so far in terms of assessment that little real learning and development is going on. I repeat the philosophy I used with my rifle company. I expect people to use their initiative and make occasional mistakes and learn from them. I promote a learning environment rather than an assessment one. As this new approach is communicated and lived out, at least in the subject areas I am responsible for, we see a big improvement in student results. The participation of staff in PT with the cadets also sees an improvement in cadet results! This isn't rocket science. Its simple humanity that I draw from my Christian faith and understanding, which regards all people as having gifts, talents and dignity. Abuse them and they will cower. Treat them with dignity and respect and they can bring out their best.

Family life continues to uplift us. We enjoy many recreational activities by the sea. In our second year of living at Portsea, Lynne gives birth to Paul on 14 April 1984 in the Rosebud Hospital on the Mornington Peninsula. We are delighted to invite Bob and Dianne Breen and Mike and Rhonda Swan to be his Godparents. Our family is complete! Marriage, family and military career are cruising smoothly together.

On Operations 1987

In 1986, I move on to be Second-in-Command of the First Battalion, Royal Australian Regiment (1 RAR) in Townsville—an infantry battalion of 850 men. Out of all the units in the Australian army, the Townsville brigade has been given the highest priority. It is designated as the first source of troops for any operational deployment. It is the premier posting location for the infantry. We arrive amidst the tropical heat and humidity and regular storms. By April it cools down to a pleasant 25 degrees with clear blue skies for all the winter months. Like a big country town, the pace of life is slower and steadier than we have ever experienced.

In 1987 my unit, 1 RAR, will be the first to respond to any crisis or emergency. There has not been a deployment for 15 years, and there are no indications that we will be required. Then history calls us forward.

On 14 May 1987, there is a coup in Fiji. I am commanding the battalion temporarily while John Salter, the CO, is across the other side of Australia with a group of officers led by the Brigade Commander, Peter Arnison, studying options for defending north-west Australia. We hear about the coup on the news. I get a very definite message from Army Headquarters in Canberra that Australia will not be getting involved. Peter Pursey, the Brigade Operations Major, tells me that nothing even looking like preparations should be made. It would be a bad look for Australia to be seen to be preparing troops to intervene while Prime Minister Bob Hawke was negotiating for a peaceful resolution of the political crisis in Fiji. Staff in Sydney tell Arnison and Salter to continue their exercise in Western Australia.

I follow the news of mounting violence in Fiji and conclude that the possibility of deployment is increasing. Peter Pursey replies to my daily calls with firm advice not to prepare for deployment. On the fifth day after the coup, Pursey calls me to Brigade headquarters in the morning and tells me to have a company group of about 120 soldiers ready to deploy within a few hours.

Operation Morrisdance

Journal entry 19 May 1987:

> While getting ready to play hockey on our regular Thursday sports afternoon, I get a surprise phone call to immediately see the Brigade Operations Officer, Major Peter Pursey. Upon reporting to Brigade Headquarters, I am advised by Peter, at about 10.00am, that the Hawke Government wishes to deploy immediately a Maritime Force, with embarked combat troops, to make a statement of disapproval to the Coup leader—LtCol Siteveni Rambuka. Violent scenes of the local police and military beating up Indian protestors are being seen by the Australian public on TV reports from Suva. The deposed (and legitimately elected leader) Dr Timothy Bavandra has also smuggled a message out of Fiji pleading for international intervention. We are to be

prepared to evacuate Australian nationals should law and order break down, and conduct other tasks as directed. I am to mobilise the Battalion and lead this first deployment of an Army combat force by air and sea to the waters off Fiji on Operation Morrisdance. This is to be the first strategic deployment of the Australian Defence Force since our pull-out from Vietnam in 1972.

There are many questions on my mind, but the first I ask Peter is, 'How much time do we have?'

He replies: 'You need to ready for immediate deployment, with the lead company and your HQ ready to fly out this afternoon.'

I am stunned. We had practised for deployments with a minimum 7 day work-up, which is needed to recall soldiers from leave and courses, conduct planning, develop our intelligence picture, gather equipment and ammunition, conduct rehearsals, and myriad other matters.

Nevertheless, I will get on with the job! I race back to the battalion HQ, grab a cup of tea, say a prayer for God's guidance, issue warning orders to recall troops, conduct planning with key staff, and issue formal orders for deployment at 1300 (1.00pm). To complicate matters, Army HQ has told us that the soldiers are to be told that this is just a practice exercise, and they can't be told our destination until the Government has made an announcement.

I have to send our Intelligence officer to the Library to get us Atlas photocopies of Fiji, as we have no maps. Overseas deployment has never been on our (or our Government's) radar. We have spent 15 years training to deploy to Northern Australia against mythical Asian adversaries. We have never trained with the Navy either, but I am told a flotilla is already training at sea, off Sydney, and is now steaming towards Norfolk island, and we are to be flown there to rendezvous with them as soon as possible. Four C130 transport aircraft have been ordered to Townsville to transport our lead elements and the entire RAAF C130 fleet will reposition to Townsville, to be ready to fly in follow-on elements. We are to be on 2 hour's notice to move from 1700 (5 pm) that evening.

In the midst of this frantic activity, I ring Lynne and tell her to bring the kids in with some extra clothes for me to pack. For security reasons I cannot talk about what is happening, but she has heard news of the Coup on radio and surmises that something is happening. At 1900 (7 pm) Prime Minister Bob Hawke makes a national broadcast announcing our deployment, and I feel a lump in my throat. I have been greatly concerned that we have deceived my soldiers, and critical stores may not have been packed by some soldiers thinking this was just another exercise. I decide to immediately address the battalion members on the Parade Ground, explaining our mission and possible tasks, and warning them for Active Service. I write the script in my diary:

> Men of 1 RAR, our time has come. As you may have just heard on the radio, the government has committed us to a response to the Fiji coup. Our destination is not a training area, but Fiji. I am formally warning you for active service. Battalion HQ and B Company are to be ready to deploy by air immediately. A Company is to be reinforced and to be ready to deploy within 24 hours. We are to be prepared to assist in the evacuation of Australian nationals, protect Australian government staff and assets, and other tasks as directed. It's most likely we will fly to Norfolk Island to join a navy flotilla, but we may need to fly direct into a Fijian airport. It's not clear what reaction the Fijian military will have to our deployment, but we must be prepared for a worst-case, opposed insertion, and we must also be prepared for chaos on the ground, with many more people wanting to

get on our aircraft than we have capacity to evacuate. It's not clear how long we will be deployed, but I want us to be self sufficient for at least two weeks. There is much to be done, and you will receive confirmatory orders when we get them from higher. This is a moment in history for the Operational Deployment Force. Let's do our country proud. Duty First!

There is stunned silence as I stop talking. The Adjutant, Captain Mex Cernaz, comes up to me and says, 'The Brigadier (Peter Arnison) has just got in, and wants to see you up at Brigade HQ ASAP, boss.' I race up to his office and he tells me formally, what I in essence I just had told the soldiers, and asks me how things are.

I say, 'We are ready to go, but there are still many things that could be done better. We haven't test-fired weapons and we don't have any maps.' He then sits me down and gives me his wisdom on how we might organise an evacuation. We have never done this in training, and my mind imagines the chaotic scenes of the fall of Saigon. Never the less I feel a quiet confidence, and am reassured by many thoughts of scripture verses like 'Be not afraid, I am with you always ... (*Matthew* 28:30)

Ready to deploy within 7 hours of being advised, we await the call forward. Preparations continue through the night and we are told at about 2200hrs that we are to be held in Townsville for 24 hours, should we need to be inserted directly from Townsville into an airfield in Fiji. Television footage coming out of Fiji shows ethnic Indian Fijians being beaten up by Fijian police and military, and the prospect of civil war between the majority Indian population and the minority ethnic Melanesian Fijians looms larger. Clearly the Government wants to keep its options open and no doubt is looking to see what reaction emanates from Fiji. The following day we conduct rehearsals and pack and repack equipment as our potential task list expands. I give instructions that family members may come into the camp to say their farewells over our evening meal.

We eventually depart for Townsville airport at about four in the morning on Saturday 21 May. Four C130 are carefully loaded equally with people, vehicles, ammunition and stores, such that if any were to not reach the target, remaining elements will be able to complete the mission. Upon takeoff from Townsville, I breathe a sigh of relief, and take a few moments to contemplate the significance of this event. The drought of expeditionary, overseas military deployments has broken. A Labor Government had pulled us out of Vietnam and it seemed as if we were going to be kept indefinitely as a 'Home Guard'. But here was a change in that policy. It dawns on me how important it is going to be that we perform well, and reinforce whatever confidence the government is showing in us.

In May 1987 1RAR responds to the Fiji coup.

As Norfolk Island comes into sight, with tall Norfolk pines prominent on the horizon, the exhilaration of this adventure revives me. Word comes through on the radio that the flotilla's helicopters are waiting on the airstrip, and we are to go directly from the rear of the C130 straight onto them. Running down the rear ramp, we are caught up in the hot rotor wash, loaded down with packs, weapons and equipment. I identify myself to a loadmaster as the Army mission commander, and I am directed into a whirring Wessex helicopter that takes me onto HMAS *Success*, a large supply ship that is already underway on a direct course to Fiji.

In what is, for all the soldiers, our first experience of naval life, we struggle through the gangways with all our kit, and are allocated floor spaces in various parts of the ship. There are no bunks available for us, as the ship was not designed to accommodate any soldiers. I am escorted up to the 'Bridge'—the ship's control room, and introduced to the Commodore of the Flotilla, Matt Taylor, a tall smiling man dressed in a neatly pressed naval white uniform.

He is very friendly, 'Welcome aboard, Gary, great to have you with us. I have to acknowledge that this naval group has never worked with embarked troops before and that this is going to be a learning experience for all of us.'

I reply, 'Great to be here, Sir. I'm sure we'll work things out just fine. It may take us a little time to work out your ship routine but we are keen to learn.'

We steam through the night at best speed. It will take us 30 hours to get to Fiji and so we set about with all sorts of training in our new environment. We practise 'man-overboard' drills, 'action stations', replenishment at sea, and ship-to-ship transfers by helicopter and 'Jackstay'—sliding along a rope suspended between two ships underway. Two frigates, HMAS *Sydney* and *Parramatta* are to close in with us by dawn.

We test-fire our weapons from the back decks, aiming at inflated garbage bags tossed in our wake. On receiving orders that we might need to secure the Australian High Commission in downtown Suva—a ten-storey building covered in radio masts, I direct training for the soldiers in 'fast-roping'—gripping and sliding down some 50 metres from helicopters held at the hover. This is high risk and even more dangerous when done in high winds at sea onto heaving and rolling decks, but quite exciting at the same time.

We plan and rehearse securing one of the main airfields or ports at Nadi or Suva. Our significant shortcoming is a lack of intelligence—not really knowing what the Coup leaders' attitude to our deployment might be. In normal Army style, we plan for a worst case—a fight—and hope and pray that this would not be required as we know that the Fijian military are quite competent opponents, having had many years of UN service in the Middle East.

Prayer is something we also do. Commodore Taylor invites the key staff to join him in a service of prayer for a peaceful resolution to the conflict on the morning of 23 May as we awaken to see the outline of the Fijian islands on the horizon. We gather in the ships hospital space which doubles as a Chapel, and Chaplain Simon Hubbard leads us in prayer. Each night over the coming two weeks I join in with the ship's MCF prayer group and we continue these prayers.

With Fiji in sight of us, and us in sight of the Fijians, we receive orders to conduct 'demonstration operations' along a steaming line between Suva and Nadi, just outside the 12 nautical mile territorial water line. The coincidental annual meeting of the Regional Prime Ministers Pacific Forum in Tonga provides an opportunity for discussion of the Fiji crisis. Possibly to strengthen Australia's negotiating position, we make our presence felt by conducting a series of rehearsal operations, flying our troops from ship to ship along the flotilla line that now numbers some eight ships. The Coup leaders send out a light aircraft each day to observe our activity and we are pleased to show them our stuff.

We keep sailing up and down this patrol line for several days, until the Coup leadership announces that it has brought ill-disciplined police and military elements under control and that foreign nationals are safe and not in need of evacuation. Just to be sure, we hold the patrol line for a total of six days before receiving orders to redeploy back to Sydney.

What we have done in military language is indeed a 'demonstration' of our capability to intervene. We think it has been successful and helped to restore peace. No doubt a range of factors were at play, but this has been a massive step in our government's confidence to use the ADF as part of its response to crises in the near region.

Prime Minister Hawke and Defence Minister Beazley come to Townsville to review a parade and to thank us profusely. Bob Hawke confides in me that he had restless sleep for the first week of our deployment, worrying that an accident might occur, or that we would need to be landed and face a confrontation with the Fijian military which could have been very nasty.

I am overjoyed to be back with my family, knowing what anxiety they must have had over the course of our deployment without any communication with me. I thank God for them, and am so proud of Lynne, who has been leading the Battalion wives group through this. A photo of us being reunited ends up hanging in Parliament House.

We have been called to undertake a mission on no notice, with no intelligence, and no prior training with the Navy, and it has still worked

I return home from Fiji to a growing family.

out. Many shortcomings in our preparedness for this type of mission are identified. Bob Breen and I write an article for the *Defence Force Journal* highlighting these. The Labor Government seems now to have a change of heart in terms of use of its military, and agrees over the next few years to send peacekeepers to missions in Namibia, Mozambique, Northern Iraq, Western Sahara, and Cambodia. No doubt a range of other factors are also at play in this, but had we had some catastrophic accident enroute, say with a helicopter crash with troops onboard, (which did happen on a later deployment) the government's confidence to use the military would have been much less.

Moving on and up

My command of the army component of Operation Morrisdance brings me to the attention of senior officers and contributes to my early promotion to Lieutenant Colonel and posting to the Directorate of Infantry in Canberra.

My faith has grown during all of the experiences over the past 15 years. Operation Morrisdance certainly exercised my faith as I faced many uncertainties and yet I was able to remain cool calm and collected, through the confidence I had in God's upholding of me. Prayer and scripture study have become part of my daily routine.

Lynne and I also get involved in organising retreats, scripture studies and participating in movements within the church. More and more I come to experience God intervening in life events in response to prayer. At a 'Life in the Spirit' Seminar in Townsville in 1986, and through the prayer of others, I experience a euphoric sense of God's spiritual presence within me. St Paul calls this, 'the fullness of the gifts and fruits of the Holy Spirit' (*Galatians* 5:22). I feel God challenging me with a mission to share his Good News, and to encourage, support and affirm those who are already following him. I would like to be involved in some sort of full-time Christian ministry, but I don't know what this could look like. But I am also on the crest of a wave in my military career. I am among the top of my cohort for promotion and postings. I pray that God will guide me in a resolution of this dilemma.

Life still has its challenges

While firm in my Christian convictions and public in my profession of faith, there is unease among some Infantry officers. These men display either a concern that Christian values weaken combat soldiers in face of the need to kill or they are just bigots who dislike Christians in general and/or Catholics in particular. My future in the Army is about to be shaped by my Christian beliefs.

Prior to Operation Morrisdance, a senior Infantry officer tells a group of his officers in the Mess that he would stop an Army posting of me, to under his command, because he wouldn't have a 'Catholic God botherer' on his staff. The posting goes through despite his public and discriminatory comments. This officer had a policy of unexpectedly insisting that his staff stay with him drinking in the Officers' Mess in the evenings. One Wednesday afternoon, he informs his officers that we are to have a session that evening. At 11.00p.m. I go up to him to excuse myself. Of course by now he is quite drunk, and he orders me to sit down. I feel as if I need to show some courage here, so I do not sit down but I say quietly to him, 'Sir, I have respected your direction to spend some time together, but I have important work to do for the unit tomorrow, and I think it only reasonable that I and the other officers be allowed to go home.'

He can see that I am not going to back down, and smashes his drinking pewter onto a table and yells out to all gathered, 'The night is over', and storms out. The following morning at about 10.00am, he arrives at my office and tells me to come into his.

Though I am a major, he orders me to stand to attention in front of him and speaks angrily to me, 'How dare you embarrass me in front of my officers! I am the Commanding Officer of this unit, and I direct what will happen and when it happens.'

I realise that I am at a moment of truth in my life and I reply, 'With respect Sir, I will serve you competently in whatever needs doing, but I don't think that keeping the officers in the Mess so long after working hours is reasonable. I participated for seven hours. I really think it reasonable that the officers should be free to go home from 6.00p.m. of any evening at the latest, and be able to have dinner with their families.'

He stares daggers at me, and an awkward silence ensues.

'That is all' he responds. I salute and march out.

I go back to my office and phone our area Catholic chaplain, Peter Quilty, for advice. Peter is a very experienced priest and a wise man who has been our pastor at the local Army Chapel. I've also learned that the Chaplain is the one person in the Army you can go to with any problem and get a reasoned and practical response. He says, 'Gary, I know this fellow. You are not going to change him. This is going to be a difficult posting for you. Just keep doing your job professionally and don't give him any reason to criticise you. I will pray for you, and you can trust in God. He will support you.'

I am conscious that at a human level this encounter may have sharply ended the career I would otherwise have had, unless I was prepared just to keep my mouth shut and comply with whatever was dealt up to me. But I have a conscience and I will give that priority, and trust that God's plan for my life will prevail.

It is a very difficult year, and I remain under constant scrutiny in everything I do. But he never again keeps the officers in the Mess after 6.00pm. Ten months later he is posted out from the unit. My consolation is that one of the officers comes up to me the day after he leaves and says to me, 'Boss there must be something in this God business of yours, because the officers have expected you to be removed long before this, and you have ended up outlasting the Commanding Officer. You have our admiration and respect for living up to your convictions!'

I imagine many people go through dilemmas dealing with difficult bosses at some stage in their lives. There is enormous pressure on people to conform, or put up with inappropriate treatment, for fear of consequences. Fear can play real havoc in our lives if we let it. We need to acknowledge our fears, and overcome them, rather than being overcome by them. For myself, I find that through my faith in God's provision, I feel confidence to be frank and honest, and show the courage of my convictions.

A new test of my faith in God that is beyond my imagining is just around the corner.

Chapter 4
Keeping the Peace on the Iran-Iraq Border 1989-1990

Salaam Allah Kum—May the Peace of God be with you
(The customary greeting in the Middle East).

In 1989 I am appointed Commander Australian Contingent UNIIMOG

In December 1987, at 35 years of age and after 18 years service in the Army, I achieve the rank of Lieutenant Colonel and begin work at the Directorate of Infantry in Army Headquarters, in

Canberra. My role is to direct the Corp's training, doctrine and capability development—how we train, why we train and what we train and fight with. The Board of the Military Christian Fellowship of Australia also puts its trust in me through election as Chairman. For two years I am a busy staff officer travelling widely in Australia and overseas to meetings in the United States, Britain and Canada, an active Chairman of the MCF and local parishioner, as well as an 'in demand' family man attending as many events in my children's lives as possible and enjoying Lynne's loving companionship. We also provide support to Lynne's mother, Marie, who struggles with depression after divorce.

Out of the blue, a few months short of my next posting, the Director of Infantry, the tall, forthright Colonel Paul O'Sullivan, comes into my office and tells me, 'Gary, pack your bags. You have been selected to deploy to the Iran-Iraq border in command of an Australian contingent of peacekeepers. You will be participating in the implementation of a UN resolution to achieve a ceasefire after 8 years of war. The mission is known as United Nations Iran—Iraq Military Observer group—UNIIMOG—pronounced UN ee MOG. From what I've heard, the conditions are Spartan, the Iranians are unpredictable, but our involvement is of strategic significance, as few other westerners have been able to enter Iran since the US Embassy was overrun by revolutionaries. It will be a fascinating experience.'

On my way home my head is buzzing with a thousand questions, and my heart is groaning a little to think I will be away from my family for a long time with little contact possible. We have been having such great family times doing things together, like camping at the coast and going on bush walks, participating in the myriad sports and social activities the children get involved in at their schools.

This mission will be dangerous. The horrors of the Iran-Iraq War have been in the news for eight years. These two antagonistic peoples have killed one million people and wounded three million more of their citizens. Saddam Hussein, President of Iraq, invaded Iran in 1979 with American encouragement, just after the Islamic fundamentalist, Ayatollah Khomeini overthrew the US-sponsored government of Reza Shah Pavlavi in a swift, bloody revolution. Iraq smashed Iran with 16 Armoured Divisions and captured Iran's oil wells in the south. But the Iranians fought back fanatically with suicidal ferocity, even using young children to go ahead of their troops to explode the millions of mines scattered in front of Iraqi positions. Ayatollah Khomeini's government called up all Iranian men for military service and sent them into the maelstrom, counterattacking in the mountainous north where the Iraqi armour was less effective.

Fearful of the rise of Muslim fundamentalism under Khomeini, the United States and the USSR separately supplied Saddam with munitions, aircraft, chemical weapons, weapons and intelligence. After both nations shed the blood of a generation of their young men in futile attacks that exhausted them, their surviving units dug in and began trench warfare along a 1,200 kilometre front. In 1988, the United Nations offered to broker and then monitor a cease-fire, while continuing efforts to mediate a permanent end to the conflict.

At the time the Australian Army did not train its officers to be peacekeepers, though it had been sending groups of officers to the Middle East to serve in the UN observer groups in southern Lebanon, Israel and Syria for a number of years. In short, the Army sent a few of its officers overseas for 12 months, gave them to the UN and then remembered them again when they were due to return to Australia and the Military Secretary in charge of postings had to find jobs for them. This was about to happen to me, but my contingent and I were going to a new dangerous UN mission rather than a well-established benign one.

Burdened with some anxiety over all this, I take a diversion on the way home to drop in to see Chaplain Bernie Hennessey, our local pastor at the Duntroon chapel where we worship. Bernie, a calm and peaceful man, affirms me in being selected for a difficult mission, and assures me that the parishioners will look after Lynne and the children in my absence. He says a prayer over me, and I head off home, much calmer and more prepared to tell Lynne the news. What a wonderful wife she proves to be when I tell her, 'Gary this is God's destiny for you—to be a peacemaker.'

I go back to work the next day and tell Paul O'Sullivan that I am 'good to go'. For several weeks I wrap things up and hand over my job. During this busy time I decide to not only to command my contingent but to also offer Christian ministry to the UN mission because there are no Chaplains posted to the mission and I feel called to do so. Bishop Geoffrey Mayne, the Catholic Bishop to the Defence Force, supports me with a letter of authorisation to conduct Communion services and gives me guidelines.

My 15-man team assemble in Canberra for a week's pre-deployment administration and training in defence from chemical weapons, and we fly out to Iran on 14 October 1989. As we fly across the Indian Ocean, I gaze out the window of the plane, pondering the uncertainty of it all. The small quiet voice of God seems to understand my thoughts and says, 'Gary, Do not be afraid—I am with you.' Professionally, it could be extraordinarily interesting to help to make peace following the most devastating conflict since World War II. During team discussions, in our stopover in Dubai, we share snippets from each person's research on the mission. We acknowledge that immersion in the life of Revolutionary Iran will dominate our whole experience and challenge each of us culturally, ethically and professionally, as well as test our resilience to pressure. We will operate on the Iranian side of the border with the Iranian military units. Major Geoff Hourn, a solid, burly Special Forces intelligence officer, briefs us in great detail about the chaos and uncertainty of life in Iran. My second-in-command, Major Stuart Cameron, a big and bold army engineer and a nuclear, biological and chemical (NBC) warfare weapons expert, briefs and trains us in how to react to NBC dangers. The Iraqis have used numerous chemical weapons against the Iranians. We will be patrolling across battlefields that are littered with these weapons and anti-personnel and anti-vehicle mines, as well as numerous other unexploded munitions that might go off at any time if disturbed.

A tarmac ringed by anti-aircraft guns and scores of Revolutionary Guards with AK47 assault rifles greet us menacingly on our arrival at Tehran's Mehrebad Airport. Chaotic traffic and sensory overload waits. Murals painted on walls, announcing 'Death to America' and 'Down with Infidels', along with gruesome depictions of war and violence, line our route. Heavily armed police and soldiers are everywhere. Along the streets all the women are wearing the black chador. The men are all bearded and wear jackets without ties. The town is filthy and in disrepair. It seems as if there are no road rules. There are traffic lights at some street corners, but nobody is following them. Cars just push into the intersections honking their horns. An hour later we arrive at our accommodation near the United Nations headquarters that has been established in the offices of a former sports stadium in the northern suburbs of Tehran.

Our early briefings at UN HQ spell out the many dangers to Westerners in this land of Islamic fundamentalism. Colonel Heiki Pirola, the UN Chief of Staff, a tall, bluff and forthright Finlander, is very blunt with me from the start: 'You Australians are allies of the US. You will be constantly monitored by the secret police and military intelligence officers. Expect the worst if you are even suspected of spying. And we don't want you bringing unnecessary attention upon the rest of us in the UN.' Wow! I reflect in my diary that night, 'this experience is going to be very challenging, when even the UN are suspicious of us.'

Pirola spells out that we will observe all the fundamentalist Islamic laws—no alcohol, no western music, no exposure of skin apart from hands and face and no contact with Iranian women—don't even look at them, he emphasises. I write on 17 October;

> It feels like we have left the planet and are now immersed in another world, where everyone lives in fear … Sitting on the flat roof of our house in Tehran, the stillness of the night is broken by an occasional explosion and bursts of machine gun fire—another secret police raid perhaps.

We are also in the middle of a bitter domestic conflict, as well as one between Iran and Iraq. The Iranian Revolution isn't popular with many Iranians. Once welcomed 'freedom fighters' have become tyrants and oppressors. Society is traumatised and many people are angry. Dissident groups abound. All of my men feel this pressure, particularly in Tehran. No one appears to be rational. Anarchy reigns. The West has become so alien to these people—and we are Westerners. Anything we do could ignite a violent response.

My education in international politics begins. Curious about how local attitudes have developed, I take an early visit to what is known as the 'Den of Spies'—the former US Embassy. The Iranian Government have transformed the premises into a museum displaying multitudes of captured Top Secret CIA documents detailing the US participation in murder, assassination and other violations of international law—dirty tricks—in support of the Shah's cruel regime. As well, there is a display of documents describing US support for Saddam Hussein, including the provision of chemical munitions and cluster bombs. Using a term that would gain notoriety later, the documents show that the United States had provided Saddam Hussein with many 'Weapons of Mass Destruction' for use in a war where the collateral damage would be thousands of Iranian civilian lives. Later in the mission I will see these weapons as unexploded munitions littering the countryside in many different locations, clearly marked as US military ordnance.

I also become educated in the politics of the United Nations. Our UN colleagues come from 26 different countries, and mainly from the Third World. Some are unprofessional and unsuited to this mission, which requires high-order interpersonal skills. It is interesting to meet such a diverse group of people, and certainly affirms the quality and professionalism of Australian military training. Our closest friends are the Kiwis and the Irish with whom we have much in common.

I come to realise that the UN has significant limitations in achieving anything more than maintaining the status quo. The UN Headquarters in New York seems unprepared to push for the resolution of serious grievances like the repatriation of 20,000 Iraqi and 80,000 Iranian prisoners, which could considerably reduce tensions. While maintaining my own impartiality and neutrality, I become aware that, with the Soviets and the US both supporting and arming Saddam at this time, there is little movement at the UN Security Council for resolving the conflict. I wonder at times if it suits some nations to maintain this impasse! The oil has started flowing again—perhaps that was all that really mattered. The US is still smarting from their Embassy in Tehran being taken in 1979 and the Americans seem to want to keep the Iranians suffering. As I read in further detail the copies of captured CIA documents from the 'US Den of Spies', I become aware that several US governments have been complicit in the installation and support of a number of brutal and corrupt regimes across the Middle East. The dealings of the CIA that I read about are far from honourable.

I love and respect Americans and value their many positive contributions to the world, but their government's actions in the Middle East have sometimes been misguided and have had disastrous consequences. I work out very quickly that most people in the Middle East (except the Israelis) are alienated by US involvement, which has shown little respect for local customs. Only truly just and genuinely peaceful intervention will have any hope of being accepted and being successful with these peoples, who are fed up with external manipulations.

Our mission is to implement a ceasefire in what the Iranians describe as the 'Imposed War of Aggression by Iraq'. Heiki Pirola splits us into teams of UN Military Observers (UNMO) located with the 15 Iranian Infantry Divisions, about a half a million men, living in trenches along the border with Iraq. The troops are mainly infantrymen, supported by tanks and artillery. Revolutionary Guard units, who are poorly trained militia and, in many cases, indoctrinated fanatics, live alongside the infantry battalions of men trained for conventional combat. The Guards are selected for their religious zeal in fearlessly defending the 'mullahs'—the religious leaders who now run the country and the Shia Islamic fundamentalism they preach. In all, one million Iraqi and Iranian soldiers face each other under arms, ready for the slightest incident to inflame deep hatred and erupt in murderous exchanges of fire.

This is an intimate confrontation. In some places trenches crammed with troops and their fanatical cohorts are only a hundred metres apart, supported by tanks 1,000 metres from each other. Young men, far from home with nothing to do but wait, occasionally take pot shots at each other, patrol forward at night, dig deeper and reinforce their defences, and capture prisoners for interrogation.

My team's mission is to contribute to the United Nations' mandate of deterring Iran and Iraq from returning to all-out war, because of some misunderstanding or incident along the 1,200 kilometre frontline. At the same time we have to conduct our peacekeeping duties in such a way as to deter either the Iranians or the Iraqis from killing us!

Australian officers are well respected in the United Nations. I have been selected to be the UNIIMOG Operations Officer, but before assuming duty Heiki Pirola orders me to spend my first month in the forward defended localities so I get to know first-hand the work UNMOs do and the conditions under which they operate.

Pirola's staff brief us for a few days' in Tehran, before we fly out in a New Zealand Andover aircraft that does a 'milk-run' along UN border positions each day. I and several others get off the plane at an Iranian Air Force base at the regional capital of Dezful. The UN sector commander, Colonel Volkan Kaplama, a big man with a big, ever-present smile from Turkey, gives me a double-handed, overly-enthusiastic, warm handshake. That is where our mutual communications end. To my surprise, he doesn't speak English. We find ourselves dependent on one of the Iranian military liaison officers, Commander 'Ali' (not his real name), who can speak Turkish,

Farsi and English perfectly. He tells us that he is an engineer who has trained in the United States, but there is no doubt in my mind that he is an intelligence officer who is spying on us.

The next day I am flying in an Iranian Army Bell 212 helicopter, down to the forward trenches in the Dezful sector that is defended by No 2 Corps—a force of some 100,000 troops. I am amazed to see the massive earthwork berms (long mounds of dirt bulldozed up to block the vision of the enemy on the flat desert floor) superimposed over a generally flat, treeless desert. Behind the front line of trenches are thousands of well-constructed tank firing positions, bunkers galore, tanks ready to go forward to a firing position at the first sign of trouble, artillery barrels pointed to the sky, and supply depots spread over many kilometres. The Iranian soldiers are all dug in deeply and protected by sturdy fortifications—reinforced concrete bunkers every 30 metres connected by two-metre-deep communication trenches. This interconnected defensive bunker system extends the full length of the 1200km border. It is a massive feat of engineering. For Australians it is awe-inspiring to see the lengths both sides have gone to in order to survive in this barren landscape. It is like a scene one imagines from France or Belgium in the First World War.

The space between and even amongst the Iraqi and Iranian positions is covered with the deleterious waste of past battles—hundreds of thousands of unexploded artillery shells and aerial bombs, mines and burned-out tanks, vehicles and probably under the sand, bodies. Volkan Kaplama takes me down through the chain of command from Corps headquarters through Divisional and Brigade headquarters to a series of Battalion headquarters—all dug-in behind well-constructed and camouflaged bunker systems.

In the course of the first week I meet many battle-hardened survivors of the war. Men in the regular Army units are generally friendly, albeit clearly suspicious and cautious. I commit myself to winning their confidence and building closer relations.

In the southern sector, Geoff Hourn visits Revolutionary Guard units whose members are unpredictable and sometimes hostile. He and all of my team are serving in dangerous areas dealing with emotionally stressed people who have and will become violent at the slightest provocation. Now dispersed, I communicate with members of my contingent at night time using UN communications. Like me, all of my men are both amazed and somewhat apprehensive of what they see, the environment they are working in, the people they are meeting and the uncertainties ahead of them.

It is sweltering hot by day when we first arrive: 50°C is normal. We are told that one of the Italian officers died of heat stroke within two days of arriving in the mission. There is no escaping the heat. There are no trees, just stony barren desert, and the battlefield trenches and bunkers and hulks of burned-out tanks for scenery. The relentless heat by day and night adds to the stress of working amidst the Iranian units. Another stressor is rudimentary accommodation. We live in portable cabins with big white United Nations signs painted on them sitting alone and unfortified in the barren desert landscape that could be bombarded any time if the ceasefire does not hold.

Patrolling and reporting dominates daily life for each of us and our UN colleagues. Our job is to look for any reinforcement or forward movement of troops or tanks, guns and vehicles by either side. We listen to complaints and try to resolve disputes over ceasefire violations. Our authority lies in the UN mandate, our usefulness and power lies in our mediation skills.

Captain Shane Caughey, a former private soldier whom I have known for 10 years through attending the same church, shares patrolling duties with me at the 21st Iranian Infantry Division, at Einkush, where I spend part of that first month. Shane and I walk along the forward defences from bunker to bunker offering the customary greeting, '*Sallam Allah Kum*' (the peace of God be with you) and shaking hands. Our job is to reassure the Iranians that we are there to monitor the peace and listen to their concerns about the Iraqi units opposite them. We share many a cup of black thick Iranian coffee—an acquired taste. Opposite us, our UN colleagues are doing the same along the Iraqi bunkers.

At night we return to Division headquarters to dine with our Iranian Liaison officers, who accompany us everywhere and act as our interpreters. Dining in the frontline of the Iraq-Iran War is comprised of two feature dishes—chicken and rice, or rice and chicken. While we work hard at learning Farsi, most of our communication has to be through interpreters who are all intelligence officers. They take notes on most things we say and do. Generally they seem to want to be helpful to us, but we are careful to never criticise their culture, and we are always conscious that their loyalty is to their people. Our well-educated minders extol the virtues of Islam and consistently defeat us at chess. Chess was invented in Persia, and they haven't lost their touch. These men provide us a fascinating insight into a remarkably different culture and the root causes of the Iraq/Iran War. They are clearly intelligent and proud of their ancient Persian culture and are at pains to point out their major cultural difference from the Arab Iraqis. They are also Shia Muslims, while the Iraqis are largely Sunni Muslims.

My overt practice of Christian religion through the conduct of Communion services in the Catholic tradition soon attracts the attention of the Iranian Liaison officers. At Einkush, the senior Iranian Liaison Officer, Captain Aziz, asks me many questions about my faith. 'Are you a Christian?' He says.

I reply 'Yes I am. I am a Catholic Christian'.

'We have some Aramaic Christians in Iran', he comments. They speak the mother language of Jesus. Do you know we Muslims respect Mary, the mother of Jesus, and we acknowledge Jesus as great prophet?'

'No, I did not know that, but I would like to know more about what we have in common.' Within a week he hands me a brochure in English about Islam. I reply by giving him a copy of our Australian Army New Testament. I'm not sure whether Aziz is just personally interested in my religious inclinations or whether he is profiling me for intelligence purposes. Both, I guess. But I think it important he knows that I am a theist—a believer in God—the same God he believes in and in whose name he and his countrymen defend themselves against the Iraqi invaders.

I am comfortable responding to many such enquiries from other liaison officers as well. One Liaison Officer, Commander Ali, stands out among the rest. He is quite friendly to us. He is tall, fit and olive skinned. We have many discussions, and I learn a lot about Persian culture. One day he intervenes to stop one of my Australian men being arrested for taking photographs in the battle area. We are very grateful for that. I have a very comfortable feeling about him.

The most dominant source of stress is negotiating with the combatants. Both sides use us as shock absorbers for their anger and frustration with each other. Clearly most of them are traumatised from years of conflict. We listen to and investigate allegations of breaches of the ceasefire from one side or the other on most days. In reality, we can offer little practical assistance to resolve breaches of the ceasefire that most often take the form of rifle shots across No Man's Land. Shots fired can hardly be recovered. We are left to sooth anger and assure complainants that we will submit reports to respective superior headquarters in Iran, and also to UNHQ in New York. In short, we fire the facts up the line, in response to either side firing bullets across the line.

While negotiation may sound not particularly dangerous, investigating the facts and diffusing tensions can be extremely dangerous. One of my men, Major Ross Parrott, a smart and confident artillery officer, earns a Conspicuous Service Cross for his actions in crossing to and fro, through No Man's Land, to investigate the loss of an Iraqi soldier one night. The Iraqis presume the Iranians have taken the soldier captive, and prepare to attack in retaliation. Ross courageously walks through a minefield along what he hopes is a cleared path with his interpreter to negotiate with the Iraqi commander to hold off until he searches all the Iranian bunkers for the man. Whilst Ross conducts his search, the Iraqis find their lost soldier behind their lines trying to desert his post and return home. The ceasefire is kept. But this incident could have cost Ross his life and possibly the lives of many others had the Iraqis not found their deserter.

After a month in the frontline, I farewell Shane Caughey and return to Tehran as operations officer. In many ways I jump from a stressful frying pan into a stressful fire. In this role I become involved in heated negotiations with senior Iranian commanders and staff officers over major ceasefire violations. Iranians respect strength of conviction. My role is to travel quickly to hot spots along the border where violations have occurred and communicate United Nations' 'conviction'. Revolutionary Guard commanders, who want to open fire on Iraqi units they see moving forward, threaten me routinely

I visit a UN team in Piranshar—it's minus twenty degrees.

when I caution them that two wrongs do not make a right. I absorb their threats to open fire and reply with firm and convincing threats of my own. In reply to their threats, I state that I will report them to the United Nations Security Council should they retaliate to an Iraqi provocation! I hope each time I do this, that they do not conclude that dead UNMOs tell no tales.

My journal entry for 10 January 1990 records;

Patrol today to forward defensive locality vicinity of Abou Zar, to investigate reported ceasefire violation. Local IRGC (Iranian Revolutionary Guard Corps) Battalion Commander complains of on going Iraqi forward movement by night. He is very angry. I note scars on his face, fingers missing on his right hand, and just a stump at the bottom of his left leg. He points out new Iraqi bunkers about 200m from his forward positions. It's steep hilly terrain. Iraqis hold high ground and overlook Iranians. Through binoculars can see signs of fresh digging. I note grid reference and try to raise UN Military Observers from the Iraqi side. Cannot get communications. CO starts yelling and tells me he will open fire, if I don't move them back within 30 minutes. I contemplate moving to Iraqi side but note numerous UXO (unexploded ordnance). CO yells and curses toward Iraqis. Through interpreter I tell him I will report this. He yells even louder at me. Can't understand him, but he is going crazy. I start yelling, telling him I am very angry with Iraqis too, and I will be very angry with him if he opens fire as more men will die. I tell him I have left my family in Australia to try to help his people, so stop yelling at me and let me try to sort something out. The interpreter struggles to keep up with the translation! He can see I have become very animated and he calms down. I return to Sector HQ and talk to UN Sector Commander, Lt Col X, from Nigeria. He shrugs and says the Iraqis are doing this all the time. I tell him to arrange a visible meeting in No-Mans-Land with UNMO from Iraqi side and protest the Iraqi forward movement. He agrees, but I'm not confident he will. Heart was pumping plenty today!

We can do a lot to simmer things down at local levels by our presence, but that presence comes at the cost of many risks. One of them is venturing into No-man's-land to conduct 'flag meetings' with UNMOs monitoring the Iraqis; a useful technique to calm both sides and give an impression that something is being done. Both sides see us discussing what has happened in front of them. But No-Man's Land is covered with nasty surprises. The next step could be one that detonates a mine or disturbs an unexploded artillery shell sufficiently to cause it to explode. Equally stressful is the habit of bored Iraqi soldiers to 'spice up' 'flag meetings' by firing shots in the vicinity. In all, it is very emotionally draining. We want to promote peace, but feel that the United Nations has limited capacity at higher levels to do much more than complain and convene meetings, while the major powers and the antagonists inch towards an end to the war.

Diary entry 18 January 1990:

Flag meeting with Iraqi UNMO today north of Marivan to discuss repatriation of bodies. Heavy snow fell last night. Snow is from hip to knee deep in most places. Set out through the wire and minefield down into valley on a line that the Iranian liaison officer says is clear from mines, towards a single tree about 500 metres distant which is to be the meeting point. Exhausting pushing through the snow. After 300 metres we enter a dip and lose sight of the tree. Have to keep looking back at track in the snow to stay on a safe track (we hope). Decide we should take it in turns to lead for 50 metres each. Realise this is crazy. We could be stepping on anything in the snow. Pray the Lords prayer repetitively. Get there and back without casualties but will never do this again. Could easily have stepped on a mine or UXO. Totally unsafe—should never have agreed to do this!

Over time, I develop empathy for the Iranian soldiers. During my flying visits in response to an alleged breach of the ceasefire, I make a point of going into every bunker as I walk along the forward defences and shaking hands with every soldier I can. My aim is to show as many soldiers as possible that the rest of the world, including the people of Australia, is now concerned about their plight. They have survived up until now— they may not survive another day. They cope by saying, '*Insh-allah*', which translates as, 'May the will of God prevail'. Many things in Iran are left to '*Insh-allah*'. It's the most common phrase you hear. So many things in life for us too must be left to '*Insh-allah*'. I'm intrigued that my compatriots all start using this phrase, even those who otherwise don't show any religious leanings. It is a cry of the powerless in the midst of overwhelming circumstances. For some it may be religious, for others superstition, but for all of us it is a cry of the soul for something beyond us.

The Iraqis have the Iranians out-gunned and have inflicted significant suffering on the Iranian Army and ordinary people, who are real survivors. I think the Iranians eventually see that we Aussies are friendly impartial people who are concerned to keep the peace and avoid further killing. We cop abuse that allows them to vent their frustration and anger, but grow to accept this gracefully as the price for keeping the peace.

I suffer weeks of hyper-vigilance and little restful sleep. I have become hyper-active and fully absorbed in my work that involves repeated confrontations that only serve to deepen my sleepless condition and increase my hyper-vigilance. The only sleep I am getting is after I have taken a strong dose of sleeping pills. I fear the side effects of this regime on my physical and mental well-being, but I am determined not to leave my men in this hellish place and return to Australia suffering from stress.

In March 1990, a major crisis leads to one of the most dangerous incidents I am to participate in that deepens my fear of being killed or seriously maimed. Troubles had begun in the Dezful Sector some months before when Iraqi commandos conducted a raid into 'No-Mans-Land' and set fire to Iranian oil wells. Opposing forces are over one kilometre apart in this area of the Dezful Sector—just outside tank-firing range. I had already been there several times, and always rued seeing and smelling the smoke from the oil wells—a tragic waste of resources caused by a provocative act of vandalism.

The United Nations Commander, Yugoslavian General Slavko Jovic, listened to Iranian complaints and wrote reports, but concluded that both sides had to maintain the territorial status quo until a general peace agreement was reached. In his way of thinking, nothing could be done in No-mans-land, not even the rational action of putting out oil fires.

The Iranians become frustrated at Jovic's inaction, and decide to put the fires out themselves. Our UN team in Dezful reports that an

Iranian battalion has moved forward during the night and surrounded the oil wells. General Jovic quickly understands the gravity of this situation and tells me to come with him to Dezful. We fly down and then walk forward to the UN team nearest to the Iranian battalion in No Man's Land at a post called Dehloran.

Looking out from the helicopter, Jovic and I comment that the Iranians are at battle stations. Iranian gunners are standing by their guns. Tanks have moved out and are positioned on elevated firing platforms ready to engage targets. Soldiers everywhere are 'standing to' in full combat gear, with their rifles and machine guns pointed at the Iraqi bunkers. As we alight from the helicopter, a Canadian officer who has flown in from the Iraqi side tells me that the Iraqis have mobilised their armoured divisions and have hundreds of artillery pieces ready to fire on the Iranians. He warns us that the Iraqis could open fire at any moment. General Jovic decides that we should drive out into No-mans-land with large blue UN flags flying and protest the Iranian movement forward, in person. In a bold and dramatic ploy

Iranians prepare for Iraqi attack.

he notifies the United Nations observers on the Iraqi side that he is moving into the site, and that any hostile Iraqi action might result in his death and worldwide shame for the Iraqis. Sitting beside him in the jeep, I am less enthusiastic about offering my life as a source of shame to the Iraqis.

We drive through a landscape littered with unexploded bombs and mines that are visible all around us. To keep safe, we are following in the tyre tracks of an Iranian liaison vehicle that is leading us forward. This should provide some security, but throughout the journey I am quietly praying over and over again, the Lord's Prayer, 'Our Father who art in heaven ...' On the plane that morning, in anticipation of the danger that this day would bring, I write a final letter to my family telling them how much I love them and how I hope that, should they read this after my death, they could be proud that I died in the service of peace. This letter in the breast pocket of my jacket reminds me of the consequences for my family if Jovic makes a wrong move and a fire fight ensues that could trigger a major battle.

The Iranian battalion commander, whose men surround the oil wells, meets us at the first burning well. Through an interpreter, he tells us that it is his mission to secure the oil wells until they are extinguished by a specialist engineering team that is on its way. I look through my binoculars towards the Iraqi forward lines. As far as the eye could see to the left and to the right, Iraqi T 72 tanks have pushed forward into firing positions with their barrels all directed at us. 'Oh, dear God.' Fear grips my body as I contemplate that just one itchy trigger finger from either side will set off a lethal engagement with us as sitting ducks in the crossfire. We stride around the immediate area with our large UN flags flying, in order to demonstrate to the Iraqis that the United Nations is taking some action. I begin to look frantically for places to take cover should shooting start. There is nowhere that will protect us from the massive firepower directed right at where we are standing. Quietly I pray, and pray, and pray. Adrenalin courses through my entire system while I struggle to maintain a calm, professional demeanour as General Jovic fulfils my worst nightmare by beginning to berate the Iranian battalion commander through an interpreter.

I am surprised and alarmed as General Jovic shouts at the Iranian battalion commander, telling him that he must withdraw as he is in violation of the cease-fire arrangements. I am bewildered and stunned. Clearly this battalion commander is acting on orders sent all the way down the chain of command from Tehran. Jovic then threatens the battalion commander by stating that the Iraqis will obliterate his men should they not withdraw immediately. My heart is pumping as fast as it was up near the Caspian Sea. I try to maintain a confident manner in this serious situation, but my head starts throbbing now as well. Shooting could break out at any moment. There is little I can say or do with the Iranians. Jovic is in charge and I feel powerless to stop him. In my head I start singing one of my favourite hymns: 'Into your hands we commend our Spirits oh Lord; into your hands we commend our hearts ...' I am preparing for death.

Jovic maintains his rage, and, much to my surprise and relief, his bluster seems to be paying off. Neither side opens fire. Having made his points about the gravity of the violation and the lethal consequences if there is no immediate withdrawal, Jovic then remonstrates that he will return immediately to Tehran to protest the Iranian move forward to the oil wells to the highest levels at the UNHQ in New York. I am relieved that we can now leave this dangerous place.

As we then move back to the helicopter, we see even more soldiers 'standing to' in their battle stations. The 21st Infantry Division is ready to repel an Iraqi attack. I pray: 'Please God, help us to have peace today; may sanity reign; may everyone hold their fire'. I look at the faces of the Iranian soldiers. They have the lifeless resignation of the 'thousand yard stare'. They know what could happen and are probably saying '*Insh Allah*'.

As we arrive at our chopper, I breathe a deep sigh of relief. At least we may survive today. We fly back to the airbase at Dezful and catch our UN Andover aircraft back to Tehran. General Jovic and I go straight to the Iranian Military Liaison office, our connection to the High Command. Word of our efforts at Dezful has beaten us there. Jovic meets the Iranians head on again. A robust session follows, with the Iranians loudly protesting the scandalous waste of the burning oil. Jovic protests their movement forward. Nothing seems to be resolved. We return to UN HQ where I draft up and issue a summary of our actions to go to UN HQ and all our stations in mission. At day's end, I take action as the Australian national commander. I fear for the safety of my men. I drive to the house of the Australian Ambassador and brief him. He is very concerned that the situation at Dezful will lead to major outbreaks of firing along the border. I contact Army HQ in Canberra on his secure satellite telephone, alerting staff there that my contingent and I are on full alert for the possibility of withdrawing from the frontline if hostilities break out and there will be no peace to keep.

The night passes without any reports of firing. I pray for protection for Shane Caughey whose UN porta-cabin is in plain sight of the Iraqis. I am sure that he and his cabin will be taken out in any outbreak of firing. Next morning everyone rejoices at the regular UN morning briefing when a report comes in from Dezful saying that during the night the Iranians have withdrawn from the oil wells back to the cease fire line. We are flabbergasted! The peace has been kept. Thanks be to God—*Al-Hamdullillah*. Jovic's remonstrations and assertive manner have worked. We have kept the peace. Lives have been saved. Our presence has made the difference.

The trauma of the incident near the Caspian Sea combined with the peak event at Dezful and numerous other stressful encounters with the Iranians has two contrasting consequences. My prayer life grows immensely as the accumulation of stress both tests, but at the same time strengthens, my faith in God. I live on prayer. My faith reassures me. I sense God saying to me, 'I got you through yesterday Gary—I will get you through today'. I recall constantly my mother's favourite hymn, 'One day at a time sweet Jesus—just live one day at a time …' and that remains with me too. My 'daily bread' is journalling—reading the scriptures, reflecting on God's presence in the previous day's events, listening and then writing down the thoughts God puts in my mind.

In addition to finding great solace in the scriptures, the only two Catholic priests in Tehran, whom I meet soon after arrival in Iran, inspire me to hold on and stay the course. Their life of persecution and privation to make the Eucharist available to Catholics in Tehran, reminds me that God will always assist Christians to endure stress and pressure. Both of these missionary priests, Father Peter from Italy and Father Manuel from the Philippines welcome me warmly. Later they tell me stories of the Revolutionaries visiting their church regularly and pushing them around, punching them, searching their premises, throwing around and smashing their property, and pouring out their 'home brewed' communion wine. They supply me with consecrated (bread) communion hosts, which I take with me on visits to the front lines and share with Catholic UNMO.

In almost every UN outpost I visit, there are Catholics overjoyed to join in prayer and receive Holy Communion. We share this privately and inconspicuously. This ministry is a great source of nourishment and comfort to me as well. It seems a natural thing for me to do. The seeds of a vocation that I planted after my ordeal by the Caspian Sea begin to germinate as I battle with sleeplessness and hyper-vigilance and turn to God to help me complete my mission and care for my men. My journey to future full-time ordained ministry has begun in Iran.

I complete my remaining months in the mission, coordinating the UN operations from our HQ in Tehran. We continue our reporting and investigation and protestation of ceasefire violations. I travel to many trouble spots. My physical and mental systems are overloaded and under stress. I am tense most of the time, as well as hyper vigilant and hyper aroused. I need to take sleeping pills every night. Stress is constant. Just getting to and from the UN HQ is a life-endangering daily experience in the traffic.

While I am not a spy in a technical sense, my Australian superiors have ordered me to provide weekly reports of life and happenings in Iran back to Canberra. This is a breach of UN neutrality that would cost me my job if General Jovic finds out. The consequences if Iranian intelligence finds out would be dire. Should even one of my reports to Canberra be intercepted, I could become a long term guest in a dark underground cell of Evin prison, just down the road from UN Headquarters. Iranian intelligence agents monitor all Australians in Tehran—both through tapping our telephone communications and surveillance by agents who follow us everywhere.

One day a foolish logistics officer in Canberra telephones me at the Australian UNMO house in northern Tehran, wanting to make arrangements for debriefing in Washington on my way home from the mission. A dart of anxiety cuts through my brain as I contemplate the grave danger he is placing me in by mentioning a debriefing by Iran's most reviled enemy. I pray that the eavesdroppers do not pick up on this stupid phone call. Before he can say anything more damaging, I quickly spit out that I am returning home via Hong Kong, and hang up abruptly. Later, I call Canberra from the Australian Embassy, alerting my superiors to this serious breach of security. Moreover, I tell Canberra that I will not be returning home via the United States, and they are to make no plans for me to be debriefed by the Americans! I would like to go home to my family alive.

Fear of being arrested adds to my stress levels and floods my daily life as the time to return to Australia approaches. I counter these feelings of dread with passionate prayer, offering my life to God, begging his protection over me. I 'sterilise' the house we maintain in Tehran. I burn anything that could be interpreted intelligence-gathering. I count the days to our repatriation obsessively.

On the last day in the mission, one of the Iranian liaison officers I had worked with in Dezful, Major Muhammadi, comes up to me and thanks me for my service. He says 'Thank you Colonel Stone for helping to bring peace to our country. We have watched you closely and have realised that you truly are a man of God—please accept this memento in appreciation for your work here.' He has somehow procured a quite ornate Christian cross. It remains one of my proudest possessions. I realise I had bridged a cultural gap and served my country, as well as my Lord, in the most honourable way possible.

I say, 'Thank you, Major Muhammadi, I am overwhelmed by your gift. May peace be with you too.' The emotions that I have kept in check below the surface after nearly six months of constant stress and battling sleeplessness and obsessive watchfulness burst forth. The cross is such a powerful symbol. To have received it as a gift from a thoughtful Muslim officer bursts the dam. Tears stream from my eyes.

On 14 April 1990, six months after my arrival, I fly from Iran after handing over to a new team of Aussie peacekeepers. My last stress test is seven checks and searches on my way onto the Iran Air plane. At any time I fear being led off to a room for interrogation. I am jubilant upon lift-off. I have survived! I fly via Dubai to Phuket in Thailand, where Lynne waits for me. Tears fill my eyes as I see her at the beachfront hotel. I have been telling her in weekly phone calls that everything has been going well in Iran, but emotionally I am a mess, and she soon sees it.

We have a joyful reunion upon return from Iran. But, although I have come home from war, the war has also come home with me.

We spend a week in Phuket and then a week in Hong Kong before returning to the children in Canberra.

I have come home from the war, and the war has come home with me. How I am going to deal with this state is beyond me. I've just got to Hope that God will get us through this. I may be on a journey to a new phase of life, but I have a new health condition to contend with, that I have to come to terms with.

Chapter 5
The Battlefield of the Mind

Yes I have a problem, but no, I can't just, 'Get over it'!

My watch dimly illuminates a soft blue glow that shows the time is only 3am. What if I can't make it to morning? What then? Suddenly, my head snaps round to the sounds coming from the darkness of the Tehran alleyway I'd only just escaped down mere seconds ago. I hear them coming. The shadowy figures have been chasing me for the last twenty minutes or so. My breath comes in short, sharp gasps. I am near exhaustion but my legs refuse to yield. Their footsteps are thunderous. I can't out-run them now. They're almost upon me. I turn again to run. The pavement gives way and I stumble, and then fall. Fear reaches out to drag me down again, but I refuse to give in to it. I can't.

Desperately I drag myself a few more steps, hoping that this is the way out of the labyrinth into which I've plunged. I feel their breath on the back of my neck as a steely embrace envelopes me. The shadowy figure has me by the throat. He's too strong. I resist but slowly I begin to lose consciousness as icy fingers crush the life from my windpipe. I lash out to no avail and feel myself choking ... gasping ... gagging. I'm going to die ... but I won't give up without a fight, and I slam my fist over my head as hard as I can in one last attempt to live. It connects with the shadowy figure's face, and for a brief moment I feel the crushing tension on my windpipe relax.

'Gary, wake up!' A voice screams to me. 'Wake up!' In the darkness of the room where I am, a sense of relief comes over me.

'Gary, please ...' a familiar voice cries out.

Slowly, my eyes adjust to the light as a ghost-like figure appears in the room, slowly coming into focus. 'What's going on ...?' I mumble as I recognize that the ghost-like figure is my wife, Lynne.

'Gary, you've just punched a hole through the wall behind our bed!'

For seconds I'm not entirely sure where I am, but then I realise the shadowy figures are gone. My body is awash with sweat. The pounding in my ears begins to subside as my heart rate starts to fall below 170 bpm. I am now awake and see for the first time the anxiety written all over my dear wife's face. Then, as I turn to follow her gaze, I see and feel my knuckles grazed and red, then a hole the same size as my fist in the plaster just above my pillow. The demons from Iran still visit me.

There are some things in life we don't know about, and are beyond our comprehension. We don't know what we don't know, and so we stumble on. The hidden effects of trauma on our minds, is one area that is still a mystery to many. For many veterans who leave a war zone, the battle continues on in their minds. Those who have not shared their experiences cannot comprehend what has gone on for them. It seems incredible to veterans, that many people aren't interested in their amazing experiences. We naturally want to appear to have our life together, so we shut out unpleasant memories as much as possible. The problem is that trauma leaves an indelible imprint on our mind, and leads to other consequences if not understood and managed appropriately. But again you don't know this if you haven't learned it somewhere, and there are very few experts in this area. Worse than that, there are plenty of sceptics in the area of mental health, so emotionally wounded veterans soldier on in silence, hoping it won't be too big a problem and hoping it will all just go away.

When I leave Iran in 1990, I expect to leave those terrifying memories of my captivity, and the constant threats to life and limb behind me. But in the first few months of being home, my life is far from normal, at least to me anyway. As a result of my recent Middle East experience, I am given a demanding job as the Land Operations Officer in the Defence Force Command Centre. The second week after I start work, we are immersed in Operation Desert Storm—the liberation of Kuwait from Saddam Hussein. We have many direct inputs from the battlefield. The coalition forces are obliterating thousands of Iraqi soldiers. I see and imagine and emotionally feel the death, destruction and suffering that is going on. The media hails the success of US power, but there can be no joy for me in the knowledge that we have contributed to wholesale slaughter of a retreating army and the devastation of Iraqi infrastructure.

In moments of pressure, I experience uncomfortable heart palpitations. Many people including the Chief of our Defence Force, General Peter Gration, and Prime Minister Bob Hawke come into the Command Centre and ask me about aspects of life in the Middle East. This just reinforces some of the negative feelings I experienced there. The pressures continue after the invasion. We are extremely busy sending peacekeeping contingents off to Iraq, Western Sahara and Cambodia. I start to have feelings of anxiety, imagining things that might go wrong. I start to get anxious at the phone ringing, imagining it may be more bad news. This paranoia infiltrates into everything.

One day I am jogging home from the Russell Offices Defence complex, along a cement path, when all of a sudden the cement stops and some broken soil appears in front of me. Without thinking my body slams to a halt as I stop myself from stepping on the disturbed earth. My subconscious is reacting to the possibility that a mine is laid here. My heart is racing even faster now. My brain catches up. I rationally remind myself that there have been no reported cases of mines being laid in suburban Canberra! Even still, I skirt this broken soil and resume my jog, but keep to a solid footing.

I visit an Army doctor and tell him, 'I really don't understand what's happening to me or why I feel so on edge all the time. I feel I am living in a state of alert without any respite. How long can I feel this way?'

'This is a normal reaction to your service in Iran. Eventually, the symptoms will subside', he says.

The placidness of Canberra does not relax me. It does not get better over time. I have difficulty sleeping—waking at every noise around the house. I am short-tempered with the children and immediately regret my aggressiveness and bad temper. I find it difficult to concentrate and focus on one thing at a time. I am hyper-vigilant, hyper-aroused, hyper-sensitive, hyper-everything! I just want to be the way I was before I went away, but somehow I can't get back to being me. We engage an Army Social Worker, who tells my wife to expect things to be different, but that things will gradually improve once everything returns to normal, or once I get used to being home and in a familiar environment.

After nine months at home, I reluctantly see an Army psychologist, who tells me I need to be 'de-briefed'. The Australian Defence Force has not deployed people to conflict zones since the Vietnam War. There seems to be no plan or corporate memory of what to do with individuals who have returned home with mental health concerns.

The psychologist puts me through a process called the 'Mitchell Method' of debriefing, named after an American doctor, Jeffrey Mitchell, who devised a therapeutic technique to deal with trauma in emergency services personnel. The purpose of the debriefing is to take the active memories of the event and 'normalise' them. He explains how, normally, our minds can bring about 'closure' to an incident that has created anxiety. But with life threatening trauma, we may fail to get closure, and tend to keep re-living the event. Debriefing is suggested to try and make sense of it, see it in perspective as a past event that won't recur, and to help us regain order and control.

For hours he puts me through the process of telling my story. Initially, he asks me for the facts, and then we go over the facts again, trying to recall the thoughts I was having at the time. Then we go over the incidents again, trying to recall the feelings and emotions. 'Thump! Thump! Thump!'

My heart pounds and my head throbs. Both feel like they are being hit repetitively with a rubber mallet. It feels at times that any minute my head will burst. The psychologist reassures me that this is normal. But it doesn't seem normal to me! For me there is not just the incident with the Revolutionary Guards on the road near the Caspian Sea. The psychologist digs up many buried stressful events. Most nights in Iran, I feared that the secret police would arrest me and charge me with spying. Most days on the roads were chaotic and very stressful. Every moment on patrol I was alert for mines and unexploded munitions. I had been living on adrenalin for six months, and I had taken sleeping pills to get to sleep on many nights.

At night I try to sleep but I fear that nightmares will return and I will be on the run again. And they do. One night I relive in a dream, a real incident at Bahktaran, where I went for a jog around the base without an

Iranian liaison officer in tow, and at one point a guard yelled out at me, calling me to stop, and raised his rifle at me. Frustrated with the many restrictions we lived under, I called this guy's bluff and kept running till he ran me down, blocked my path, letting forth an angry response. In the recurring nightmare, he fires the rifle at me. I feel the bullet hit me in the chest. I sit bolt upright in bed and feel a real pain in my chest!

I toss and turn throughout the night. The next day in therapy, the psychologist presses me to tell the stories again, and then yet again on the next day. Weeks pass. I am no better. I actually feel more anxious and more reluctant to tell the stories. I'm tired of it. The psychologist warns me that I could be medically down-graded and discharged if I can't make this therapy work. He becomes another source of stress! There is no scope to stay serving in the Army and not be fully fit for deployment to operations. In effect, he is saying that the career I love and have committed myself to over the past twenty years may be coming to an end. I go back to my doctor who offers me medication, but with it the consequence of immediate medical restriction, and preclusion from any training courses or posting until re-classified fit. That is a definite career stopper!

This makes me even more distressed. I do my best to hide the shocking emotion of what I feel from the psychologist. To be told that I may not continue to be in the Army scares me. This is my vocation, my life, and my identity as a person. I decide that for next session, I'll just pretend that I am feeling better. I will also pray for God to heal me and give me peace. 'Dear God, please take this mental torment away'. Every morning I pray a similar prayer. I get some sense of tranquillity, but my weak link is confrontation, that results in a loss of temper. I quickly realise I'd do better to avoid situations that might aggravate my condition.

I did not know it then, but the Mitchell Technique deepens my anxiety rather than removing it. I and many other troubled veterans become victims all over again with this method. In years to come, the medical profession will acknowledge that the Mitchell Method of Debriefing increases distress in most veterans. But in 1990, the Army just does not understand how to assist it's members suffering from Post-Traumatic Stress.

Compounding the distress of veterans suffering from traumatic stress, too many people are sceptical of the illness. This scepticism forces veterans to have to deal with feelings of rejection and disrespect. Many poorly-informed people don't even consider this an illness. They characterise those suffering stress as 'weak' or as malingerers who should 'harden up' and 'get over it'. The prevailing attitude among my peers is that officers who can't handle stress are liabilities and need to be discharged. I decide to keep my stress a secret, and seek some other way of dealing with it.

Ironically, the upside of traumatic stress is hyper-vigilance that assists with multi-tasking. I find I can do many things at once. My heightened arousal gives me energy, but only for a period—before exhaustion floods my system. I find I am very productive at work but when I go home, I crash and burn. I have little energy for Lynne or the kids.

Generously, my family are patient and understanding, but none of us really comprehends what's going on with me. I am unable to be a good father or a good husband whilst I am travelling with all this baggage. My family become victims of my service along the Iran-Iraq border. A diligent and loving husband and father left them for seven months and he has now returned as a short tempered, distant and unsociable workaholic.

Nightmares and flashbacks take me back to a world of insecurity, uncertainty and despair. I can't get rid of them. Increasingly, anxiety grips me whenever I am challenged by someone. A new fear that my marriage is slowly falling apart magnifies my paranoia. Lynne and I try to keep it together through a series of counselling sessions. Lynne longs for a life of normalcy. Nothing seems to work for me. I'm terrified of losing her, but I can't seem to get a grip on this demon who keeps invading my life.

Soon after my return I act on my promise to God in Iran and apply to become a Catholic deacon and serve as an Army chaplain. Providentially for us, being accepted into the Banyo Seminary gives me a reprieve from the pressure of work at Headquarters ADF. We move to Brisbane in December 1991. Lynne and I look forward to settling in Brisbane so the children can settle into their schooling and I can start theological studies. We hope and pray that we can work out how to live a normal life again.

I think back to what Mum used to say about Uncle Jack's coming home from the Second World War. I ponder that many veterans must have struggled with these demons, and I resolve that I will not let them beat me. My only hope, though, is faith in God's assistance. I dare not share what's going on with any more Army psychologists. Besides, this is my calling. I was born and destined to be a soldier, and I have been a good one. I feel there is still a lot more I can contribute, especially if I can become a chaplain. My experience with traumatic stress will enable me to empathise and show understanding of what soldiers, especially veterans of nasty peacekeeping operations, go through. Perhaps with time I may even be able to turn this wound into strength. I sense that God has allowed me to have these things happen to me, and He will use them for His purposes in due course.

Moving Forward

The experience in Iran, the struggles with my mental well-being, and the commencement of my studies at Banyo Seminary transform my life and take me in a different direction. On one hand I will continue to serve proudly as a commissioned officer in the Australian Defence Force. On the other, I will do so as a peacemaker ministering to people whose job is to defend the nation and its interests in some challenging parts of the world. My experience in Iran has given me a firsthand understanding of the great tragedy of conflict between peoples, and the need for nations to avoid war or any violent resolution of disagreements. Iran also illustrated how different cultural paradigms can distort thinking, attitudes and behaviour towards others. For me this has been a great insight into Islam and Muslim people, who generally are peace-loving, and at their core, little different to us in the West. They want to provide for their families and be free to live comfortable and harmonious lives.

I vow to study and respect cultures different to my own, and show humility in dealing with people of other cultures. I want to live my life as an advocate for peace, and continue to do whatever I can to avoid the insanity of the war I have just witnessed, which, although initiated by Saddam Hussein, was then fuelled by superpower arrogance and political convenience, to rein in a rising Iranian nationalism. The cost in human life in the Iran-Iraq War is a crime against humanity. Superpower support for Saddam (and Israel) has upset the balance of power in the region and will have longer-term consequences beyond the First Gulf War.

I feel a paradigm shift in my world view. I have reached a point of transition within myself. Up until this point I have generally been comfortable to sail along within the institution of the Army, accepting what they put in front of me and getting on with the job at hand. Now I feel a newfound need to spread my wings and fly freely, liberated from the absolute norms and restrictions that the military likes to impose on people to keep order. In Australian military history there are many cases of 'mavericks' that push the boundaries and take things to new heights. They might 'ruffle feathers' but they are part of our tradition.

I am also ready for such a change of approach. I have commanded two contingents of Australians on two very different missions. I don't feel particularly excited about 'driving a desk' in Canberra for the indefinite future, which is what promotion to Colonel will precipitate. I have particularly enjoyed the lay ministry of bringing communion to the soldiers in Iran. The vow I made during the interrogation near the Caspian Sea turns me towards greater involvement with Christian ministry.

Postscripts to Service in Iran

In one tragic postscript, my second-in-command in Iran, Major Stu Cameron returns to the Middle East on leave from the Army one year later to assist in humanitarian relief operations with Care Australia in Iraqi occupied Kurdistan. Stu was a good man who cared for the suffering people we had seen. In an incident similar to mine, his vehicle is stopped at a militia roadblock near Sulehmayniah, and he is shot dead. Vale Stu Cameron—you served with honour!

I find my Christianity is often tested by a challenge to seriously follow the second most important commandment, *Love thy neighbour*. In 1995, five years after returning from Iran, I receive a phone call at my new home in Brisbane, from former Iranian Liaison officer, Commander Ali. He is calling from Turkey, and tells me he has been forced to escape from Iran with his family of wife and two young girls, after coming under suspicion of subversion. I am amazed he is able to establish contact with me in Australia. Clearly the Iranian military have ways and means of finding people!

He admits to working as a double agent. He has been secretly supporting a dissident group of military officers wanting to depose the Ayatollah and return the Crown Prince to rule Iran. But he gets a tip-off that he has been found out, and escapes Iran with their secret police chasing him, even now in Turkey. He asks me if I am able to get him political asylum in Australia. He has approached the American Embassy who debriefed him and put him back out on the street!

From my work in HQ ADF, I have developed a range of contacts in other Government departments. I ring many people, including our Embassy in Ankara. I find that our quota for accepting Iranians is zero. It's seems just too difficult. Ali contacts me by phone every night. I sense he is both genuine and desperate. I write up a submission to the Minister for Foreign Affairs, pleading his case on the basis that he protected the life of one of my men who was caught taking pictures in the combat zone. I suggest what an asset he might be in future dealings with Iran. I also pray.

A week later, I get word that his family will be accepted as asylum seekers. Thanks be to God. Something has moved them. Within two weeks of him contacting me, I greet them at Sydney airport. We are all in tears. He subsequently sets up a business and is a model citizen. We have kept in regular contact ever since.

Like 'Ali' and his family, I am about to step into a new life. I am to transform from Christian soldier, to a Soldier of Christ. It is a huge step of trust as I close one chapter of my life to open a new one, in the uncharted territory of being a married catholic cleric.

Chapter 6
Army Chaplain–Soldier of Christ

Saint Paul encouraged his friend, Timothy with these words, 'Be strong through the grace that is ours in Christ Jesus. Take the teachings you have heard from me, and share them with others, who in turn will teach others also. Be a loyal soldier of Christ'.
(2 Timothy 2:1-3).

On 9 December 1994, a ceremony in the Assembly Hall at Enoggera Barracks, Brisbane, marks my change from Christian soldier to a front-line Soldier of Christ. Twenty-five years soldiering has prepared me well for the next two decades of military service.

In the presence of hundreds of friends and family, Bishop Geoffrey Mayne stretches his hands over me and prays that God's Holy Spirit will consecrate me for a life of service to God and humanity. He says (in part), 'Send your Spirit upon this man who is now set apart as a minister of Jesus Christ ...Gary, receive the Gospel of Christ whose herald you now are: Believe what you read, teach what you believe, and practice what you preach...'

As with my wedding day, my ordination day is the launching pad for a life of ongoing service. We have a wonderful celebration in the centre of the 'market place' for my future ministry. Vested in a white garment, I lie prostrate as the community prays for me. The Bishop leads me through vows, and eventually lays hands upon my head and prays the prayers of consecration. The community greets me with rousing applause. I feel on cloud nine—perhaps it is a foretaste of heaven!

I am ordained a Deacon at Enoggera 14 December 1994

Few Catholic people in Australia have received all the sacraments of the church as I have experienced now. I am one of a pioneering few who receive the sacrament of Holy Orders, superimposed on the sacrament of Marriage. I hadn't even been aware of this possibility a few years before. Though there are about 25 married Deacons in the Catholic Church in Australia in 1994, this evolving innovation grows to 160 deacons serving the Lord in Australia by 2014 and 46,000 deacons worldwide.

Progressives in the Catholic Church welcome deacons as a way of getting more ministers into the mission field. Conservatives are suspicious about married men joining the celibate ranks of the priesthood. But from the beginning, the people who I minister to are extraordinarily affirming of this innovation, to the point where I can scarce keep pace with their willing engagement and requests for assistance.

Many people are intrigued that I would leave a successful career and forego a Lieutenant Colonel's salary for a Lieutenant's wage. What motivates me to make this change?

Invitation

An Army chaplain at Enoggera, Father John Tinkler, sows the seeds early in 1989, before I go to Iran. He tells me of his vision to introduce, train and ordain married men as Deacons for Catholic Defence chaplaincy. Known affectionately as 'Tink', he is one of the best chaplains the Army has ever had. Tink is always cheery, and active in sports. Soldiers love him. He is also practical and looking to the future. Tink still has a lot of work to do to fulfil his vision, but he sows a seed of interest in me and it germinates in prayers asking God if this is to be my destiny.

My faith deepens, and thoughts of undergoing studies to become a deacon, mature in Iran and turn into action during my subsequent attendance at the Joint Services Staff College, and the busy appointment as the Land Operations Officer in the HQ ADF Command Centre. Tink tells me that things have progressed. He has the Church's agreement, but is still struggling with some opposition from some of the Anglican and Protestant chaplains who are not comfortable with either having married Catholic deacons as chaplains, or having Army men trained to be chaplains, or both!

This is quite a revolutionary concept for its time. Up until now, any soldier interested in being a chaplain, had to leave the military altogether, fund their own training, get ordained in a civilian church, get at least two year's full-time civilian ministry experience and then re-apply to join the Army. Tink is proposing that the Army sponsor and fund the entire process, in the same manner as Army's in-service recruitment and training of doctors, lawyers and other specialists.

In the meantime I seek out and begin what is formally known as 'discernment' with the Catholic Bishop to the ADF, Geoffrey Mayne, a gentle former navy chaplain (and mad keen South Sydney Rugby

League supporter). We meet monthly for over a year, and he gently asks me many questions about my faith in God, and my capacity and desire to love others. He invites me to study the life and ministry of St Francis of Assisi, a deacon of the 13th Century, who gave up life in a wealthy family to serve the poor, and lead others into a ministerial life (now known as the Religious Order of Franciscans). At each meeting, I also bring along a series of questions about matters where I need greater understanding, such as the many rules and regulations of life in the church. I get to understand that many things are not as 'Black and White' as one might imagine, and that accomodations can be made through 'pastoral sensitivity' and applying the 'Spirit of the Law' when the 'Letter of the Law' does not really address the complexities of a person's case. We pray together, and lunch together. He becomes a spiritual mentor and father to me. I complement this process by beginning theological studies part-time at Australian Catholic University in Canberra.

In July 1991 Bishop Mayne formally accepts me as a candidate for training towards ordination, and I ask the Army to post me to Brisbane to commence studies under Tink's supervision. It's made very clear to me that I can have no guarantee of ordination or transfer to Chaplaincy. I will have to prove myself and complete a Theology degree.

By this time I am convinced that my Christian soldier mission has been completed and God is calling me to be a Soldier of Christ.

The Diaconate

Deacons were very prominent in the early church, and are frequently mentioned in the scriptures. Broadly speaking, in the early days, before there were priests, bishops ministered to the gathered and 'the converted', and deacons ministered to the 'scattered' and those on the margins of the church.

As the church institutionalised, an order of priests or presbyters, was established to undertake some of the functions of both bishop and deacon. The innovation of priests proliferated into dedicated missionary religious orders of priests such as the Jesuits and Dominicans. Concurrently, the missionary dimension of the role of deacon diminished. By the tenth Century deacons became a transitional ministry on the way to priesthood. At about the same time, the Pope decreed that all clergy in the Western or Roman Church were to remain celibate. This edict did not extend to the Eastern rites of the Church.

At the Second Vatican Council, 1962-1966, the Pope and his cardinals restored the distinctive missionary ministry of deacons as a permanent and enduring ministry in the church, and decided that married men over the age of 35 would be admitted to this traditional order. The reasons were:

The Church needed a renewed engagement with those outside it—deacons are to lead this outreach.

The laity within the Church needed a renewed model and inspiration for service to the poor and marginalised—to quote Bishop Anthony Fisher of Parramatta, 'Deacons personify the servant heart of Jesus, as Icons of Charity.'

The Church concluded that the sacrament of Marriage could be complementary to Holy Orders, and not an impediment to it—deacons give expression to this duality.

Deacons compensate for the need for more ministers, considering the dwindling numbers of men aspiring to celibate priestly ministry.

The Pope leaves bishops to introduce deacons at their discretion. North American bishops embrace the diaconate quickly and recruit, train and ordain thousands of married deacons. Australian Bishops decide to wait to see how the North American dioceses fare.

Formation for Ministry

Bishop Mayne ordains his first deacon, Major Graeme Ramsden, a Vietnam veteran, in December 1992 after he completes his Theology degree at the Banyo Seminary. I study with Graeme and will become the ADF's second deacon. The staff at Banyo Seminary—including Rector Father Frank Lourigan, Academic Dean and Father (later Bishop) Michael Putney, and Director of Formation, Father John Chalmers—are excellent guides and mentors to me.

Before I am to get into fulltime military ministry I am to do an internship—'on-the-job' training. I am particularly fortunate to have my first years following ordination in parish ministry at The Gap, in Brisbane, supervised by Marist Father Seamus McMahon, a tall Irishman with a warm smile, who has spent most of his ordained ministry in the mission fields of PNG and Fiji. I enter a threefold ministry: preaching and teaching at Mass and in faith education; celebration of the sacraments of baptism and marriage, as well as conduct of funerals; and exercising ministry of pastoral care—being present to people in their trials and tribulations, offering advice and providing a listening ear.

Whilst undergoing my internship in parish, I also commence part-time military chaplaincy at Enoggera. Deacons can be employed in a range of ministries, and military chaplaincy is just one of them. Chaplains work where the church has minimal presence, such as hospitals, prisons, police forces and schools. These institutions employ chaplains and pay them for their services.

Military chaplaincy is the oldest form of this ministry. It dates back to the ministry of St Martin of Tours. Martin was a soldier in the Freanch Army, about 350 AD. One day he was riding back from battle and saw a wounded soldier, shivering and begging for help. In these days there were no arrangements for caring for the wounded—they normally were just left to die. He looked with compassion on the soldier, and tore his cloak in half and wrapped him in it. That night in a dream, he had a vision of the wounded soldier looking up at him, and saw in him the face of Christ. He concluded that God was calling him to care for the wounded as an official ministry of the church. He presented himself to his local bishop for some training, was ordained a priest, and returned to battlefields and began organising care for the wounded. Soon military commanders were asking bishops for more chaplains because their work with the wounded and encouragment of others had a significant positive impact on morale. Progressively, all militaries in the Western world began to employ chaplains for these reasons, and chaplains are now integrated into defence forces around the world.

Chaplains arrived with the First Fleet, and with all subsequent British regiments that came out to establish and protect the new Australian colonies in the late 18th Century. Australian chaplains deployed to the Boer War at the turn of the 20th Century and every subsequent conflict. Chaplains serve with every battalion or regiment in the military. My family and I get to know many chaplains over the first 25 years of my military career. I am absolutely convinced of the value of this ministry and excited at the prospect of getting involved in it.

The die has been cast, the foundations laid. The Holy Spirit is guiding my path—my new phase of life is taking shape.

Transition from soldier to minister

Many people ask me how difficult it is going to be, to transition from being a soldier to being a minister. I reply that it isn't too difficult at all. While I have to gain extra knowledge and skills, my basic attitudes and underpinning values are no different.

The official ethos of the Australian Army is summed up in one word—*Service*. Jesus embraced this attitude in his statement that 'He came to serve—not to be served'. (*Luke* 12). That is foundational for ministers as well. Indeed, in many respects the vocations and professions of soldier and church minister have much in common—requiring commitment, courage and compassion for engagement in a mission. Clearly a soldier may also be required to kill people, but in the Australian military this only occurs with 'Just Cause'.

For me the transition from Christian Soldier to Soldier of Christ turns out to not be a significant change in direction. I synthesise the fruits of two careers. Years later, my Brigade Commander in the Army Reserve, Brigadier Peter Jeffrey, proudly tells people, 'I benefit from having a 'Padre squared'—a competent minister, as well as an advisor who has a wealth of military experience, to assist me and our soldiers'.

Perhaps the biggest change is that I have to surrender my Lieutenel Colonel's salary, and start again on a Lieutenants salary! This is to have impact on my family but they graciously accept it. 'God will provide for us', my daughter Catherine says.

Yes, some sacrifice is necessary in order to achieve anything significant, but we never go in need.

Life as a Chaplain

Good chaplains, often called 'Padres' (Spanish for Father) are constantly on the move visiting soldiers in all manner of places, offering a cheerful smile and a listening ear. They accept a soldier's situation, no matter what it is, or how bad he has been. They represent the soldier's interests and can bend the commander's ear if the soldier needs special consideration. Just when a soldier thinks he has no options left, a wise Padre can put things in perspective, and help him think of another way of dealing with a situation. In a system that sometimes seems like it is out to crush the individual, a Padre can be a 'get out of jail card'. Actually the so-called 'System' doesn't seem to mind this—the Padre helps keep the System honest. Indeed having the Padre's objective perspective is part of 'the System'. The Padre also provides the 'pressure relief valve'. People can 'vent' with the Padre in confidence, and sometimes this is the only help they need.

Many soldiers develop a special rapport with their unit's Padre. He may have celebrated their marriage, baptised their children, or buried one of their mates or even their Mum or Dad. Many Padres are father figures to members of their unit. Normally the Padre is a generation older than the younger diggers, has possibly been a soldier in their earlier life, and has seen it all before. Nothing is too much of a shock to Padres with a military background, and they can be trusted with secrets even when someone has 'stuffed up' something awful. The Padre is the soldier's friend.

In my preparation for Chaplaincy, I interview and study the ministry of many chaplains, to gain insight into the best practice I can adopt. Some Padres are firmly etched in the history of the Australian Army. Eugene Harley, Gerry Cudmore, Les Thompson and John Tinkler were famous characters of the 60s Malaya/Borneo/Vietnam War era. They are famous because they are 'characters', always able to turn up at the most critical times with a cheery word or joke. In the 1980s and 1990s a new cohort of Catholic chaplains emerge, who make their own indelible marks, including John Butler, Mick Taylor, Glynn Murphy, Graeme Ramsden, and Mick Lappin. As with their predecessors, they are comfortable on the sporting field or in the 'boozer' (the soldiers club). Soldiers appreciate their presence, interest and sense of humour. At the same time they are deeply spiritual men with an unshakable faith in their God.

Spiritual moments in Regimental life occur throughout each year. The Padre will preside over Battalion anniversary and memorial services, ANZAC Day services, and the presentation of new Colours. Weddings and baptisms provide joyous celebrations, but the Padre really becomes indispensable upon the death of a soldier. The Padre knows how to support grieving family and friends. The dignity and honour of a military funeral ceremony is unsurpassed. Chapel communities like St Joan of Arc at Enoggera, and All Saints at Townsville, provide a spiritual home for soldiers and their families. Regimental Colours are laid up there, and units have provided items like the brass Tabernacle presented by 3 RAR to St Joan of Arc Chapel, Enoggera.

I study how the Padre has a unique role on operations. Padres go to war with their units. Chaplain John Tinkler, served as the Padre of 1st Battalion, the Royal Australian Regiment, at the battle of Fire Support Base, 'Coral', in Vietnam in 1968. He is remembered for moving around the battlefield under fire, anointing the wounded, encouraging the living and praying for the dying in their final moments of life. Some Padres carry weapons, others don't, but all affirm the soldier's right and obligation to use lethal force in combat with the enemy, and to protect the lives of the innocent.

I ponder how Chaplains carrying weapons has always been contentious. ADF policy provides Chaplains a choice. Some chaplains maintain they could not in conscience kill anyone, even in self-defence. Others wish the option to defend others in situations of grave danger, especially the wounded. Of course the chaplain is not expected to perform guard duties or to engage the enemy.

2 RAR Chaplain in Timor in 1999, Glynn Murphy, spends his whole tour moving from company to company, keeping up spirits, celebrating Mass for soldiers and locals alike, as well as providing a bridge of confidence to encourage terrorised Timorese to return from hiding, including their priests and nuns. The battalion chefs bake 2000 communion breads a week for him to keep up with demand for Holy Communion! Glynn carries a 9 mm Browning pistol on his belt. Morgan Batt, chaplain to Fifth Battalion, the Royal Australian Regiment in Iraq in 2007 is well known for blessing of all the patrols as they leave the base each day and being there to welcome them back. He doesn't carry a weapon, but instead carries a staff, symbolic of the Good Shepherd.

A year after my ordination I become a chaplain to the 6th Brigade in Enoggera, with priority of effort to the Second Combat Engineer Regiment. This is to be my 'bedding-in time' as a chaplain. In order to get to know as many people as possible in the shortest amount of time, I plan a regular routine of visitation. A tragic event overtakes this systematic introduction. Less than a week after my arrival, a motor vehicle accident claims the life of one of our sergeants. Presiding at his funeral introduces me to the regiment. I am the only Catholic chaplain in the Barracks, and so I also celebrate baptisms and weddings and conduct funerals for Catholic members of every unit. It is fascinating working with the 'sappers' (engineers)—hard workers and highly skilled. I develop great respect for them.

Back to Duntroon

I had hoped to stay in Brisbane until all our children had finished high school. The Army has a different idea, and posts me as Chaplain to RMC Duntroon, my *Alma Mater*, for 1998–99. I am the first graduate

Celebrating Marriage at Duntroon Chapel 1989

to return as a Chaplain. Lynne stays in Brisbane, to see our younger children, Paul and Christy, finish school in one place after having had our eldest two, Michael and Catherine, change schools too often. We are to have to spend two years apart. I immerse myself in the limitless ministry opportunities at the College, but it doesn't make up for the many lonely nights. We do manage to get a weekend together every 6 weeks, but I miss her terribly.

My time at Duntroon is nostalgic and meaningful, particularly as our eldest son Michael is undergoing his training there. I spend time on countless exercises, walking miles with the cadets, and supporting the staff that have their share of personal issues. I particularly enjoy conducting Character Development—training in ethos, values and ethics. My thesis is that the Army values of courage, initiative, respect and teamwork don't just emerge in soldiers because they put on a uniform. Shared experience and reflection has to nurture and internalise these values.

I develop a presentation called 'The Spirit of the Aussie Digger,' that reflects on Army history and my own experiences. I believe that true Digger Spirit is very much sourced and nourished in and through the Divine. I am determined to encourage people to become more aware of what that Divine nature means for them. Ideally I want to help them to grow in relationship with God and the Christian community. I don't pressure people, but let them progress at their pace. It is amazing to discover the many spiritual experiences people have already had—but have kept them a secret. God has been at work in their lives long before I have.

There are occasional crises requiring action. One night a knock on the door of my quarters next to the College chapel wakes me. A tall and gaunt looking cadet, dressed in a track suit is at the door, shaking, seemingly uncontrollably.

He says in a shaky voice, 'Padre, I was just about to kill myself out in the forest. My army career is over. I've injured myself, and they are planning to discharge me after three-and-a-half years of training'. He sobs, 'There is nothing else I've ever wanted to do. I don't want to have to face people back home as a failure. I was about to gas myself in my car, and a thought came into my mind about you. I remember you telling us that we could always see you about anything. I'm just a bit worried that I might not go to heaven if I commit suicide. Could we talk about that?'

I say to him, 'Wow, I am so glad you came to see me. Please come in. Let me put the kettle on.'

This cadet was not one I had got to know well. I don't ever remember talking to him. He did not attend chapel, but I clearly had been with him on the many exercises we had at the college. My presence had made some impact upon him, and in my mind the Holy Spirit had prompted him to see me at this late hour.

I sit and listen to his story. I affirm him for coming to see me. I help him clarify what it is he fears in facing his family and friends, and help him develop some other options in life. I offer to pray for him. I put my hand on his bowed head and pray, thanking God for his life, asking God for his blessing on this young man, praying for his family and friends' understanding.

I look him in the eye and tell him, 'God has a plan for your life. He loves you and so do I. There is something in life that you are going to be able to do that will bless others. Together we can work that out in due course. You can choose to die or choose to live. You have developed many skills here that will be foundational for another career. Can you choose to go on living?'

He hugs me like I was his father, and in tears and choking voice says, 'Thank you, thank you, thank you. Yes, I want to live. I thought there was no hope. But you have given me hope. I want to believe in God. I want to have faith like you.'

His body slumps on mine, exhausted and perhaps relieved. I am exhausted too. My heart is pumping. I guide him onto my lounge and tell him to lie down. I lay a blanket over him and tell him to sleep. I go back to bed and say my thanks to God. A life has been saved. In the morning I take him up to the Duntroon hospital, and see the doctor with him. We develop a management plan and get him on some medication. We call his family and invite them to come to see him. He is to start a new life.

There are many challenges like this at Duntroon. The place is a 'pressure cooker', with almost half of the cadets in each cohort, called a 'class', becoming injured or failing tests and being discharged. I act as an advocate for cadets who I think are being treated unfairly. I also challenge staff that are abusive. Some of them don't like that, and make complaints about me. Their accusations are soon found to be false, but it hurts just the same.

My Commanding officer at Duntroon in my first year is a Lieutenant Colonel John Cantwell. Like me, he had served on exchange with the British Army, and served with the allies during the First Gulf War in 1990. Man to man, we privately share some of the adjustment problems we both have from having been traumatised in the Middle East on operations. We also acknowledge that our peers and the Army system neither understand what we are going through, nor show much sympathy for us. We just have to 'soldier on'. (In 2012 John will release his own book 'Exit Wounds' detailing his long and agonising journey).

My busy schedule, confrontations with some staff members, and separation from my family takes its toll. My system cannot take it. After 9 months I 'hit the wall' and become chronically depressed. I wake up one Monday morning, and just don't want to go to the office. The trigger had been a problematic weekend, when a number of cadets came to me complaining about being harassed by staff and not released in time to come to our programmed chapel services. Another confrontation in the offing tips me into depression.

I ring up our Coordinating Chaplain, Andrew Sempell and tell him, 'I'm stuffed, mate. I'm over it. Too much bullshit going on. Minimal support from the staff. I would like to give some of these instructors a piece of my mind, but I just can't face up to it.' My anxiety level is through the roof. I have lost the ability to function.

Andrew, who was an Armoured Corps officer before he becoming an Anglican Church minister is very understanding. 'No worries Gary. You need a good break. It would be good for you to see Doctor Michelle Barrett'. She gives me two week's sick leave and suggests Lynne and I get together. Lynne flies down and we have a week at a country retreat centre. We then come back to Canberra and have another week in my quaint little cottage in the College grounds. We go for lots of walks and have a nap after lunch every day.

After this 'time out', Michelle, a veteran from peacekeeping operations in Rwanda in 1994–95, questions me thoroughly. She tells me, 'Gary, you are displaying symptoms of Post-Traumatic Stress Disorder (PTSD), most likely related to your time in Iran. It's manifesting itself in anxiety and depression after being triggered by further stressors at the College.' She then does a stocktake of all the stressors that have been affecting me.

Life as a student for three years and in parish for two years has distracted me from some of the pressures of military life. Frankly I don't understand what mental health really involves. I have been a changed man after Iran. Lynne and I had never settled back into the same intimacy we had before. My mind is always racing—I used to think it good that I could do so many things at once. But I am not really present to Lynne and the children. I've had numerous visits to doctors and physiotherapists due to stomach pains, muscle spasms, and problems sleeping. But no one has diagnosed PTSD. But now, after 'hitting the wall' I cannot deny that I have a serious mental illness any longer. Providentially, my Commanding Officer, John Cantwell, understands, because of his own challenges to cope alone with PTSD. He gives me the space to work things out.

My weak link is dealing with confrontation. At this time, I am also clashing with a senior military chaplain and cannot fully enjoy my Chaplaincy, due to the anxiety of pressure to conform to his expectations of me.

Michelle Barrett helps me, because she understands PTSD. But she also wants to help me rehabilitate rather than get rid of me as a perceived weak link in the chain. She suggests I go to the Department of Veterans Affairs (DVA) and undergo a series of tests. DVA doctors diagnose me as a person suffering from PTSD and give me a health care card so that I can access treatment outside the Army. I am medically downgraded, but given six months to improve before the Army contemplates a discharge on medical grounds.

Michelle, my amazing life-saving angel, enrols me in an intensive six-week DVA-funded PTSD program with other veterans in Brisbane. Ten years after returning to Australia from Iran I finally receive treatment that will do some good.

Towards Healing

During this course, I discover that when I was in Iran, my mind and body were simply responding to the life-threatening experiences I faced. My mind reprogrammed my body to maintain a state of constant alert as a survival mechanism. My mind is also numbing me emotionally, making me feel detached. My hyper-vigilance is causing me to see many things as potential threats to me. The negative messages from TV, newspapers and living in the military are many. I suck them all in and trigger depression.

The DVA six-week program is brilliant. Every day I join a group of nine other veterans at the clinic to undertake a broad range of therapies. Most days start out with an hour of physical activity. We go for a walk and do a range of physical exercises. This releases endorphins into our system. We then have an educational session with a psychologist. I am intrigued how clearly and simply he explains what is going on in our heads. It is so heartening to get this information, and simply understand what is going on within us. Certainly we're not crazy, we are just different. And it appears that there is a simple reason why we are reacting as we are. I wonder how so many doctors, psychologists and social workers I had seen in the previous ten years had been unable to explain this phenomenon to me before this six week course?

The baseline PTSD condition is simply hyper-vigilance and hyper-arousal. This is the body's normal protective mechanism when in danger. The trouble for us veterans is that the dangers we faced, both real and perceived, persisted for long enough, and peaked so intensely at times, that our bodies programmed in hyper-vigilance forever. We are on alert for any potential threats 24/7 for the rest of our lives. Sights, sounds, smells, or feelings that are similar to those that we experienced on operations trigger the body and mind to a state of hyper-arousal. Hyper-arousal is fine for short periods, but staying in the hyper-aroused state for long periods is exhausting and debilitating. The psychologist explains that we must minimise hyper-arousal if we are to avoid developing anxiety and depression. Anxiety and depression are separate illnesses triggered by PTSD. They are 'co-morbid' conditions that will get worse unless we can control and minimise hyper-arousal. Accordingly, another component of every day is relaxation. The psychologist teaches us how to relax using various techniques of meditation, and resting and breathing to quieten our minds.

Another psychologist takes us through cognitive behaviour therapy. We are now naturally hyper-vigilant people, who need to retrain our bodies not to react automatically and obsessively to stimuli that the body perceives threatening. We have to discriminate real threat from irrational imagined threats. We have to stop allowing our bodies to be on the lookout for danger when no danger exists. The challenge is to stop irrational fear translating into a physical reaction of fear, increased heartbeat, or perspiration.

A psychiatrist supervises the whole program, and normally spends a short session with us each day as a group, and then once each week conducts a detailed interview with each of us to see how we are going. He suggests and prescribes medication for each of us, to try to slow down the activity in our minds. Up until this point I have been resistant to taking any medication. I finally agree to take a medication designed to restore the chemical balance in my brain in order to allow me to minimise hyper-arousal and hyper-vigilance. It is not addictive or dangerous. Amazingly, within several weeks my mind is clearer, calmer and more relaxed. I don't know how long I will need to take the medication, but the doctor reminds me that I have had over ten years of programmed behaviour. I cannot expect to get better miraculously in the short-term. Indeed, he says that some people might need to be on medication for many years, if not for life.

Within a few weeks, Lynne notices positive changes. For a start, I am positive that I can improve my condition because I understand what is going on in me for the first time. Prior to this I have been unable to name the demons, and understand some of the strategies that will be needed to combat them. I am also sleeping better. I seem to be able to relax more and not worry about so many things going wrong. It's early days yet, and this is intensive therapy without any stressors, but I am delighted.

One aspect the program doesn't address is the area of faith, spirituality or hope. Throughout the program, I have been continuing to try to reflect and listen to what God has been saying to me. More than anything, I am living in hope and the confidence that I am going to come through this situation well. For some of the other men on the program, this is not the case. Some of them have done some things that they regret, and feel guilty or remorseful. Even though we are getting some good education and information on how to manage PTSD, there are clearly other life matters that are adding to their distress that this program is not in itself addressing.

I share my own faith with them and some of the wonderful things that I have seen in life-like the warm friendships of our church community, and the generosity of ministry groups like St Vincent de Paul, where ordinary people like them help the poor and disadvantaged. I hope this will be of comfort, or perhaps something for them to contemplate in the future.

I reflect how I am the only Post-Vietnam veteran in the programme, and how my fellow patients have struggled for more than 30 years to get to this point of treatment. I am saddened to hear their stories of marriage breakdown, alcohol and substance abuse, and social dysfunction, let alone the tragedy of suicide and early death of so many of their mates. Clearly PTSD has claimed many more casualties than enemy bullets. Those of us receiving treatment are the fortunate ones. It seems far too many veterans are just soldiering on in silence. I hope and pray I can be a part of turning this around and helping more veterans into treatment, but frankly I can't trust the military hierarchy at this point, and must be most circumspect in who I tell, and what I say about my condition.

The programme continues Monday to Friday for six weeks, and then I return to Canberra. Over the following six months I get to return to Brisbane for one day's follow-up session each month. This serves as a healthy checkup for each of us. At this point I see a local Brisbane psychiatrist who, incidentally, is also a parishioner in our church in The Gap. We agree to meet once every six weeks as a regular checkup on how I am travelling.

I have to say how grateful I am to the Department of Veterans Affairs for providing this program for veterans. It doesn't fix our problems completely, but it certainly helps us to understand how to manage the conditions that we have.

I am not alone. The program has made me realise that I am not hopeless. What I am experiencing is something many other veterans have experienced before me. I have to learn how to manage what is happening to me and understand what triggers set me off into a state of despair and depression, and how to avoid those triggers.

I return to Duntroon after the course, and start putting into practice the skills I have learned. Perhaps people give me a bit of space too, but I seem to be able to hold things together.

Moving on

I throw myself back into training Christian leaders by running some retreat weekends and mid-week meetings for the cadets who are interested in growing in the Christian life, and learning some basic ministry skills. Lynne and I had facilitated a similar programme called 'Antioch' in our parish over four years.

Our son Michael, who is a cadet at Duntroon, invites many of his mates along. We have 60 cadets attend our first weekend. We follow up each Wednesday night from 5p.m.to 7pm, with a meal, a talk and some prayer time. I get a massive covered pergola built on the back of my house to accommodate everyone. The Cadets Mess provides 60 TV dinners each week. My spirits soar. I see lots of growth in faith. This is the best ministry I can be involved in—training more ministers who will share the load!

I get another big boost when my daughter Catherine moves to Canberra to keep me company. She moves into my cottage and gets a job with a computer company. God bless you Catherine! With both her and Michael at Duntroon I am no longer as homesick.

Time seems to pass quickly. My new regime and medication have worked wonders. After six months Dr Michelle reclassifies me as fit for ongoing service. Hooray! I am conscious that I will not rid myself of PTSD, but I can manage it and have learned I will need to be quite disciplined in managing its symptoms to try to avoid further breakdowns.

My treatment for PTSD is absolutely timely, for the ADF in 1999 is about to see its biggest test for 30 years with a whole series of crises requiring response forces being deployed. Much good work will be needed, and many more casualties will need to be treated. I am to be involved on both fronts.

I train and commission Lay Ministers at Duntroon 1999

Chapter 7
East Timor – 'Loving our Neighbour'

East Timor–'Loving our Neighbour'

> *'The Spirit of the Lord is upon me, because he has chosen me to bring good news to the poor. He has sent me to proclaim liberty to captives and recovery of sight to the blind...and announce that the time has come when the Lord will save his people'*
> (Jesus in *Mark* 4:18)

East Timor comes onto my destiny radar in mid-1999. Australia's tiny neighbour is heading for a massive ordeal after the Indonesian President B. J. Habibie invites the United Nations to supervise a ballot to decide whether East Timor should accept autonomy within Indonesia, or become an independent nation. The Indonesian armed forces that have occupied East Timor since their invasion in 1975, respond with a violent campaign to terrorise the East Timorese using recruited, trained and sponsored pro-autonomy militia groups. This leads to systematic human rights abuses that create a humanitarian crisis, prompting worldwide calls for international intervention to stop the violence. The Australian media is full of appalling scenes of militia thugs at work intimidating, brutalising, assaulting and killing innocent people. Australia wrestles with the requirement to maintain good relations with its populous northern neighbour and a moral obligation to join the world in condemning the violence.

The Australian Broadcasting Commission alleges that despite Australia's obligations to share intelligence with the Americans, the Australian Government wants to appease Indonesia and keep the United States in the dark about the complicity of the Indonesian armed forces in the violence. The Americans had been pushing for peacekeepers to be deployed in the country in the lead-up to the referendum, but Australian Foreign Minister Alexander Downer opposes this after assurances that Indonesian troops and police would keep the peace.

The moral dilemma of what to tell the Americans touches my life in a very personal way on 10 July 1999, while I am still Chaplain to RMC Duntroon. At no notice, Sandra, the wife and now widow of one of my Duntroon classmates, Merv Jenkins, calls, telling me that Merv has died, and asks me to assist in conducting Merv's funeral at the Duntroon Chapel. Merv had given his country outstanding service. A patriotic Western Australian, Merv was a real gentleman and a man of integrity. At the time of his death he had been serving as the Senior Australian Defence Intelligence Liaison Officer in Washington.

The Anzac Memorial chapel of St Paul is packed with hundreds of family and friends. We are in grief at the loss of a mate. Sandra has lost her husband and her children have lost their Dad under the most tragic circumstances imaginable. We just can't understand what has happened. In the frantic preparations for the funeral, Sandra tells me that Merv took his own life by hanging himself at home in Washington after being threatened with charges under the Official Secrets Act by senior Defence officials sent from Canberra. Apparently he was passing on intelligence to the US Government on the extent of the Indonesian criminality in the lead-up to the referendum in East Timor. I can't believe what she is saying. It is shocking. It doesn't make sense. Has my government intimidated a loyal Australian to commit suicide?

We struggle to give Merv a great send-off, but the circumstances just don't add up. Has he had a nervous breakdown? What could East Timor have to do with his death? For the last 25 years the ADF has hosted Indonesian officers on military career courses. Our senior officers and intelligence briefs have thoroughly indoctrinated ADF officers that the Indonesian armed forces have blocked Communism from developing in our region and are 'the good guys'!

After the funeral, Merv's wife goes public with her anger and disappointment about Merv's treatment and the Defence Department 'cover-up' over East Timor. The ABC *Four Corners* programme puts the evidence together in two episodes shown later in the year.

Sandra alleges on the program that Merv had been troubled all year that things were going really bad in East Timor, and that he was aware through telecommunications intercepts that the Indonesians were committing terrible atrocities and were planning to destroy the place. Superiors in Canberra allegedly direct him to hide this inconvenient truth from the Americans. This was unethical to him, and he passed the intelligence to his American contacts in Washington, who challenged their Australian counterparts in Canberra.

Senior Defence officials sent from Canberra allegedly advised Merv that he was to be charged with breaches of the Official Secrets Act, effectively ending his career in Defence in disgrace. Within hours, Merv hangs himself. As I watch the show I am enraged.

After the arrival of the UN electoral mission in May 1999, the violence in East Timor gets worse and international pressure mounts on the Indonesian President to invite international intervention. On 1 September, the United Nations announces that 78 percent of the Timorese people have voted for independence. The Indonesian military and the militias they sponsor begin systematically destroying the country's infrastructure and forcibly displacing thousands of East Timorese internally and deporting thousands more to West Timor. From my house in Duntroon I watch with disbelief as Dili burns to the ground. Tragic scenes show babies being thrown over barbed wire fences into the UN compound in Dili as UN staff flee the country.

Merv's predictions have come true. I am incensed at our Government's betrayal both of Merv and these tortured people. I frantically read up on the many stories that have been told of East Timor, but have been kept from the general public, and start to see things in a new light. In Desmond Ball and Hamish McDonald's book, *Deaths in Balibo and lies in Canberra*, I read of a quarter-century of deceit and shameful diplomacy. Allegedly, the Australian Government knew beforehand that five Australian journalists were to be killed in Balibo in 1975 and did nothing to warn them in order to protect technical intelligence gathering capabilities. The Government was then complicit in the Indonesian cover story that the journalists had accidentally been caught in crossfire between the Indonesian soldiers and East Timorese rebels.

I join many others from the Catholic Church and other groups in silent protest (in civilian clothes) outside the Indonesian Embassy in Canberra. Unable to control the Indonesian armed forces in East Timor, on 12 September President Habibie invites regional troops to enter East Timor as quickly as possible. Eight days later on 20 September 1999, Australian troops land in Dili. They are three weeks too late. Destruction is almost complete.

As part of the ADF's mobilisation for a longer term commitment in East Timor, I receive a posting order to my old battalion 6 RAR, which is to be re-raised as a regular battalion to relieve 5/7 RAR at Balibo in April 2000. Before I am able to join the battalion, the posting of the incumbent Chaplain is extended. I am redirected to 2/14th Light Horse, Queensland Mounted Infantry, an armoured cavalry regiment, also being reconstituted as a regular unit for service in East Timor. My son Michael is due to graduate from Duntroon on 11 December and leaves for Timor the following day to join 2nd Battalion, the Royal Australian Regiment, on the border.

There is euphoria in the air. Helping the Timorese is surely God's will. It may involve significant stress, and my capacity to manage my PTSD will be fully tested. Lynne and I talk and pray about this, and we receive peace that this is definitely a moment in history when we must do our best, no matter what the risks. In any case, I am to get eight months in Brisbane with family and friends before I am to deploy.

It is said that 'Absence makes the heart grow fonder.' I don't agree. Two years away from Lynne and our youngest two children has just been awful and has dampened my relations with Lynne and the kids. I quickly get back into routines that had been life giving in the past. Once a fortnight we invite the extended family over to a Sunday roast lunch. Lynne excels at hospitality and can cater for 12 people without blinking. Lynne and I get back into tennis competition of a Tuesday night—actually Lynne has not left this. I enjoy the concentration that tennis requires—needing me to blank out all other thoughts to just focus on the ball and what I am going to do with it. Tennis reminds me that every throw of the ball is a new possibility. It's still possible to win from being down 40-love in a game, or even 5-love in a set. One just has to concentrate on winning the point at hand.

Catherine delivers us baby Brianna in September 1999 and we become grandparents. It is such a joy to have this wonderful young girl in our family. Brianna's father is not ready to accept responsibility for her and so Cath and Brianna move in with us, while Cath also starts a University course in Information Systems.

Michael has a month overseas and returns from East Timor with his battalion, to Townsville. We go up there to witness their welcome home parade in January 2000. He is full of energy and has certainly hit the ground running in his first command of soldiers. He shows us photos of the destruction of Timor and the poverty of the survivors of the Indonesian occupation. His battalion is to re-constitute and be ready to deploy again to East Timor in one years time, as Indonesian militias crossing the border continue to challenge UN forces. Successive governments have run the Army down to just five regular infantry battalions and much work is to be needed of all of them to meet commitments to concurrent crises in East Timor, Bougainville and the Solomon Islands.

Christy graduates from Mount St Michaels College in Ashgrove, and commences a degree in Commerce. She has been a very well balanced young lady, and has a wonderful circle of friends. She accepts a part time job in the Catholic Archdioceses' Human Relations office which is to develop into a full-time job. The Church assists her in completing her degree.

Our youngest child, Paul, is progressing through Marist College Ashgrove, participating in rugby, soccer, cross-country running, tennis, and martial arts. Following his Dad, and brother Michael, he is also a successful member of the local Army Cadet unit at Enoggera. His heart is set on a fulltime Army career, but rugby injuries to both knees are challenges he will have to overcome before doing so.

It is just great to be home. My nightmares are under control. My day to day lifestyle helps me manage tendencies for hyper-vigilance and hyper-activity. I continue meditation and regular exercise and positive thinking. I also get myself established in Chaplaincy at Enoggera, principally to the men of the 2nd /14th Light Horse Regiment, as they prepare to deploy to Timor.

Conducting a field service at Shoalwater Bay for Cavalry troops preparing for Timor deployment.

Army Chaplaincy in East Timor

On 16 August 2000 I arrive in East Timor aboard a RAAF C-130. As I gaze through the portholes with the plane crossing the southern coastline, I am amazed to look down upon village after village that has been razed to the ground. The lush green of the mountains seems out of place surrounding countless villages where only blackened cement walls rise up from the ground, and partially-burnt roof beams have collapsed in. We circle Dili before landing. It reminds me a little of Khoromshar in Iran which had also suffered total destruction. I shake my head in disbelief that the Indonesian military could have been so bloody-minded to cause this wanton destruction. No doubt the perpetrators were following orders from higher up their chain of command, for this was not just random acts of ill-discipline. A 'rogue element' cover story is promoted by the Australian Government in order to avoid directly confronting the Indonesian Government and its errant armed forces. What I see is a comprehensive, systematic logistic operation to steal and remove everything they could, and then burn and destroy everything else.

Scene of the massacre of 75 civilians in Maliana on 2 September 1999.

The tropical heat of Dili hits me as I alight from the plane and make my way to the Australian base in a burned-out school nearby. Major General Mike Smith, the tall and smiling UN Deputy Force Commander, who was two years ahead of me at Duntroon, greets me warmly, 'Welcome to Timor, Gary. Great to have you aboard!' Mike and I know each other well from several postings and he was in the same class at Command and Staff College. He now has responsibility to assist with the command and control of 15,000 troops from several regional and international armed forces. Mike invites me to dinner with him that night, much to the surprise of the other reinforcements I had flown in with. He apprises me of his frustration with the classic mandate of UN forces, which is to maintain the status quo, when this situation needs immediate and massive humanitarian relief and re-construction. Despite the massive numbers of UN personnel, including several engineering battalions, they appear to be uninterested in alleviating the needs of a people who have lost everything.

After a few days in Dili, I take over from Chaplain Mick Lappin, Chaplain at 6 RAR, who is also a Catholic deacon. Mick is a legend among the 6 RAR diggers who he knows intimately, and visits constantly. Mick takes me around the 18 posts we are manning across about 80 square kilometres of the western districts of East Timor. It takes three days to do this, stopping and offering a service at each location and spending time chatting.

On patrol in Bobonaro District East Timor August 2000.

In recent weeks there has been the accidental death of one of the armoured crewmen, Corporal 'Monsta' Jones. His rifle accidentally discharged in the back of an armoured vehicle. Another soldier is accidentally shot by his mate whilst cleaning his weapon in the week prior to my arrival. Additionally a New Zealand soldier, Private Leonard Manning, has just been shot, killed and mutilated by a militia patrol. Four Aussies have also been wounded by grenade explosions and are in hospital.

Mick departs and I settle in with my old battalion, 6 RAR. It's been 18 years since I served there as company commander. Some of the privates that once worked for me are now sergeants and warrant officers. It is great to catch up with old friends from not only 6 RAR, but also 8/9 RAR and 1 RAR days.

Chaplaincy on operations is exciting, although in many respects is not too different from the ministry I conduct on our exercises in Australia. People want to talk about their hopes and fears, concerns about loved ones, and affirmations or complaints about their bosses. They are particularly interested to hear what is happening in other platoons and companies. I develop a routine of visitation and conduct services at company and platoon bases. Indeed the Chaplain is the one the Commanding Officer relies on to find out what is really going on with the soldiers, and the only one in a unit who sees everyone regularly.

Communion Service Maliana East Timor.

At one remote platoon post a young soldier says to me, 'Padre, I'm worried about my girlfriend. We don't get any chance to communicate other than letters. About every 6 weeks we get to use a satellite phone for 10 minutes, but then she just tells me she's fed up with me being away. I'm worried I'm going to lose her.'

I reply, 'I'm happy to give her a ring and explain your circumstances.'

He replies, 'Please could you do that, as she can't understand why others in HQ are getting to ring home every night.'

Hope is what he is looking for. But I can't give him false expectations so I say to him, 'Relationships are two-way streets. We can't control them. We can just do our best to love each other.'

I then share with him the challenges that Lynne and I faced during our separations. After some discussion he concludes by thanking me, and then saying, 'I feel much better now having talked this over. I guess if she is the girl I'm meant to marry she will still be there when I get back.' (I do ring her up and meet her on my return, and they go on to get married, by me, a year later.)

With 6RAR diggers on patrol in Maliana August 2000.

There have been several militia attacks on isolated outposts in recent weeks, and although no-one is physically wounded, the guys have been shaken up by rifle fire and grenade attacks—eight explosions on one post. It is great to spend time with these men and bring a smile to their faces.

At a Section post in a village called Aidabasalala, which had recently been attacked, (and where our son Michael had spent several weeks over Christmas), a soldier boldly says to me, 'Padre it is a miracle none of us were killed or wounded.'

I reply, (with a smile), 'I'm sure it was, so I hope you thank God, and will start coming to church now!' I then spend hours just sitting with these guys chatting and listening. Humour is one way soldiers deal with some stressors, and where appropriate I joke and offer cheeky comments. Of course there are other situations, where I just sit quietly and listen. Sometimes without me hardly saying a word, soldiers will thank me so much for coming to see them, at a time when they just needed to vent or have some company. My presence seems to remind them of a reality and a hope that they hadn't thought of for a while. Privately, many soldiers share with me that they believe in God, but seem to have lost the practices of regular worship. Most are embarrassed and admit to feeling guilty that their lives have strayed from a moral base. I reassure them that God loves them and they can turn back to him at any time, just like the Prodigal son (Luke 15).

The most common request is, 'Padre would you say a prayer for me /my family /my mate?' I stop and pray there on the spot, aloud, and mark them with the sign of the cross. Afterwards they will grip my hand and frequently shed a tear.

With so much travel involved, I am conscious of the danger of a real enemy. Six 'shoot outs' with militia patrols, occur during my tour of duty. Numerous Militia groups of about 10 men are moving throughout the border area, trying to intimidate the local population, and proclaiming that they will take back the border districts in due course. Clearly there are several thousand militiamen just across the border. They have made bold attacks at our bases, and constantly put out propaganda of threatening major attacks upon us until we withdraw. They know this countryside better than us, and we are spread very thinly over a vast distance. We don't know how this situation is going to develop. In any case, I decide to carry a 9 mm Browning pistol in my pocket to protect the driver who takes me from base to base. It certainly feels good to have that weapon as an option.

In Iran we were not permitted to carry weapons, and I found it quite disarming (please pardon the pun). The powerlessness of that circumstance clearly added to my distress. But we were third parties to that conflict. Here in Timor we are on a mission to protect the population from criminals who had killed thousands of innocent civilians, and they are trying to kill us as well. The Catholic Church has long maintained a position that Christians have a right *and obligation* to protect the lives of the innocent as well as themselves, using the minimum force, but up to and including lethal force, if necessary. (*Catechism of the Catholic Church* paras 2302-2312).

I am travelling around in areas where militias are known to be active, and I consider I have an obligation to protect anyone I am travelling with. The driver has a rifle but he couldn't use it when driving, and if we are stopped or shot at, we need two firers to cover each other. Of course I am 100 percent convinced that the soldiers are on a 'just cause' mission and no one would be killed unless they were threatening someone else's life.

Every trip we undertake requires detailed orders and contingency plans in the event of enemy ambush. I joke with my drivers (they change daily), that I have already been taken captive once, and I am not going to let that happen again. In any case, I don't need to use the weapon, but am very happy that I have it. The drivers tell me that they are happy too, especially when word gets around that I am qualified as a marksman!

The predominant experience for me is the interaction I have with the local populace. The Timorese are wonderful welcoming people. They have suffered interminably from Portuguese and then Indonesian occupiers, and yet retain a dignity and resilience. By far their greatest strength has been their strong faith in God. Their faith has not only sustained them, but given them the courage to resist oppression until they achieved independence. Despite that, they are still in a desperate situation economically.

They have experienced total destruction of their infrastructure, and the United Nations is not going to fix that any time soon, and the army of emergency aid agencies in East Timor are moving very slowly—the UN effort is focused on security and conducting an election.

I am intrigued and disappointed that little is being done to meet basic infrastructure needs. Indeed it annoys me that several UN Engineer Battalions sit idle or play volleyball when there are so many needs they could meet. Others would advise me that of course they are there to support the UN force commander. They get paid the same for standing idle or for working. They don't work in order to preserve machinery and not have to spend money on fuel, maintenance and spare parts.

The prevailing official Australian Defence policy line, allegedly from Canberra, is that the soldiers shouldn't do anything to help the locals as they will become dependent on us, and we are in a process of drawing down and planning to pull out as soon as possible. Humanitarian Aid (HA) is allegedly the province of Non Government Organizations (NGO) but in reality there are none actively present in this area, as it is dangerous and still being contested by the militias. The HA policy is interpreted in a range of ways by various commanders, from some who tell their diggers they may not even give out lollies from their ration packs, to others who quietly ignore the policy and help the locals with school repairs and transport. My attitude is that we are human beings first, and if someone is in need and we have spare capacity to help them out, we should. All battalions have a civil liaison section that does engage with the locals, but their capacity to undertake HA is very limited.

This matter is perhaps the most controversial issue amongst the soldiers who on the whole want to help out. I think that I can do something to assist the local people from my parish in Brisbane, no matter what others are, or are not, planning.

East Timor–'Loving our Neighbour'   163

Friends and Partners with East Timor (FPET)

I record in my diary how, on my departure from the border, the parish priest of Atabae, Divine Word Missionary, Father Andreas Hane tells me, 'We are going to need your help for the next 15 years.'

I say to him, 'I will tell the people of my parish of your needs.'

In a tone of desperation, he simply asks me, 'Please don't forget us.'

I wonder how many others have said they will do something to help, only to be never heard from again. I will be true to my word, in sharing the story, but I wonder what we can realistically get done from so far away.

As I am leaving Dili, I go to the National Hospital to check on a lady, Madaleina, and her new-born child, Bendita de Sina, whose birth I had assisted with in Maliana several days before. The survival of the child is a miracle in itself. There had been significant birth difficulties—the baby just wouldn't come out and the waters had been burst for almost a day. A doctor from 'Medicines Sans Frontiers' who was assisting with many emergency treatments in the hopelessly understaffed Maliana District Hospital thought the child may have died within the womb, and the mother was also likely to die from blood loss. I was called up to give the last rites. With the mother lying on a stretcher on the floor, I introduce myself to her as 'the Padre.'

My diary of 7 September 2000 records:

> I pray over Madaleina, and then see her eyes light up as she has a massive contraction and the baby pops out! It is limp and blue and scarcely breathing; so I pray some more and hold its tiny hand—it kicks into life with crying. Thanks be to God. I ask the Army to fly them both by helicopter to Dili, which they do.

Upon finding them in the hospital, they are both doing well. She says to me as I am leaving, 'Please don't forget us!'—the same phrase that Father Andreas had used. The words haunt me—it is as if *forgetting* is what they thought we had been doing for the previous 24 years!

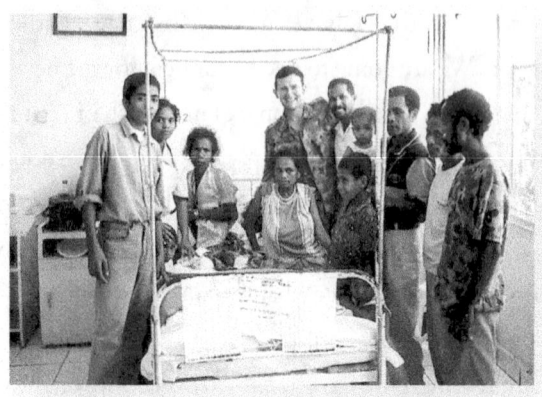

Madaleina with her miracle child I helped her deliver—she appeals to me, 'Please don't forget us'.

Early steps in humanitarian assistance

On numerous retreats I have been reminded that, come Judgment Day, we will not be asked by God how many medals we have won, how many degrees we have to our name, or how much money we have made, rather we will be asked how we have cared for the poor, clothed the naked, given water to the thirsty, and fed the hungry.

And so, upon return to Australia I share my experiences, and the needs of the Timorese in formal talks at Masses in various parishes around Brisbane. In Atabae, as in most villages, the needs are immense— they have no clean water, their schools have been destroyed, their electricity generators have been stolen by withdrawing Indonesian units, and they have no medicine or doctors. We raise about $10,000 in late 2000 from parish talks that I give, and in 2001 I take back two ex-army mates, Peter de Haas, a communications engineer, and Peter Fitzsimmons, a technician and tradesman, to survey what else we could do to help.

In faith we fly to Dili, hire a vehicle and take off for the border. The locals do not know that we are coming—we have no way to communicate. We arrive at the burned out shell of a parish school, where children are sitting on the ground. I ask a teacher in my limited Timorese language (Tetum), 'Where is Padre?' Within minutes we are surrounded by a hundred children, all intrigued to see and touch us.

It appears that the parish priest has changed over, and the new one, Father Marsellus Banoule, is brought to us. He is delightfully astounded that I have come back. Fortunately for us he can speak some English. After explaining what we are offering, he says to us, 'You are truly an answer to our prayers. I have only been here a few weeks and I have felt overwhelmed with the needs. Just last weekend I was telling the people in Mass that we must pray that someone will help us. And here you are!'

I return to East Timor in 2001 to initiate a humanitarian mission— meeting with Brother Hendricus, Peter de Haas, Father Marcellus and Francisco (Atabae village chief) to discuss priorities.

For the next two weeks we travel with him around the expansive rural parish—with no radio, no electricity, sleeping in village huts, eating local food with the villagers, (and getting sick from it), and all the time learning more about their situation. Out of this visit, in consultation with the Timorese, we agree on establishing an association called *Friends and Partners with East Timor*, with me as its spiritual director. Peter de Haas agrees to be our first President, and we meet monthly at his home in Brisbane—with, on average, about 12 faithful apostles wanting to improve the lot of the Timorese.

These early days are challenging, as we have no easy way of communicating with the Timorese parish from Australia. We have to rely on hand-written messages passed on by soldiers coming and going. We raise awareness and money through talks I give around Brisbane, using PowerPoint presentations with lots of photos I have taken. Priority for our early donations goes to financial assistance to widows and orphans, medical supplies, and emergency food supplementation. Jesus would be proud.

Concerned about developing the relationship in the absence of communications, in September 2002 I conduct my third visit to the border, this time alone, taking our collected funds with me in cash. Our partner parish of Atabae has approximately 10,000 people (all Catholic) living in 17 communities spread throughout the area. Father Marsellus Banoule, Br Hendricus Ulan, Parish Catechist Ms Fatima Soares, and two Catechists in each village provide spiritual leadership and points of contact. The Catechists lead daily prayer in the villages, provide pastoral care to their people, prepare candidates for baptism, confirmation and marriage, and preside over funerals. The confidence and responsibility placed in Catechists and their daily witness to their people provides the model of Christian living to the villagers. Father Marsellus conducts a 'patrol' around the villages for two weeks of every month. Participating in this patrol is the highlight of my visit this year, and a feature of each subsequent visit. The roads are rough beyond imagining, and my back aches from all the bumps we experience in a small Honda four-wheel drive. At one point we lose braking power, and discover that the front left disc brake assembly has come lose and is trailing on the ground! Father Marsellus somehow puts it back in place. I find myself praying about personal safety through the rest of our journey.

Travelling to each village, we are met joyfully by the parishioners, welcomed formally in a ritual of sharing betel nut and drinks of coconut juice (which invariably gives me diarrhoea). We have a community meeting, where Marsellus asks all groups within the village to share their achievements and needs. I take copious notes in my journal, but also tell them that it will take many years for all these needs to be met.

I ask them, 'What is one small thing we could do for your village?' Some ask for a generator, some for a few lanterns, and some for a medical kit. One village, Aidabasalala, asks whether we could provide them with a metal tabernacle where they could reserve the Blessed Sacrament—the consecrated bread signifying the presence of Jesus. I am impressed by their frankness and honesty and commitment to improve the lot of their people.

Following the community meeting, we celebrate Mass, during which I preach, affirming our love for them and our desire to be in a long-term relationship with them. During some of the masses we also have baptisms or marriages. At the end of each Mass I sing them a hymn in English, 'I will never forget you my people, I have carved you on the palm of my hand. I will never forget you, I will not leave you orphaned, and I will never forget my own.' It is a popular hymn of the time, putting in music the words of the prophet Isaiah (Chapter 49). Afterwards Father Marsellus explains what the translation is, and they invariably break out in clapping and cheering, bringing tears to my eyes. A community meal follows—with rice and chicken being the norm (and a new wave of stomach pain and diarrhoea).

As the sun goes down, the light goes out as well, and we experience life in a society that no longer has electricity-good for dialogue, but difficult in every other respect. No way to pump water, no communication, no refrigeration, no use of electrical appliances, TV or radio—all services that they had enjoyed pre-1999. As a military man I am particularly conscious of the absence of access to emergency medical treatment.

I come to realise these people are our brothers and sisters-the neighbours Jesus talks about in the Gospel. They are extremely grateful for our friendship, but they deserve our financial support to help them re-establish basic services. They have no money, their Government has no money, and other aid organisations have come, done a little, and left. I am delighted we can now share in paying the price for their freedom. I return to Australia with a renewed fire in my belly to win them some more support.

Getting serious about loving our neighbours

On one Sunday in late 2002, in our Catholic parish of The Gap in Brisbane. I am merciless in my preaching to see some serious charity delivered.

> *'These people are the neighbours Jesus asks us to love. We can make a big difference to their lives. We can save the lives of some of their children who will die without medical support and transport. I will not rest until we have assisted them in their time of crisis. Please join us in this mission! Give as generously as God has been generous to you!'*

East Timor–'Loving our Neighbour' 169

I raise $70,000 in cash after preaching at four Masses!

The parish in Atabae asks to have a four-wheel drive pick-up truck as their first priority. The 10,000 people of the parish need a reliable vehicle to help them with any medical emergency, let alone transport key supplies. We purchase a Toyota twin-cab tray-back, from our donations and pack it with medical supplies. Our first treasurer, Jack Brady, drives it to Darwin and gets it on a ship to Dili. On my next trip later in the year, I see it carrying about twenty students in the small tray! Other funds go to materials to rebuild chapels and schools. Some good work is commenced but much more needs to be done. 30 years more work at least is my estimate!

I reflect that the Holy Spirit is richly blessing this particular missional work I have initiated between the people of East Timor and Catholic parishioners in Brisbane. Indeed, I believe the power of the Spirit can make a difference in whatever we do to make the world a better place. I am deeply engaged spiritually by what is happening here. Up until this point I have been working all my life within the framework and protection of the military and then the church hierarchy. Now I am launching out without this 'top cover'. Indeed my 'top cover' is coming from God alone. I don't go anywhere to get permission for these trips, and equally when in country we don't have the luxury of radio communications, helicopters or doctors to support us. We are 'flying on faith' and this is the most enervated I have ever felt in my life. I am sensing that this mission of love to our neighbours is becoming central to my life's work for God at this point.

My ongoing experience in Timor seems to be fulfilling many of the words of sacred scripture, including where St. Mark (Chap 16) records the words of Jesus:

> *'Go throughout the whole world and proclaim the good news to all creation. In my name lay hands on the sick and they will become well'.*

Much more is to follow, but in 2001 other tasks beckon—the Army wants me to go to Bougainville on another peacekeeping mission.

Chapter 8
Peacekeeping in Bougainville

'Me alright now—I got Jesus in me!'—A Bougainvillean lady's response to ministry.

On 6 June 2001, I am peering down from the porthole of a C130 transport aircraft at the lush green forests and mountains of central Bougainville, Papua New Guinea's (PNG) most eastern island province. Circling Kieta airfield, I can see outline of trenches that were dug by the Bougainville Revolutionary Army across the tarmac during the Bougainville Civil War to deny its use to the PNG Defence Force (PNGDF). New Zealand peacekeepers filled them in and restored the runway in November 1997. The pilot is circling now so he can be certain that there are no animals or obstructions on the runway to endanger our landing. He comes in hard and we have a bumpy touch down on this remote war-torn tropical island. A wave of hot, steaming, almost claustrophobic, humidity hits me as I walk down the ramp to begin a three-month tour of duty as a chaplain with the Peace Monitoring Group (PMG).

This place is significant both personally and historically. My uncle Jack fought the Japanese in Bougainville with the 61st Battalion during the last months of the Pacific Campaign in 1945. This is where he really started struggling with mental health issues as he and his mates were pushed forward into the jungle against an unseen enemy who inflicted many casualties, in what was really an unnecessary campaign at this late stage of the war. I have longed to see that terrain he fought over and contemplate what it might have been like for him.

We are here because of the Bougainville Crisis that erupted in 1989 when Bougainvillean saboteurs forced closure of a huge Australian-owned copper mine. The Crisis has claimed thousands of lives and ruined many others through physical and mental illnesses. The Crisis threatened the sovereignty of PNG, as well as its nationhood, and cut deep divisions between PNG's political leadership and its armed forces. The elderly, and women and children, suffered the most through displacement and lack of medical services, as well as the intimidation and violence of the PNGDF and marauding gangs of young Bougainvillean men.

After eight years of suffering and isolation from the world, New Zealand facilitated a peace to keep in Bougainville, and military and civilian peacekeepers from Australia, Fiji, New Zealand and Vanuatu landed at Arawa in central Bougainville in November 1997. They spread out among the people and set up five remote peace monitoring camps to monitor and facilitate a journey to a peace agreement that is due to be signed in a few months time in August 2001.

I am well placed to make a difference. Brigadier Mike Swan, the PMG Commander is a close friend from my Duntroon days in the early 1970s. We had played hockey together, and we both made Christian commitments whilst we were cadets at Duntroon. We deepened our friendship over the year we spent together at the Army Command and Staff College at Fort Queenscliff in 1983.

Also, I had got to know the former Commander of the Bougainville Revolutionary Army, General Sam Kaouna, at Portsea, located on the tip of the Mornington Peninsula south of Melbourne in 1985 where he completed officer training for a career in the PNGDF.

It will be great to support Mike and the men and women he commands and to meet up with Sam and encourage him in the peace process. Mike has told me in advance by phone, that while I am in Bougainville he expects me to coordinate PMG support for the celebrations of 100 years of Christianity in Bougainville. He hopes that 20, 000 people, almost one quarter of the population of 80,000, will attend Mass at Loloho, a few kilometres north of Arawa.

As I walk down the ramp of the C 130, and onto the blistering hot tarmac, a smiling Phil Anderson, the PMG chaplain I am relieving, meets me with a cool bottle of water saying, 'Welcome to Bougainville Gary. You are going to love it here.' We jump into a Landrover and head off in convoy to the PMG's home base for 180 members located adjacent to the old copper wharf at Loloho, just north of the main town of Arawa. 10 years before, this had been a bustling paradise, carved out of the jungle by Con-Zinc Rio-Tinto. Modern houses, a golf course, a modern hospital and sealed roads allowed expatriate staff to manage the huge open-cut copper mine and extract copper for export to the world. The mine's royalties provided almost 50 percent of the PNG budget.

The devastation of eight years of civil war is everywhere. The hospital and town centre at Arawa have been destroyed. The mining facilities, hotels and houses have been stripped, and the steaming jungle has consumed and grown over the skeletons of buildings that remain. The PMG is sustained by resupply from Australia. A weekly RAAF C130 transport aircraft flies in food and other supplies. Australian Army helicopters fly peacekeepers around the island. By the time I arrive in 2001, the Loloho camp is well set up, although everyone lives in tents under a huge mining shed.

Phil and I have a very strong resemblance, and also a similar cheery, positive attitude. He is a Uniting Church minister who had been a barber before a minister. His barbering skills enabled him to get to know everyone quickly. But I will not be providing haircuts every afternoon at 1600hours like he has!

Phil says to me, 'Gary, this has been a wonderful experience. We've a great bunch of people, and there is so much to do here. The Fijians and the Vanuatans really know how to engage with the locals. The Aussies and Kiwis are better at administration and logistics. I've been trying to get out and about as much as possible.'

I reply, 'Show me what you've been doing and I will continue in your footsteps.'

My first port of call after dropping my bags at the chaplaincy tents is to go to the mission headquarters to catch up with my new boss and my great friend Mike Swan. Wearing the trademark PNG yellow T-shirt and khaki shorts, Mike greets me with a beaming smile, a firm handshake and a strong hug. It has actually been several years since we have seen each other, but it doesn't seem that long at all, as we catch up on happenings in each other's families and what we have been doing personally in the military. Mike says to me, 'Gary this is the best job I have ever had in my army career, and it will probably also be my last. I have been here four months already and four more to go, and I plan to enjoy every day of it. We have made some really great progress in facilitating dialogue among the various parties in this dispute and please God, will have formal peace agreement signed within a few months.'

I ask him, 'What would you like me to do for you chaplaincy wise?'

He replies, 'Well you are the Chaplain, mate. What do you think you should be doing ?'

I respond, 'The very first thing I would like to do is to get out and about and certainly get to meet all of our Peace Monitoring Group members, but I also would like to liaise with the various church leaders.'

He replies, 'Gary, develop your own plan and go for it. It is just so good to have you here. I'm going to appreciate your friendship and company. I will be present at all of your church services. And I would appreciate you being my eyes and ears out on the ground, and keeping me informed of the good things that are happening and the potential things that might cause us grief. Oh, and by the way, Sam Kauona came down to see me from his mountain village retreat last week, and he looks forward to catching up with you in due course. We can have lunch together on his next visit. Sam is such a gentleman. It is hard to imagine the negative press that he got some years ago. He is a definite supporter of the peace process.'

After meeting and greeting numerous other people on this busy first day, and after saying goodnight to Phil, I sit on a chair outside my tent, taking in the stars and the coolness of the evening, and am overtaken by an emotional high. Yes this mission is going to be great. After all the stressors that I have had in recent years, it just seems like I have found an ideal situation to be a good servant of God, and his people in a wholly supportive environment.

In the first few days Phil takes me on a helicopter tour to the five remote sites where we have peace monitoring teams of about 12 people-a mixture of military monitors from Australia, New Zealand, Vanuatu and Fiji and a twenty-strong contingent of Australian civil service monitors from Defence, Foreign Affairs, Australian Federal Police and AUSAID.

After a one-week handover, Phil flies out on the weekly courier and I set to work developing my own ministry in this new mission.

A little background

As I sit at the altar in the local Catholic church at Sunday Mass at Arawa, on 28 June 2001, looking out on a sea of pitch black, smiling faces, I reflect on how my involvement with Bougainville goes back to 1984 at the Officer Cadet School, Portsea, where I was the Senior Instructor. Sam Kaouna was one of two PNG students, doing the course with the Aussies and Kiwis and two Fijians. It was tough going for Pacific Islanders. They had to cope with our language and the cold weather and still pass in all subjects to the standard of the Aussies. Most years one or two Pacific Islanders would be returned home 'NUTS'—'not up to standard'.

I got to know Sam better than most, as he came along to church and Bible study. He was a man of faith. He powered through the course and graduated into the PNGDF Engineers. He was different and more capable than his peers. He was also black as black can be. I didn't realise at the time the significant cultural difference there was between the 'Bukas' of Bougainville and the 'Redskins' from mainland PNG.

Just a few years later, I hear that Sam has left the PNGDF to raise a group of separatists known as the Bougainville Revolutionary Army (BRA) who sought independence from PNG. I am a bit puzzled at this. The media are portraying Sam's 'BRA' as a group of thugs. I just can't work out how this faith-filled Christian man is now being portrayed as a violent criminal. Of course there are two sides to every story and it isn't till I get to work in the ADF Command Centre in 1991 that I become aware of some of the facts behind the Bougainville Crisis. By this stage the Australian Government has been supporting the PNGDF with helicopters, arms, ammunition and all sorts of other equipment to stamp out this secessionist movement. I had remained puzzled about the negative propaganda about Sam.

When I meet him again in July 2001 he hasn't changed much at all. Indeed from his perspective, he has followed his conscience to defend his people against the brutality of the PNG police and military that had started beating and killing people in response to the sabotage of the mine. Sam and his followers were also taking up arms against the corruption of a PNG government that was receiving massive royalties from mining operations but was not providing adequate services to Bougainvilleans.

My developing awareness of international affairs in our region leads me to the conclusion that Australia has misread, misunderstood, or perhaps ignored the genuine aspirations of Pacific Islanders who are fed up with the inadequacies of post-colonial government models.

Working at the ADF Command Centre in Canberra gave me some insight into Australian thinking about the South Pacific. The Departments of Defence and the Department of Foreign Affairs and Trade had different interests and approaches. In the 1980s and early 1990s, Australian governments did not want to get into practical intervention and risk being seen as a neo-colonialist despite deteriorating political, economic and social conditions. Australia was not a good neighbour to these struggling new nations.

PMG Bougainville is the watershed in positive Australian responses to crises in the South Pacific. Military and civilian Australians deploy together to support peace for the first time. Personal contact releases a mysterious peacemaking power that emanates from human beings of different cultures when they come together in common purpose. People look each other in the eye, acknowledge the truth of a situation, and encourage each other to find solutions.

Chaplaincy to the troops

Setting up a routine is important for being a chaplain to troops on operations. It is particularly helpful that the troops know when you are going to be visiting. I sketch out a simple weekly plan that Brigadier Mike endorses.

I will conduct services in Arawa and Loloho on Sundays. Sunday mornings, I co-worship with one of the local Arawa denominations-Catholic, Anglican, United, Pentecostal (x3), or Seventh Day Adventist-at their local churches, and take some of the PMG people with me. Sunday lunch is for 'communion' with the non-churchgoers at Loloho PMG base. Sunday afternoon I wander round the Loloho base and catch up with folks in recreation mode. Sunday evening I lead a service in our open-air, grass-roof PMG Peace Chapel. Starting with a core of a six or seven, over time we build up to about 25 regulars. We have a joyful celebration singing, preaching and distributing Holy Communion.

I am to be the last full-time PMG chaplain. The ADF wants to 'down-size' its numbers in Bougainville. Following me, the ADF will just send a Chaplain for one week every month or so. Right from the start I develop a plan for laypeople to lead worship after I depart. The mission Chief of Staff, Lieutenant Colonel Warwick Jones, a tall, handsome artillery officer, is to remain on after me, so I ask him if he could lead weekly worship after I depart. He agrees, and I start weekly training sessions with him on a range of ministry functions.

Monday is to be my weekly day off. I have learned that I need to have measures in place to minimise the chances of the PTSD 'monster' biting me. Right from the start I consider it is important to maintain my own health and spiritual fitness and recreation. So I do my morning physical training, have a swim in the bay and then head off by dinghy with a few of the off-shift medical staff to a small beach on the other side of the bay. The place has been named 'Bonnie Doon', and it is perfect for relaxation. We snorkel on the reefs, explore the jungle, read and rest on the sand, and prepare our own lunch. Returning in the afternoon, I send emails to some friends and family, and I even complete a major article for the *Australasian Catholic Record* on 'The Married Catholic Deacon in today's church.'

Monday night is also my scheduled time to ring Lynne and the children in Brisbane. PNG members are permitted to make one ten minute phone call every week to their families. The restricted outside contact is the result of the remote location of this mission and limited and expensive satellite linkage that is needed to communicate back to Australia. I find it difficult to have a really good conversation with Lynne throughout the mission, as the limited time to say hello to each of the family members, makes it difficult to talk about anything substantial. We supplement this contact by writing a long letter to each other each week, in which we can get more intimate, but the absence from each other is still difficult. I distract myself from this by immersing myself fully in the mission at hand. I realise as before that I will need to be making a substantial investment in my marriage and family upon return.

Tuesdays, I head off by helicopter to the remote team sites. One week I go north to Buka and Wakunai. The alternate week I go to Sirikatau and Kanga in the central mountains, and then Buin in the far south. Basically we have set up a monitoring team in each location where the BRA had a company of soldiers—five locations in all. Each team has a Lieutenant Colonel in charge of a mix of civilian peace monitors, supported by a military operations and administrative staff. They live in houses near the local people, and have only military radio contact with us at Loholo, and no contact with Australia. For most monitors this is a great cultural shock, and they welcome my visits. I spend one night at each site before catching the helicopter back to Loloho.

Invariably people have concerns that they ask me to listen to. In the remoteness of the mission, and the absence of any team-building prior to the mission, there are numerous tensions among the diverse groups we have in place. On my first visit to the Kanga patrol base, a female defence civilian monitor calls me aside and tells me of a range of difficulties that she is having in working with the particular army major who is the operations officer for the base. I listen patiently to her story and then explore what other issues might be of concern to her. She acknowledges that she is very homesick, and missing any regular contact with her children. I offer to dialogue with the army major and should there not be subsequently any improvement in relations, to raise the matter with our headquarters staff. I also offer to pray with her. I gently put my hand on her shoulder and say a simple prayer of blessing. At the end of this she bursts into tears and gives me a big hug. 'Thank you so much Gary I really needed that. I do have a faith and realise now I should be exercising a little bit more. Thanks so much. I really appreciate you coming to visit us.'

Later, I get some time with the major, and before I can say anything, he launches out saying, 'No doubt 'so and so' has had a whinge to you about me. I am not the problem, she is!' He then details a list of concerns that he has, about her. After listening patiently, I ask him, 'Well mate, I can see this is a difficult situation for everyone, but is there anything that you can do that will ease the tension here. He replies, 'The only thing that will improve the situation here is for her to leave.'

I reply, 'My experience is that the only people that we can change in life are ourselves. I just had a chat to her. I think you both can take a slightly different attitude to things. Can you please give her another chance? I'll be back in two weeks and if nothing has improved by then we can elevate the situation for the headquarters to look into.'

I return two weeks later and amazingly both of them, whilst not 100% happy, tell me that they have worked things out a little, and would like to get on with the job without getting the headquarters involved. Wow, I feel good about that. I reflect how amazing it is to just give someone a listening ear, to let them unburden and work out a solution for themselves.

It also makes me reflect that in the difficulties of this austere environment, our Defence and Foreign Affairs monitors are to get valuable insight into the lives of soldiers that will be of benefit to all concerned for years to come, as we see much greater co-operation and interaction between the various arms of government. It is just as valuable to have the civilians see the benefit of Chaplains too! I am to help many of them out as they struggle with separation from family, and the culture shock of this very isolated post.

I make a point in each location to also engage with local church leaders and hear their stories, whilst sharing how the PMG could help them. I have to educate our team members about the importance of the church in the lives of the local people. Many secular Australians overlook or do not comprehend the importance of religion in the lives of others. It has been a deficiency in all the missions I serve in, and something that I have worked hard at explaining, in training that I subsequently conduct.

In Bougainville and elsewhere the churches have been the key players in both peacemaking and reconciliation. They are going to be still doing this after we leave and we cannot really do our job well, without collaborating with them. Some Aussies still seem to have a cultural aversion to working with the churches, which is a great disappointment. It is a real blind spot which our Pacific Island brothers and sisters can't understand.

Buka is my favourite team site. Major Greg Walker, a tall Military Police investigator, is the Operations Officer there during my time. He always asks me to conduct a service and takes me around his patch, showing me off to the local people. He values religion and religious leaders, and I feel that as a result of his work and approach, this is a more peaceful area than the others, where random acts of violence and drunkenness are more common.

A visit to Buka also enables me to catch up with the local Marist Fathers, whose religious order priests care for our parish in The Gap in Brisbane. The Marists have been in Bougainville for 100 years. I love to listen to their stories and gain their perspective on what has happened here. Whilst always on the side of Peace, they are critical of the earlier brutal behaviour of PNGDF soldiers and Australia's earlier support for them. The Marists have been the primary providers of education and health care here throughout the last 100 years. During every visit I have long conversations with Father Kevin Kirley, a frail, thin priest from Brisbane, who has spent 50 years on the island. He has agonized over the violence perpetrated by all parties, and has shared in the starvation and isolation that the PNGDF blockade had caused. I am cautious of not wanting to dig too deep into his trauma knowing how much my own recollections have further distressed me at times. He knows all the key players intimately, but has been ignored in diplomatic dialogues. I pass on much of the information he shares with me, to PMG Headquarters staff, but I am disappointed that little comes of it initially. Subsequently I tell Brig Mike about this, and with agreement of the chief civilian monitor, the PNG commences an engagement program with the key religious leaders.

I return from the remote team sites on a Friday and visit our team in Arawa, which is also our area of greatest problems with the locals. Arawa has become a ghetto town with 'rascals' coming in from the mountains, getting on the 'jungle juice' (home-brewed alcohol) and getting into criminality. The victims of rape and assault regularly present themselves at the Arawa medical facility that I visit weekly. Our PMG vehicles are occasionally hit by stones, and theft is commonplace. There is no effective police or judiciary in Bougainville at this stage. Members of the PMG are unarmed and have no powers of arrest or detention. We have to leave the community to respond to the criminal behaviour of gangs of young men. Most villages have a self protection system where elders mete out tribal justice to miscreants. This form of justice is brutal. Someone found guilty of a misdemeanour will normally be beaten with sticks, and sent out of the village for a certain period to fend for themselves.

Personal safety for peace monitors is stressed and practiced. We have the right to defend and protect ourselves in self defence. Every week we participate in several sessions of self-defence training, using boxing techniques and riot batons with plenty of gusto. We only travel in groups of two or more. There is no movement by night unless in an emergency. In the physical training sessions I seem to always get teamed up with an SAS Sergeant who has been a contestant on the *Gladiator* television series. He gives me really solid workouts, a few bruises, and I lose plenty of sweat.

Saturdays start early with a 10 km 'fun run', and a refreshing swim in the bay. I then get around Loloho and drop in on people in their workplaces. In the afternoon I prepare my services for Sunday. And so the cycle rolls on ...

Work with the health team

My tent in Loloho is co-located with the Combined Health Centre. These people are a major component of our team, and critical for the local people as well. We have to be able to provide the highest level of life-saving health care for peacekeepers. Indeed there are no other immediate options available on the Island, and we have no on-site fixed wing aircraft to evacuate anyone to a proper hospital. Any major evacuation aircraft would have to be sourced from Cairns or Townsville, at least three hours flight away. We thus have on-site, a range of surgical, pathology, X-ray and in-patient nursing staff. I take particular note of the preventative health staff, who conduct training in health awareness and disease prevention. I am to learn a lot about health from the staff, which is to be of great value to me later in Timor. I witness numerous injured locals being brought in with broken limbs, machete wounds, burns, and concussion from falling coconuts, and I observe their treatment.

A Miracle?

One night, the senior army medical officer (SMO), Dr David, comes to my tent and asks me, 'Gary, can you come in to theatre to give the last rites to a dying man? This man is named Cornelius, and he has a gunshot wound to the head'. Andrew Bourke, a 26-year-old Australian volunteer doctor who is running the Arawa government clinic with almost no equipment and little medicine, has brought him in.

Doctor David explains to me, 'He has taken a bullet in the jaw, smashing it, and it has ricocheted upwards. The bullet is now inside his skull and inoperable in terms of our capacity. He will possibly die very soon. We don't have any intensive care life support equipment for a case like this. There is little that we can do for him except keep him comfortable. He also has lost an enormous amount of blood'.

The operating theatre is just a tent with portable equipment around the walls. A local friend named Michael is comforting Cornelius, who is lying on the gurney in the centre of the tent. He appears lifeless, lying there in just a pair of shorts and nothing else. About six theatre staff are around us. Their faces are downcast.

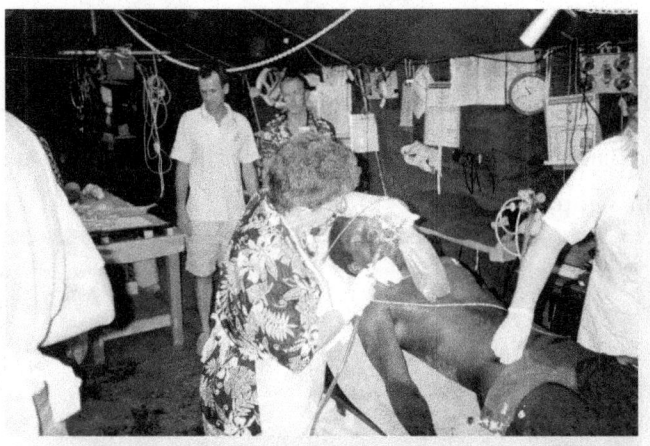

In Bougainville 2001 — Cornelius is near death.

I ask Michael, 'What would you like me to do?' Michael replies, 'Father, please pray that he would live.' He catches me out with this request. I think that even if he does come through, he will most likely have brain damage. His desire challenges me and I am conscious that any prayers to keep him alive might not be successful.

At that moment, I remember that wonderful statement in the scripture where Jesus tells us that if we have faith even as small as a mustard seed, we could move mountains (*Luke* 17:6). I realise I have to put away the prayers for the dying, and begin praying for him to live. I lay one hand on his head, and with the other hold his right hand and pray for life to return to him. I look up to see that he is almost 'flat-lining' on the heart monitor. I ponder, 'What else can I do?' For a Catholic, the most life giving experience is to receive Jesus in Holy Communion. I clearly can't do this for Cornelius, as a tube fills his mouth and he is comatose. But I get out a consecrated host from my pyx and bless him with it and then give it to Michael to consume for him.

I give Michael the host, knowing that he is also praying for his friend to live. The heart monitor jumps into life. I keep praying and in a few minutes a normal pulse resumes! The staff are amazed. I am ecstatic. My heart starts to race, but with excitement this time, not with anxiety. I really am so excited. I believe I have witnessed a miracle! Thanks be to God!

Cornelius alive seven days later—thanks be to God.

Of course Cornelius isn't out of danger yet. He still has a broken jaw and major tissue damage, and could possibly have infection. A nurse puts him on a drip and gives him a blood transfusion made up of blood that the staff donate on the spot. He is lying there in a coma, and I leave him for the night. Providentially, on the resupply plane coming in on the day following, there is a facial-cranial specialist, who is able to put his jaw back together.

Amazingly, seven days later, Cornelius is discharged. The bullet remains inside his skull. Clearly Michael tells Cornelius of the prayers that had been said for him, as on discharge he comes up to me and hugs me and says, 'Thank you so much for praying for me. My wontok, Michael, tell me you save my life.'

I say, 'I think God and the medical staff saved you Cornelius. God loves you and wants you to be a peacemaker in this place. We should pour out our gratefulness to God.'

I see him at Mass at the local Catholic Church at Loloho every time I go there subsequently.

I believe this was a miracle. This was an extraordinary medical event to say the least. Certainly no further medical intervention was going to be given to him at the point I was invited in. There was nothing more medically that could be done in this remote location for a man with a bullet inside his skull apart from comfort him. I had always heard of miraculous healings, and there are many listed in the Bible. In this, I think I witness one first hand. This is truly a moment of grace that has subsequently encouraged me to pray boldly, even in the most difficult of circumstances ever since.

Over the coming days and weeks, I ponder this incident frequently. In humility I certainly don't want to take on some aura of being a miracle worker. But reflecting on the images I have in my mind of standing over Cornelius and holding his hand and from the depths of my heart wishing, hoping, praying, desiring, that he live, I feel some satisfaction that my presence in some way made a positive difference in the outcome of his circumstances.

I go through my Bible, and reread some of the healing miracles of Jesus. There were no magic formulas, no specific sets of words or actions that he used, other than his loving presence and desire for healing of the people who were in need of help. The image that comes to my mind of what may have happened here, is that I was simply a channel of God's grace where God's love in life giving energy, passed from God through me to Cornelius. God wanted him to live and he used my hands to touch him into life. Jesus says frequently in the Bible that we should pray about all manner of things, and surely praying in faith and hope to save the life of another person is an entirely natural, normal, and appropriate thing to do.

Meeting with General Sam Kaouna and Brigadier Mike Swan.

Meeting up with General Sam

About four weeks into the mission Mike tells me at our Sunday service that General Sam Kaouna is about to come down from the mountains, and would like to meet with us. I am excited at the prospect of this. A few days later we meet for lunch in Mike's bungalow in Arawa. Sam is already there when I arrive. At first sight he appears to have changed very little in the 16 years since we last met. Dressed simply in shirt, shorts and sandals, he gives me a firm handshake and a welcoming smile where his bright white teeth and eyes contrast markedly to his jet black face.

There are so many questions that I would like to ask him in relation to how he left the PNGDF, how he raised the Bougainville

Revolutionary Army, and how he survived over the many years of conflict, but he leads the conversation by telling me, 'It is so wonderful that you now are a Minister of the Catholic Church. We need more married Catholic clergy like you! My wife Josephine is Catholic but my village is almost all United Church people and we rarely see a Catholic Minister. I have told my wife about you and she is looking forward to meeting you at the 100 year celebrations.'

I reply, 'Thank you Sam. It is so great to see you looking so well. I have prayed for you many times over the years, and have been so impressed that you have had the courage and commitment to provide leadership to your people. I can't imagine how challenging the years of conflict must have been.'

He replies, 'Gary I have put the past behind me. There are too many bad memories for me to dwell on, and now I just want to see us move towards peace, and an autonomous political situation for us, and personally I would like to just enjoy time with my extended family in my village in the mountains.'

I can sense he does not want to talk about the conflict and so I don't bring it up. We go on to have a cordial time at lunch where he asks me about various staff and students that we both knew at the Officer Cadet School Portsea. Contrary to the earlier media reports of him being some fierce, out of control, out of his mind, criminal thug, the Sam that I am sharing with just seems to be little different to the gentle giant that I had known some years earlier. As we end our lunch, he asks, 'Gary would you pray for us now, praying for peace and prosperity for the people of Bougainville.' I respond with a heartfelt prayer, and tears streaming down my face, contemplating how God has brought us together, and how our shared faith unites us as brothers in Christ.

Collaboration with the local ministers.

I identified earlier how I considered that minimal church engagement has been a particular 'blind spot' on the part of Australian Peacemakers. Brigadier Mike and I reflect that Australians and most Westerners generally see a particular distinction between church and state in society, and are unaware that this is not the case in all societies.

In any case, I see, and Mike agrees, that this is an area I can fruitfully contribute in, particularly with the relationships I have with the Marist fathers, who had brought Christianity to the island. I start off by contacting by satellite phone, two priests in Australia who had spent long terms here—Father Seamus Mc Mahon and Father John Begg. They apprise me of key characters in the society, the characteristics and divisions amongst the churches, and of the importance to build relationships.

I then set about contacting all seven church leaders in Arawa and invite them to a meeting, so that we could all meet each other, and I could explore how the PMG could support them. I get support for this from the Catholics, Anglicans, United, Apostolic, Pentecostal, and Assembly of God pastors, but not the Seventh Day Adventists (SDA). I don't fully understand why the SDA won't participate, but apparently in this area they just don't mix with others. In any case, we have a fruitful gathering and some shared prayer. The United Church minister is full of praise for this initiative and indicates it is the first time they had all got together since the start of the crisis over 13 years before! I am really quite astounded that he would say this. Clearly there are tensions among these groups that I do not yet understand, but I know that God would bless any unity that we could achieve.

Having established contact at the grass roots level, I then seek to make contact with the Provincial church leaders. Our Fijian team

Leader in Buka, Lieutenant Colonel David is delighted to assist with gathering the Provincial leaders in Buka, and is able to arrange a meeting at Buka PMG team site. It becomes clear to me in the meeting that these men have been deeply grieved by the events of the crisis, and desperately want peace to be returned. They also struggle with the behaviour of some of their own church members and some clergy who have been perceived to have taken sides in the conflict. The complexities of reconciliation become even clearer to me as I ponder the loyalty issues in this society.

The fundamental loyalty one is expected to honour without compromise is loyalty to your *wontoks*—your tribe and clan and language group. This loyalty can supersede national law and natural justice. One of my Marist Father friends, John Begg, reminds me that Christianity has *only* had 100 years of influence here, after thousands of years of tribal 'custom'. Whilst an outsider would see these people and imagine they are all Bougainvilleans, the reality is they are members of disparate clans, who do not have the sense of nationalism or federalism that we in Australia take for granted. I feel so blessed to get these insights-I feel that they will also assist me in my ongoing ministry in Timor.

We have a great meeting. We all share stories. We share some prayer. And we share a meal. I encourage them to continue meeting on a monthly basis, and assure them of my ongoing prayers.

Another Miracle?

On 10 July 2001, on a trip to the south of the island, after catching up with our Peace Monitoring Team, I visit the sole Australian working at the Buin hospital. The members of the team tip me off that she would appreciate a visit before I have to leave. They take me to meet Barbara Allen—a petite volunteer doctor, in her mid-20s.

She and Andrew, who is working in Arawa are the only doctors for the 80,000 people on the main island. She seems very happy to see me. We exchange our stories and she asks whether I could make a visit to a lady, Josephine, who is dying of Tuberculosis—a deadly disease where the lungs are infected and eventually cause breathing to cease. Barbara thinks she will die within the hour. I am also quite conscious that tuberculosis is highly infectious, and I am taking some risk by entering the tuberculosis ward. But I am feeling spiritually alive—I am doing what God wants me to do, and I will trust in Him for my own health.

We go into the ward and find Josephine barely breathing. I kneel down beside her bed to get eye contact. I show her my cross and tell her, 'I am a minister of the Catholic Church'. Her eyes open wide. I show her the Blessed Sacrament from a pyx I carry with me. She pushes herself up, and pushes her tongue out and slowly consumes the host. Placing my hand gently on her shoulder, I say some prayers with her and she sits upright. She seems to have gained some new energy!

She says to Barbara, 'Me alright now. I got Jesus in me!' She takes me by surprise with this comment. I ponder for a moment the amazing theology this woman has just uttered. Of course she has Jesus in her. That's what we Catholics believe. I feel like the student minister being taught by the teacher! She shows a beaming smile, and I beam back at her. What a blessing it is for me to have met her and see her faith.

Barbara gives me a hug and says, 'Thank you so much. I was feeling helpless, and you have brought some joy to all of us.' I then receive a radio call to return to the helicopter which is required back in Loloho for another task. Wow! I feel this is such a privilege to be able to be involved in such ministry. Thank you God.

Two weeks later I visit Barbara again. I ask her, 'How did Josephine fare after I left'. She tells me, 'Gary, something amazing happened.

Josephine's breathing improved and she returned to her village. She survived. I can't believe it.'

I say, 'Thanks be to God. She has Jesus in her!'

End of mission

I am to leave Bougainville in September 2001, on the day following a three-hour open-air mass in which 20,000 people participate, celebrating 100 years of Christianity on the Island.

Months of preparation have gone into this celebration. Whilst I have been a liaison person for the PMG, the locals have organised this all themselves, and done a marvellous job. Representative groups come from every part of Bougainville. The service is led by more than 40 priests, most of whom are locals themselves. Rain showers come and go throughout the service, and the singing, the dancing, and the smiles on faces bring joy to my heart. Many of the people are dressed in traditional grass skirts and multicoloured tops. The people sit on the ground in orderly groups, with small signposts indicating the parish that they come from.

Many of the PMG members come along and participate in the service. I am invited to proclaim the Gospel reading, and subsequently I, along with the priests, give out Holy Communion to the thousands of people. Feeding 20,000 people takes a while!

The jubilation and energy of the people is truly uplifting. They clearly want to put the past behind them. In various speeches at the end of the mass, gratitude is expressed to the members of the PMG.

I feel we have made a major contribution to peace. Moreover I have this strong sense of oneness with these people. Yes they are my brothers and sisters in Christ. Indeed we are 'all one in Christ Jesus' (*Galatians* 3:28).

The euphoria of the day is pegged back a little, and I am reminded of the longer-term challenge ahead, when on returning to my vehicle after the mass I find it has been broken into, and some of my possessions stolen. I take some comfort in knowing it would not have been robbed by people participating in the Mass, but by 'rascals' who still present a problem for a peaceful future of these neighbouring islands. I'd like to say we fixed the problems here, but it's better I acknowledge that Peacemaking is a very long process.

Reflections

The day following is my end of mission day. A group of about 20 of us say our farewells down at the headquarters area, receive a certificate of service, board some army trucks, and make our final hot steamy journey to the airfield at Kieta. I have mixed feelings within me. I feel sad to be leaving some good friends like Mike, but I am keen to be reunited with my family. As I fly back to Brisbane via Townsville, while almost everyone else seems to be dozing, my mind is buzzing with many thoughts, and I review my journal notes and write up with some key reflections on this whole experience.

I record that I think this Regional Peace Monitoring Group involvement in Bougainville has been one of our most successful Peacekeeping interventions. I am honoured to have been a part of it. I manage to serve in the mission without any major health problems. This is a delightful reflection for me, but I note that I have been implementing some healthy measures, in getting plenty of exercise, eating a good diet, and keeping some strong spiritual support through my daily prayer and journaling. Clearly having my boss in the mission being my close friend, Mike Swan, I didn't have anything to worry about from the hierarchy. There are only a few confrontations with some staff members about my frequent requests for transport, but I deal with them satisfactorily.

Compared to Iran or Timor, the security situation is safer and I never feel threatened or in fear of my life. I have had to agonisingly witness a number of deaths of babies and adults in the clinics, and I have dealt with this in faith and through prayer. I have had to continue to ponder the mystery of life and death and how God fits into this and I imagine that I will still be contemplating this for some time to come.

I have had a specific purposeful mission to engage in, without any distractions, and a good routine, with adequate rest and recreation. I don't experience any significant PTSD symptoms. I have not been on medication, and I hope this is a sign of an end to these problems. (Alas, it isn't!)

Once again, as in Timor, I feel totally affirmed in my ministry as Chaplain. I am thrilled to see the growth in faith of a number of the staff in the mission. Years later I am to celebrate marriages for several of them.

Ooops! I realise that I have forgotten to mention my family! Of course I must confess that they have had to take a 'back seat' in my life whilst I have been enjoying this experience.

As the C130 briefly stops in Townsville to refuel and to drop off some passengers and then flies on to Brisbane, I continue to reflect on what has been, and what must happen now. This mission has been all consuming. I have immersed myself in it, but I realise that it has been at the expense of yet another separation from family. I do miss Lynne and the children very much. I don't like being away from them for long periods. I am blessed that Lynne is so resilient and resourceful. During my absence, Michael is to deploy to Timor a second time, and our other children and grandchild keep growing and having their own challenges. Lynne bears more than her fair share of the parenting. I know I must make this up on my return.

As I stare out the porthole of the noisy aircraft, I recall that while I am a minister of the Church, my first vocational sacrament is to marriage. Time and time again I have to keep reminding myself of this and deliberately carve out time for us to be together. I have now served 32 years in the military. I have made many sacrifices and my family has made many more.

Lynne meets me at Brisbane airport after a very long flight. She is alone and we experience a long hug. By now all the children have completed school and university. Catherine has a career as a Project Manager in Information Technology. Michael is serving in Townsville with the Army. Christy has a job as Human Relations Advisor with the Archdiocese of Brisbane. Paul has taken up work with Suncorp Insurance.

As we drive from the airport back to our home in the suburb of The Gap, I am feeling a little uncomfortable. I have not given my family and especially my wife, the attention that they deserve. The Defence Force is committed on many fronts and I have an intuitive sense that some change may be ahead for us as a family. The Army is overcommitted and so am I. Something needs to change.

Chapter 9
God's Call to Follow my Conscience

> *'God has given you wisdom and a conscience ... and we have freedom to follow our conscience and not be a slave to others who would quench our spirit.'*
>
> Spiritual Director, Father Peter McHugh

The pressure mounts

After the challenges and enjoyment of life on operations for three months, I return to a job as the Coordinating Chaplain of the 7th Brigade in Enoggera. But a number of interwoven and overlapping threads are beginning to unravel, as our nation, the military, the church, and I, face a number of developing pressures.

Firstly I am responsible for providing chaplaincy for nine major units (about 4000 soldiers) with only one other full-time chaplain and two part-time chaplains. Frankly, the task is beyond our capacity to manage satisfactorily. I believe that it makes sense to train mature Christians to take on part-time roles as lay ministers to ensure that no one is left without support because there are so few chaplains. The United States military has been doing this for years. On my own initiative and with my local Brigadier's approval, I engage an Army Reserve soldier who is already undertaking his own part-time studies in ministry as my 'chaplain's assistant'. He helps me in a number of administrative roles, and assists me in responding to the more simple requests for assistance, of the very many demands and needs that are being placed upon us at this time.

But some people in ADF Chaplaincy do not support my calls to appoint the good Christians I know of in uniform, into part-time ministry roles. More significantly they are also opposed to my efforts to assist the East Timorese. The Australian Government's policy at this time is one of disengagement from Timor and rapprochement with Indonesia. This is interpreted by some staff in Army to mean we are to leave the Timorese to help themselves.

The pressure comes to a head when on 2 August 2002, I receive an email from a higher headquarters staff officer telling me, 'You are to cease your involvement in charity work in Timor. Your request to travel to Timor on leave is not approved.' I despair. Can't they see that my work there is contributing to peace?

This interference incenses me. A wave of anxiety washes through me. At first I am unsure of how to respond to this confrontation. I think this must be some small-minded junior staff officer blocking me, and I plan to counter him, in an appeal in an email to the Senior Chaplain at the higher headquarters.

The Senior Chaplain responds with an even more terse response, saying, 'You should be fully immersed in working in Enoggera, and we don't expect you should have any spare time to help out the Timorese.' I feel so angry. I am working my guts out for the Army. I am probably doing at least 50 hours per week in chaplaincy, and any work that I am doing with East Timor is coming out of my own time.

As a professional soldier, and one who has been trained at the higher defence colleges, I think it bad enough that the military hierarchy cannot see the strategic importance of supporting the transition to independence in this fragile country without a further crisis. But to then have someone in the chaplaincy hierarchy try to block some charitable action on my part, just blows my mind. I am angry, disillusioned, and disgusted.

My mind is buzzing with so many thoughts. In relation to my travelling to East Timor and assisting in humanitarian efforts, I must accept that some people in authority will not share my concerns and will want to avoid any potential problems. No doubt some would see risks in having me wandering around East Timor on my leave. But I have a strong sense that I am reaching a watershed in how I want to live out my life, and my call as a Christian. I have reached a point where I don't want to live in the 'shackles' that fulltime Army service imposes on me. Institutions like the military are classically resistant to change, and uncomfortable with 'mavericks' who want to take independent action.

From the time of my studies at Banyo seminary I have been wanting to develop initiatives in lay ministry. The Catholic Church's Second Vatican Council (1962 to 1966) had commended a wide range of initiatives in empowering the laity to play roles in ministry, and many local churches of all denominations have started using lay people more actively in lower level ministerial roles. But in the military, at this time, I am in an institutional situation where some leaders are ultra-conservative and want to maintain the traditional ways we have done things.

I have many friends and supporters among the junior chaplains, who support the initiatives and approaches I have taken and am proposing. We talk and share, but they have little confidence that the military and chaplaincy hierarchy in Sydney and Canberra will accept the developments I propose. I am experiencing the normal resistance that institutional powerbrokers have to any changes that they haven't initiated.

Hierarchies can embrace renewal, or they can grip firmly onto power and control and maintain the *status quo*—which is institutionalism at its worst. Frankly, I have had a gut full of it. I would be delighted if these characters would come and see, and talk about what I am doing—what I feel God is calling me to—but no, I have to suffer being managed by emails, and telephone calls.

Eventually my Brigade Commander, Richard Wilson, a big 'Bear' of a man, who also has a PhD, and is very supportive of my initiatives, asks the Senior Chaplain at Land Headquarters, in Sydney to come up and dialogue with us. To my delight Richard gives him a thorough briefing on the benefits of my actions thus far, and recommendations for future developments, and he especially affirms the contribution I am making in East Timor. In a classic beaurocratic play, the Senior Chaplain is cordial and assures us he will take the Brigadier's comments to the most senior staff, but of course we hear nothing further.

My anxiety is now through the roof. I can't stop negative thoughts coming into my mind. I can't sleep properly. I have pains in my stomach. I feel I cannot abandon the Timorese. I see my doctor, and she tells me this working environment is not healthy for me. She directs that I cut back my working hours by half, for a month, to give me some relief. I try to do this but it is hopeless. There is no-one else to do the work I don't do when I am not in the office, so I just have to frantically try to squeeze things in. But there is no cut back I can impose on my overactive mind. It is in overdrive '24/7', stewing over all these matters. I reflect how bizarre it is that I am able to cope satisfactorily with going on operations in Timor and then Bougainville, but back in the absolute safety of Australia my anxiety levels have increased dramatically. (No doubt in both places I just had a singular focus of attention.)

As if this isn't enough, at the same time I become concerned that our Government is wanting to follow the US, in supporting and participating in an invasion of Iraq, and I feel that I must publicly oppose this on military, strategic and religious ethical grounds. I am intrigued that the Australian public seems to be accepting the propaganda that the US government is putting out. The Anglican Bishop to the Defence Force publishes an article in support of invasion. I am staggered. Our Catholic Bishop is seriously ill at the time and soon to die. No official Catholic position seems to be forthcoming from our military Bishop's office, although it is clear from international media, that the Pope and many people in the broader Catholic Church are opposed to an invasion. No-one within the Catholic Church in Australia has yet spoken up publicly on this matter.

At the forefront of my passionate engagement on this issue, is my recollection of the passive and misinformed attitude our government had taken in the months leading up to the destruction of East Timor in 1999. I feel I cannot stand by idly and see us slide gradually into an involvement, without making a contribution to a national dialogue on this issue, especially when I am one of only a few people in Australia who has had first hand experience of dealings with the Iraqis.

After considerable prayer and reflection, I write an article which I circulate among military friends. I plan to publish it in the Brisbane *Catholic Leader*, before the Australian Government announces its intention to participate in the invasion. This is a poignant moment in my life but, having had peace through prayer, I feel I must follow my conscience. God is gently leading me on a new path, but I know not quite where, other than back to East Timor!

Decision Time

Since 1986, wherever I have been, I have always had a Spiritual Director, normally a priest or nun, who I have gone to on a monthly basis, to seek guidance and affirmation in living the spiritual life. This is long established Catholic tradition, and personally it is a great sounding board to help clarify that the inspirations one receives are from God and not from elsewhere. My spiritual director at this time, Father Peter Mc Hugh, a gentle Augustinian priest with a warm smile and soft silver hair, helps me reflect on what I'm struggling with. He says, 'Throughout church history, people like you have faced similar dilemmas. They see things that could be improved and they experience resistance. Most Religious Orders, like the Franciscans and Jesuits grew out of the inspiration and courage someone had, to renew the church, and make the world a better place.'

He reminds me that, 'God has given you wisdom and a conscience. There are some absolutes of faith that we must always comply with, but there are many rooms in our Father's house, and we have freedom to follow our conscience and not be a slave to others who would quench our spirit.'

I realise I have to make the choice to follow my conscience, and really God's call to me at this time.

There is just no way that I can drop the work that I have initiated in East Timor. This is a classic situation where Jesus' command to love your neighbour requires some sustained effort and attention. I know in my heart, God is calling me to do this as my priority activity for the indefinite future. I have seen from the work that I have already undertaken, that the efforts of the group we have established can make an exponential difference to the lives of these people. Thus to free me up to engage in this humanitarian activity, but also to make a serious statement about the ethical issues of an impending war, to disengage myself from the obligation to serve in an unjust war, and to liberate me from the shackles and frustrations that full-time army service is binding me in, on my 50th birthday, 17 September 2002, I submit my transfer to the Army Reserve, and trust in God as to how my life will develop from here.

I consult with my 'Friends and Partners' team, and book flights to East Timor.

2002 is to end with four big issues that have emerged in my life at this time:

- I want to promote greater Lay involvement in ministry.
- I feel compelled to be helping the people of East Timor
- I feel I must protest against the government's plans over Iraq.
- Post-Traumatic Stress Disorder is debilitating me.

Managing these issues has potential to lead to disastrous consequences for my health. And of course I am quite realistic in considering that my protestations over Iraq are unlikely to have any significant effect on government decision-making. But my God-given conscience compels me to speak up.

The decision of anyone to follow Jesus and be a member of his community always comes at a price. Integrity demands that we make choices to follow our conscience, and I am a man of integrity.

Much of what is to happen to me in the next 15 years, including many extraordinary experiences in life beyond the military, are to flow from this decision I make in 2002. I follow my Holy Spirit-inspired conscience and leave the Regular Army which is preventing me from continuing my missionary work in Timor, and coincidently, I remove myself from a moral dilemma pending the invasion of Iraq.

The issues involved for me, with the developing Iraq situation are complex, and I will now explain them in greater detail.

Just War

I am a patriot, a proud Aussie digger, but I am also a follower of Jesus, first and foremost. So I spell out my thesis publicly, *before* our Government announces their intention to go 'All the way with George W Bush'.

On 21 January 2003, in the Brisbane *Catholic Leader*, the 'Centrepoint' article records my stance and appeal with the following introduction:

> I write today as an Australian citizen concerned at the threats to world peace and the need for us to courageously confront evil, even using lethal force in circumstances that are morally justified. I believe Saddam Hussein must be confronted, but I am concerned that a unilateral pre-emptive assault on Iraq without UN mandate has not yet been justified and may result in dire consequences ... I consider the war on the terrorist activity of the al Qaeda network, necessary and morally justifiable, but as the spectre of a new war against Iraq looms closer each day, I have grave reservations about involvement by us, on military, strategic and ethical grounds ...
>
> Chaplain Gary Stone.

This article quickly reverberates around the Internet and is reprinted in numerous International forums. I am deluged with affirmations of support and remarkably little opposition. Vatican Radio interviews me at length in a broadcast that goes worldwide. Amazingly, my military superiors are silent. The most senior officers in Army all know me very well; some of them are classmates from RMC. I suspect that they are thinking what I am saying, but for any of them to agree with me would mean an end to their careers. (All senior promotions to Brigadier and above have to be approved by government.)

Of course even as a Defence Reservist I could have been called to account, even charged, for not having cleared my article with Defence Public Relations. I did not do that because I know how risk-averse these people are, and the article would not have seen the light of day. Nevertheless I will, from now on, be seen as a 'Maverick' by people in authority, particularly people in the Defence Chaplaincy hierarchy. Perhaps everyone is waiting for someone else to bring me into line! My peers keep ringing me up to check whether I have been hauled over the coals. This is reassuring, and part of the traditional army culture that I love.

I reply, 'No-one has said anything. Maybe their consciences have been touched also.'

I have made a committed stand on an issue of international significance. In good conscience, I just couldn't remain silent on a matter with such grave consequences.

It really feels good to have made this stand and 'drawn my line in the sand.' In transferring to the Army Reserve, I will not be required to participate in what I believe to be an unjust war. Over the years as a soldier, I had often wondered whether I would have to make an ethical choice to not agree with a policy of the government of the day, and that time has come. Certainly for me, this is a matter of integrity and moral courage. There is a long history in Christian tradition that bad things should not be allowed to develop because good people stand by and do nothing. Who knows where this situation is going to lead us. We are already committed to war in Afghanistan. We can't find Osama Bin Laden, and I am absolutely sure that opening up a 'second front' in the Middle East is going to inflame the Islamic fundamentalists. By speaking up I maintain my honour, and I hope that I might give many other Christians in the halls of power in Canberra a wake-up call that we need to be, in the words of St Thomas More, 'the King's good servants but God's first!'

Tragically my concerns of the consequences of the unilateral Bush Government action will subsequently play out with the loss of hundreds of thousands of lives and a continuing unstable situation which has led to the spectre of even further conflict with Iran. No doubt there are a diversity of opinions on this situation and some will disagree with me. But the lack of a plan to 'win the peace', and the disastrous decisions to disband the Iraqi military and police, leading to widespread looting and unchecked sectarian violence, display reckless and uninformed decision making. Some will say that we are better off now without Saddam Hussein. I would agree, but the hasty and ill conceived plan to get rid of him by an invasion, was not the appropriate way to deal with the situation at this time. Moreover a time tested, ethical framework for consideration of going to war, the so-called 'just war' doctrine, was overlooked. In one sense all that I was doing was reminding people of the historical and theological lessons that we have learned from the past.

My appeal for peace

The fundamental thesis for my stance lies in the words I use in the 2003 article:

> As a Christian soldier deployed to 5 conflicts I have taken great solace in adhering to the long established 'Just War' doctrine which has informed ethical action in conflict situations since the time of St Augustine. It is not just practical wisdom. I consider it is divine wisdom. It obliges all citizens and governments to work toward peace and the avoidance of war, but acknowledges the right of legitimate defence by military force in circumstances where, at one and the same time:

- the damage inflicted by the aggressor is lasting, grave and certain;
- all other means of resolution have been shown to be impractical or ineffective;
- there must be serious prospects of success; and
- the use of arms must not produce evils and disorders graver than the evil to be eliminated.

Catechism of the Catholic Church, 1994, Para 2309

This doctrine has been tried and tested over hundreds of years and remains just as valid today. Troops sent to restore peace in a conflict vitally need to know they have both moral legitimacy and parameters on their use of lethal force. Readers might be interested to know that the Australian Army, in its most recent re-write of our keystone doctrinal document–The Fundamentals of Land Warfare, 2002–specifically endorses the criticality of adhering to the 'Just War' precepts, for the long term restoration of peace to be achieved.

I hope our military leaders will not be asked to turn a blind eye to this doctrine, and commit our soldiers to an unjust involvement which may haunt them for years to come, in order to satisfy the demands of our US allies' urgency for action.

From my first-hand experience, the politics and culture of the Middle East are complex issues that most Westerners would have great difficulty understanding. There are no simple or quick fix solutions there. Hastily devised, externally imposed, and short-sighted 'Western' solutions have led from one problem to another in the Middle East throughout the last century. Both Saddam and Osama bin Laden received substantial support from the US in earlier ill-conceived strategies. People in the Middle East continue to be outraged at the meddling by Western governments, in those affairs that suit them, (like the economics of oil), and their indifference and intransigence in matters of justice (like restoration of a Palestinian homeland). Serious attention to demands for Israeli compliance with UN resolutions unfulfilled by them, which could restore justice to the Palestinian people, would draw much of the sting out of the tail of Islamic extremism.

The US has weapons of 'massive' destruction that will be able to bomb Iraq back into the dark ages, but real peace requires more than military might. Peace will only be achieved when the root problems of justice in economic, social and political terms is provided for. It is morally scandalous that inestimable billions of dollars will be found to fund this conflict and its aftermath, when these could have been more fruitfully directed to health and human development in the poorest countries of the world where the seeds of discontent are sown. Strategically, we need more thinking and action in the ways in which we can provide justice to peoples, and nurture and sustain long-term peace, rather than the prevailing short-sightedness of seeking military solutions, which have limited prospect of sustainment. It is my great fear that unilateral action against Iraq by the US and allies like us, will greatly swell the ranks of Islamic fundamentalists and unleash forces of evil that it will be extremely difficult to contain.

What is needed in the Middle East is justice, legitimacy and integrity. The majority of Islamic people expect it just as much as we do. It is a non negotiable pre-requisite for peace.

The so called 'War on Terrorism' which has involved the pursuit of the Al Qaeda network, has in my mind, a legitimacy based on a just response to acts of terror perpetrated by an aggressor who seeks to engage us in indiscriminate conflict. A 'War on Iraq' is not in this same category, and can only be tenuously linked to the war on terrorism. Many media reporters are saying that war is now inevitable. It may be in the mind of the US administration, but it doesn't need to be. Despite the morally reprehensible conduct of the regime of Saddam Hussein, no ethical justification has yet been established for engaging in a pre-emptive war against the people of Iraq. None of the

Just-war criteria have yet been satisfied. No Iraqi, US, British or Aussie soldier should have to shed their blood over the oil fields of Iraq until they are. Continued containment of Saddam or his surgical removal, short of invasion, remain as valid options.

Should a 'just' case emerge for conflict to be initiated by us, please God it will only employ 'just' and discriminate use of force. I hope the Australian people and Christians particularly, will have the courage and wisdom to continue to speak their minds to their politicians on this issue, and not just assume we must follow the US party line and timetable. World peace is at stake here. Our integrity as a nation is at stake.

History will judge us by our actions and inactions, but more significantly God will judge us. We may well ask whether God would want us to be bombing Baghdad in a few weeks time, or pursuing other means to achieve peace. I suspect his answer might be an echo of the words of Micah that we should: 'do (only) what is just, and show mercy'. *Micah* 6.8

By Gary Stone—a Deacon of the Catholic Military Ordinariate, currently based in Brisbane.'

The Army and the Church have trained me well in the lead-up to this pivotal moment. I am able to analyse the information available and test it against the doctrine and theology I have learned. Moreover, I have formed a conscience, and in prayer I am confident that this is the stance I have to take. I suspect this may not be the only time I need to take a major stance against the establishment.

No doubt many others in uniform at the time, as well as retired senior officers, would have been having similar thoughts to mine. I hope next time, more of them, and especially those retired senior officers with the experience and understanding of matters strategic, will have the courage to speak up and inform the debate upon the best way forward.

Some months later in an article in the West Australian Anglican Church newspaper, *Market-Place*, Reverend Alan Mathieson in an article titled 'Church compromised by silent chaplains', writes:

> The Iraq war was built on lies and deception. But only one Australian Catholic chaplain, Father Gary Stone, of the more than 200 chaplains in the ADF warned that a unilateral pre-emptive assault, without UN mandate has not been justified. He went on to condemn the US weapons of mass destruction and the moral scandal of the spending of billions of dollars to fund the conflict. That's one chaplain who won't make it to Brigadier! ... The silence and acquiescence trade-off by officer clergy is no longer appropriate or defensible.

Alan was right of course, my fellow chaplains chose not to get involved in this debate, but realistically few of them, if any, had any experience in Middle East affairs, or the operational side of higher defence and national security processes. I spoke to a number of close friends in chaplaincy about the situation and they indicated that they intuitively agreed with me, but did not feel competent to enter public debate. I had received training and experience in these areas and consequently felt honour bound to make comment, and certainly not remain silent.

Perhaps I will never be promoted again, by an institution that would certainly see me as a 'Maverick' who is likely to continue to speak his mind. But I am no 'loose cannon' or rebel. I am simply a man with a conscience, and a vision for what might be better ways of doing things. I'm sure many of the chaplains would have agreed with me. Nevertheless one chaplain subsequently says to me, 'The problem for you, Gary, is that when you speak out like a prophet, you have to expect you are going to be treated the way they were—by being stoned and treated with contempt.' Of course I don't see myself as a prophet, but on this issue, my life experience had given me a particular perspective that needed to be aired.

Actually I'm quite proud that people see me as an innovator and a man who will speak up when it's needed. I hope it will make others in the military and chaplaincy hierarchies think deeply over ethical issues, knowing that I, or others like me, may speak out again in future. Moreover, this is part of our proud Aussie tradition in both the military and our church. We need to have a robust dialogue on many matters in national and international life and not just leave matters to the beaurocrats. Of course at this time my close friend Jim Wallace is himself in a transition from full-time army service to taking a role as the executive director of a new advocacy group known as Australian Christian Lobby. At this point their focus is on domestic matters of a moral dimension and only later will they expand into the international arena.

Some may wonder why continuing to serve in any form of military service is still satisfactory for me in the circumstances. Of course I hadn't ceased to be proud of being an Australian soldier and making a contribution of service to my country. Service in the Regular Army requires one to be available to serve unconditionally anywhere in the world. But the Army Reserve can only be 'called out' in Defence of Australia. Serving in other conflicts is voluntary for Reservists. In any case as a Chaplain I am still concerned for our soldiers and want to be able to be of service to them. I can continue to do that from a permanent base in Brisbane. I have no doubt that the multiple conflicts we are engaged in by now—Timor, Bougainville, The Solomon's and Afghanistan, let alone Iraq, are going to exact a heavy emotional, spiritual and psychological toll on our soldiers and I would like to be in a position to be able to help them, from the experience that I have the developed in struggling with my own issues with PTSD.

Having made the decision to withdraw from full-time service I am able to spend the next two years combining part-time Army Chaplaincy with development of a lay ministry programme in the Archdiocese of Brisbane, and significantly an expansion of my efforts to assist in East Timor.

Throughout this period I face the conundrum of dealing with the stress and anxiety that following my conscience entails. The anxiety 'demon' nips me and bites me painfully in my thoughts and in my dreams, and I find myself in constant battle with him. He brings to mind all sorts of consequences: of being charged by the military; of being estranged from my peers; of having my faculties (authorisation) to be an army chaplain taken from me and so on ... Rationally, all these negative thoughts can be tested and challenged, but PTSD means that my mind is hyper-active, and I am hyper-sensitive to criticism. The emotional and physical feelings are unpleasant. Once again I am exhausted.

My doctor and my spiritual advisor counsel me to 'live to fight another day', rather than being hooked and struggling to respond to people and situations that I have had to be dealing with in full-time service. Of course, this reorientation of my ministry involvements is to become a blessing in disguise, even though I don't realise it at this point. I am released to take up a range of ministry and life experiences I could never have imagined—thanks be to God again. And hopefully I can stay on soldiering as a proud Reservist!

My struggle with PTSD at this time requires priority attention. By this stage I have come to realise that the PTSD condition affects a person's body, mind and soul. Managing the condition requires a range of strategies to be employed in all of these dimensions. No one clinician has the time or capacity to be supervising or guiding me in addressing the diverse range of symptoms that I am experiencing. I have to be very disciplined in developing my own health management plan. I ponder how it must be so difficult for others with PTSD to understand what is going on in them and to develop and maintain appropriate coping strategies. In any case, my broad plan is that I increase my exercise, go back on an increased level of medication, submit to regular counselling, including cognitive behaviour therapy, and intensify my prayer life. I manage to avoid another breakdown, like the one that I had at Duntroon in 1998, but I wonder what long term effects this is going to have on my health. Am I going to die in my early 60s like so many of the Vietnam veterans I have buried? How many beats has my fast running heart got left?

Certainly in any society there needs to be solid workers that can get on with the job, but there also needs to be people who contemplate the future and identify ways that things can be done better. God seems to have developed me with gifts and convictions to try to contribute to making the world a better place at whatever level of capacity I have. I am certainly not going to be able to rebuild East Timor, but day by day I know I can make a positive difference in the lives of some of the people we are in contact with. All innovators experience resistance and that is what I have been experiencing. But I have been trained as a soldier and I will 'soldier on' no matter what the cost.

I contemplate often in my journalling, the character of Eric Liddell in the movie, *Chariots of Fire* who in conscience refused to run on a Sunday in the Olympics, in his preferred event, and was then given an impossible task of running on the Monday in a race that was beyond his normal capacity to win. The movie recalls his reflection at the start of the race, 'It says in the Good Book, that whosoever honours me, I in turn will honour. God made me to be true to him, and God also can make me run fast, and I will run for his glory!'

Against all odds Eric wins, and so will I, or perhaps it's more appropriate to say that God will win, and God's will, will prevail.

Facing the loss of a significant portion of family income, I take it as an affirming sign from God, that within days of my transfer out of the Regular Army, I get a call from the Brisbane Catholic Education Office wanting to engage me two days per week to develop a Lay Ministry training programme for the Brisbane Archdiocese. I accept the offer and get to work developing some Certificate level (Three and Four), nationally accredited lay ministry training programmes.

But foremost in my mind is my concern for the desperate straits of the Timorese. I throw myself into exploring how we can make a significant difference in their standard of living. No one can stop me from doing what God has placed upon my heart, and I don't need anyone's permission to get more heavily involved in this great work of compassion. The positive results and outcomes that will unfold in coming years are to exceed my wildest imaginations, at this time.

Chapter 10
Friends and Partners with East Timor

Friends and Partners with East Timor are awarded the 2005 RSL Anzac Peace Prize for making a significant contribution to World Peace.
National RSL President Bill Crews, Anzac Day 2005

Having made the choice to follow my conscience, a great burden is lifted from me. I have forfeited possibilities of a more substantial pension from the Army, and I have launched out in faith, trusting that I will be provided for by God, to get enough income for us to live on. More importantly, I can get involved with helping the Timorese without having to get 'permission' of beaurocrats.

Developing the Relationship

At the start of 2003, having addressed some of the immediate 'emergency' needs in Atabae, we are now able to look further into the human side of the relationship. We arrange visits to Australia by the Atabae parish priest, Father Marsellus, and parish council chairman, Alfredo Leite, so that they can get to know us better, and more importantly show our donors and indeed all our parishioners the human face of the Timorese. This is followed in 2004 by bringing to Brisbane a representative group of Timorese youth. I arrange to bring them back with me at the end of one of my visits and we host them in our house. Coming to Australia is an enormous culture shock for them. They are frightened by the escalators at Darwin airport, and quickly get sick eating our rich food. Nevertheless they interact with our people and share their stories with us. During this period we also send more of our FPET members over to Timor, including a young adult delegation, to help them catch the vision of what is needed to be done and to experience the life of our friends and partners still living in poverty. Communication problems continue to hamper us, and we realise we need full-time representatives on the ground to manage some of the more significant projects that are needed. This is something our committee struggles with, and later solves.

For Easter 2004, Lynne and Michael join me in visiting the parish. By now we have provided Father Marsellus with a Toyota trayback 4WD, so we are able to travel a little more safely around the rough roads, albeit with Michael and I and up to 10 others sitting in the exposed trayback. One night Father Marsellus drops us at Aidabasalala, about 6 hours drive from the main parish centre. There are Easter celebrations by candlelight and lantern, but otherwise we are in total darkness. We have no communications. There is no emergency vehicle within hours of here even if we could notify them, which would have to be by runner. Lynne asks me, 'What would we do if we get bitten by a snake?'

I say, 'We will need to pray that we don't get bitten because there is no plan B.'

We stay overnight in the house of the Cathechist, Senor John Reinado. It has cement walls and iron roof that is absolutely peppered with bullet holes. I ask John through an interpreter, Domingos, why there are so many holes.

Domingos says, 'Senor John is very brave man. When election result announced, Indonesian soldiers come and tell Senor John that

Delivering some power to Aidabasalala, December 2007.

he must lead all village people in walk to Indonesia. Senor John refuse, and they start shooting all around him in house to scare him. Many people run and hide in forest, but Senor John tell them he is servant of God and must stay to look after chapel. They have already shot dead eleven people in village, but he tell them they will answer to God for their actions. He walk calmly over to chapel with them shooting all over place, and he stay in chapel till Indonesians leave and we come out of hiding.' I realise that we are in the presence of a saint.

We return to the main parish church the next day by a pre-arranged pick-up from the Army in armoured personnel carriers led by Lieutenant Colonel Shane Caughey, one of my men from Iran and now commander of 6 RAR, the last battalion to serve in Timor before our pull-out of troops later in the year. Shane is a big man and has a big smile and welcomes us warmly. He takes us to his camp and gets us hot showers and fresh meals, then drives us to Atabae. Back in Atabae we start through the Good Friday, Easter Saturday and Sunday services. Thousands of people have come in from the villages and camp in the church grounds for three days. The services go for hours each, in extreme heat and high humidity and we are pooped, but sustained by the amazing singing. I am dressed in my white vestments and absolutely dripping wet with sweat.

In a break, Divine Word Missionary, Brother Henrikus Ulan, a gentle man with badly bowed legs, aged in his seventies, says to us, 'Over many years, many people from different parts of the world have come here, seen our poverty, and said they will do something, but they have never come back. You are the first ones that have. I think I am now experiencing for the first time that I really am part of a truly Catholic-Universal church. And it is your relationship with us that makes it truly Catholic because you care for us from far away.' We embrace. Tears flow down my face. No words are necessary.

Back in Australia, the day to day work of FPET is done by a wonderful committee of volunteers. My lifelong friend and Duntroon classmate Peter de Haas serves faithfully as our Inaugural President. Shirley Roiter from Bardon parish commences as our Vice President. Accountant Jack Brady agrees to be our Treasurer—a big job, considering the many donations and disbursements we have to process. Former agriculturist Nick Delaney offers himself as our projects manager and webmaster. Another former public servant, Mike Dooley, scours the internet to give us daily news on happenings in Timor—a service that is also later to be utilised by President Ramos Horta and his staff! Young adults, James Johnson, Joel Hodge and Mary Hodge are active on youth matters and liaison with the local Timorese community. A group of about 15 others assist as secretaries, newsletter editors, hosts or taking up smaller projects. In 2004 Peter de Haas moves north to Ravenshoe in North Queensland and hands over Presidency to Jim Johnson, a radiographer with a fine eye for detail and a long history with the scouting movement.

After consultation with the Atabae parish council, a decision is made to fund the placement of two lay missionaries—a community nurse and a project manager. Husband and wife couple, Nick and Jane Eager, in their late twenties, are identified for us through the PALMS (Catholic Lay Missionary) organisation, and I take them to Timor in January 2005 to settle them in. Nick has previous service as an Army engineer, Jane is a nurse, and they are wonderful generous folks. We arrive in Atabae during a torrential rainstorm, and I share a week with them, by candlelight, no electricity, no refrigeration, and no means of communication, save travelling three hours to Dili in an overcrowded bus.

At the first Sunday Mass that we attend, Father Marsellus invites them and me up the front and tells the people in Tetun, 'We have been blessed that this couple, our brother and sister, have come to live in our situation. You are not to treat them as foreigners. They are the neighbours that Jesus says we should love. They have left behind a comfortable situation in Australia to share their lives with us.'

The congregation bursts out in applause and cheering. After mass, hundreds of people swamp us and shake our hands. It is very moving.

Nevertheless I leave them with some trepidation, wondering how they will cope. This is an extreme situation and I can imagine it will be very challenging

They commence assisting with health care and project identification, but experience a lot of sickness. The absence of electricity and electronic communications, the extreme heat, and diet of almost exclusively rice and a little chicken would have been difficult for any Australian to endure. And then, shortly after they arrive, almost all the chickens in Timor die from bird flu! In

April, Nick contacts me from Dili with the good news that Jane is pregnant, but fears they are unable to bear the child safely in the conditions they are living in. They return home, have a healthy baby, and we are grateful for the pioneering work they did. We realise what a challenge this project really presents.

Recognised for our efforts

Our disappointment at this hiccup in finally getting some serious assistance delivered, is ameliorated to a small degree within a few days, by the surprise award by the Returned Servicemen's League (RSL), on Anzac Day 2005, of the RSL National Peace Prize.

The citation reads in part;

> The Friends and Partners with East Timor continue to fly the Australian flag of goodwill and friendship, in the remote areas of East Timor. They continue to promote peace and reconciliation among peoples still largely divided by the past. They make a most valuable and lasting contribution to international peace and goodwill.

This is wonderful recognition for our work. About twenty of us gather at RSL headquarters in Brisbane for this presentation. The prize itself is a very large (twenty centimetres diameter) silver bullion medallion, with a bust of Simpson and his donkey carrying a wounded soldier. The medallion is inscribed:

> The 2005 award is made to Friends and Partners with East Timor, for making a significant contribution to World Peace.

It's a wonderful symbol of what we have been doing.

We immediately start the search for replacements for Nick and Jane, and PALMS identifies for us David and Margaret Hall, a couple in their sixties. Originally from the UK, they have extensive experience working in Aboriginal communities in the Northern Territory. Margaret has a vision for training community health workers, and

Receiving RSL National Peace prize, April 2005.

David's background as a soldier and policeman is ideal for managing the projects needed in this remote area. In January 2006 Lynne and I head off again to Timor to help David and Margaret settle in. They set up home in a small cottage made from palm fronds woven together, and as we sit with them by candlelight in the dark, I reflect what true missionaries these people are, to offer themselves for this Spartan lifestyle. I ask Margaret what motivates them to undertake this work. She says, 'This is what we do. This is our calling. God has given us all gifts and he has gifted us to be able to live in remote situations. These people are our family now.'

I am awe-inspired by their commitment.

David gets quickly to work in managing the installing of water tanks and wells. He supervises and manages the selection and funding of students we sponsor at Teachers College in Baucau, and Technical College in Dili. Margaret commences providing nursing care and the identification of potential community health workers. With this team on the ground we are able to pull together many projects we want to deliver. We source vehicles, generators and a water supply. We manage the rebuilding of four schools, and fund their teacher's salaries for four years until the government takes over this responsibility.

With the children outside the school we build in Atabae.

Meanwhile, the Timorese government is making very slow progress in addressing the many needs of the people. Poverty and unemployment are rife and getting worse. In Atabae people are grateful because of our help, but in many other areas they are starving and desperate. In April 2006 Lynne and I visit again and I have a strong sense that things in Dili are not good. Timorese soldiers unhappy with their treatment by the government go on strike and then are sacked. Others subsequently desert. Police are on the streets in force with machine guns. Many groups start protesting against the government. At one protest, police open fire and rebelling soldiers return fire. Ironically I see the Timorese Police start using the same brutal tactics the Indonesians used on them. A convoy of troops loyal to the government is ambushed by the rebel leader, former army major, Alfredo Reinado.

Crisis erupts in Timor

Whilst we return to Brisbane, anarchy breaks out in Dili. Police desert their posts and in many places looting and criminality fills the gap.

Our son Michael, by now on duty as an advisor to the Timorese Defence Force, is in the midst of this, saving lives and attempting to restore order. His heroic efforts are recorded in an episode of the ABC *Australian Story* programme that goes to air in April 2007. In a dramatically recorded scene, he rescues a journalist team caught in crossfire between rebels and Government troops. From May to November, Michael becomes the face and voice of the Australian Defence Force on Dili television. His perfect Tetun language and appealing manner touches people in society. Everywhere he goes in town, he is recognized by the locals. He doesn't carry a weapon and is able to meet with disparate groups and dispel rumours. We are so proud of him.

I return on several visits in 2006 in my role as Chaplain to the Australian Federal Police. We send about 250 officers to deal with the violence in Dili, which goes unabated till November. (More about this in the next chapter.)

Our humble efforts to restore basic services are reflected in there being no problems of violence at all in Atabae. There, the people are quite peaceful and appreciate our presence. In so many other parts of Timor, desperately poor people resort to stealing. My strong sense in 2000 of the need to meet basic human needs is justified. Our friends in Atabae are living in hope. By contrast, in the minds of so many other Timorese, there is a frustration with the indecent haste with which the UN and Australia have drawn down their forces and left the country after granting independence. They have left without having done enough to restore basic human services or develop the institutions that are needed to see this new nation function effectively. Meanwhile in Dili, Michael is working exhaustively with leaders of martial arts groups who are contributing to most of the violence, and a movement toward peace starts with a peace parade in November that we both witness.

The *Australian Story* episode captures at the parade some footage of dialogue between Michael and me.

Michael says, 'It's great to see this reconciliation occurring.'

I add, 'And I'm proud that my son has been the one who got this process moving!'

Meanwhile, our parish schools initiate projects to connect with the schools in Atabae, sharing posters and forwarding education materials. I assist with giving awareness briefings to the various classes and connecting them. Once people in other parts of Timor hear of the preventative health activity we are offering, the demand for our health services increases beyond Atabae-to neighbouring districts, and even to Atauro Island. Under Indonesian rule, health services worked on a 'sickness' model, where only treatment services were provided. Margaret is introducing a 'wellness' model, where our focus is on preventative health and the training of community nurses, who would promote hygiene and healthy practices, and a system of check-ups for the youngest and oldest. We are saving lives by early intervention. The signature testament to our best work is the Atabae Health Centre. The building is funded by our donors, constructed by the local community under David's supervision, and operated daily by community nurses trained by Margaret. In April 2007, Lynne and I travel to Atabae to see operations in full swing. Hundreds of people present at the clinic each day, all delighted to learn and see their children growing healthily.

We have made an enormous difference to the lives of people like Mara Regina, born with an inability to walk. Until we find her, she has spent 12 years lying in the back-room floor of her family hut. She has now been integrated into society through therapy and the use of a wheelchair. One day, Miguel, aged one, is brought into the clinic almost lifeless. His parents tell Margaret that he has a demon in him. Margaret diagnoses a form of malaria, and acute dehydration. He is hydrated and treated for malaria, and now is a healthy young boy.

During this visit Lynne and I travel around the remote villages of the parish with David. It's very difficult going, bouncing up and down in the back of an old Army Landcruiser that has been gifted to us. The roads are all dirt, washed out in many places, and it is unbearably hot and uncomfortable. As we drive along, everyone we see, waves to us and says, '*Bondia* (good morning) or *Botarde* (Good afternoon).' We return the greeting and also say, '*Diakalae*' (Are you good?). They reply, '*Diak*' or '*Diak Los*' (Good or very good) Cheery smiles reveal teeth stained by betel nut. As we arrive in the mountain village of Rairobo, the catechist Vincente comes out to greet us.

Vincente bows and grips my outstretched hand with both of his, and then hugs me in an embrace. His wife Maria does the same with Lynne. He speaks no English but in Tetun I make him out to say to us, 'Thankyou Padre Gary for coming to visit us. You are our best friend. You visit us so many times. Not even our own government leaders come to visit us.'

I reply, 'We come to see you because you are our friends and partners in life. This is what Jesus has called us all to do.'

We sit down to some black coffee and dried banana. I invite him to identify some students that we can support to be trained as teachers. He is so grateful. I give him cash for the widows and orphans of the village.

Our work in Timor is very much focused on capacity development. We need to help the people develop the skills to help themselves better. To this end our work in the health programme has shifted to training them to continue our work. Maria and Lepa, two petite young mums with bashful smiles, have been our most successful trainees in this area, who we sponsor to complete nursing degrees. We sponsor numerous other students to go to teachers college in Baucau, and to technical college and university in Dili.

When I undertake a sabbatical programme in the Holy Land in 2006, I learn a great deal about various cultures, but the fundamental learning I achieve is to understand Jesus' command to 'Love your Neighbour.' It is his summary teaching, so necessary for civilised living, but the least practised even today. In my experience in East Timor, I realise that these are our neighbours and they are going to need our help for a very long time, even just to restore basic human needs. It is a lifelong work for me now, as this truly is a mission of '*Caritas*'—Love in charity—that I as a Deacon should give witness to and encourage others in.

A unique aspect of this ministry has been working in tandem with our eldest son, now Major Michael Stone, who after completing three years as an advisor with the Defence Cooperation Programme in March 2007, returns to Timor as Advisor to President Ramos Horta, in October 2007. (President José personally petitions Prime Minister John Howard to make this happen). Michael continues to be 'Mr FIX-IT' in Timor doing numerous tasks for the President, many well beyond the remit of his task as military affairs advisor. He chairs a task force on eradication of poverty, and engages the youth in programmes to get them out of violence and into community development. The ABC '*Australian Story*' records the story of our family involvement in East Timor in a second episode that goes to air on 21 September 2009. This itself leads to many speaking opportunities to share the Good News that God has been doing in Timor, particularly through 'Friends and Partners with East Timor.'

I have discovered that God blesses massively what God delights in. By July 2014, other PALMs volunteers—Anne Chapman, Ian Gray, Sharon Hearns, and Heather Henderson have all done two years development placements for us, and a new FPET executive committee of Lindsay Stokes, Eric Muir and John O'Hara has taken over the reins of management. We have raised over $1,250,000 for local capacity development projects. I am to make 29 visits to Atabae. Lynne has accompanied me on six of the visits, and the whole family has visited twice.

With Atabe youth group on my visit in January 2011.

While this humanitarian work has been developing, another dimension of ministry has been opened up for me by my transfer to the Army Reserve. I find myself 'headhunted' by the Australian Federal Police.

Chapter 11
Ministry with the AFP- Tsunami, Solomon's, Timor

16 January 2005, Phuket, Thailand.

On this national day of mourning, behind me on the beach, AFP Chaplain Gary Stone has conducted a service of remembrance for victims of the tsunami. For the past two weeks the APF's Disaster Victim Identification team has had the gruesome task of examining thousands of badly decomposed bodies with a view to returning them to their families. They have had to get on with this most difficult task with a professional detachment, but this morning Chaplain Gary Stone has offered them this time to grieve. The tears were flowing as a massive wreath was walked into the sea by the AFP members, blessed by the Padre and cast upon the waters, to the beautiful strains of Amazing Grace...We remember them...This is Damien Ryan, National Nine News

A surprise start

On Boxing Day 2004, a massive tsunami hits the coastlines of several of Australia's Asian neighbours killing hundreds of thousands of people, injuring countless others and devastating seaside towns and villages. Lynne and I watch the first news reports with horror as the scale of this tragedy overwhelms us. Australia responds immediately with humanitarian aid and a naval task force assembles to sail to neighbouring Indonesia. Prime Minister John Howard promises a billion dollars in assistance over the coming years. The Australian Defence Force (ADF) and the Australian Federal Police (AFP) mobilise contingents to fly out to assist. The AFP has specialist teams to identify human remains. This difficult but essential part of post-disaster assistance had come to the attention of the Australian people after the Bali bombing in October 2002.

A few days later, AFP Commissioner Mick Keelty's Executive Assistant calls me explaining that the Commissioner is seeking a chaplain to go immediately with his Disaster Victim Response team to Thailand. I had met the Commissioner and his family in the early 1990s when they had been parishioners in our church in the Gap.

I am in shock, but am honoured to be asked. I ring Lynne and she once again shows the quality of her character and compassion by encouraging me to go where God appears to be calling me. I catch a flight to Canberra the next day and am met by AFP chaplain, Catholic Deacon and former Navy officer, Roger O'Donnell.

Roger tells me: 'So great to see you Gary. We are delighted you can assist us in the Asian operation, as I am fully engaged by other ministry, following the recent murder of one of our AFP officers, Adam Dunning, in the Solomon Islands.'

On my way into town to be sworn in as an AFP chaplain, Roger takes me to a clothing store where I am measured up for police uniforms. I'm starting to realise that things in the AFP happen very quickly!

I go straight to the Commissioner's office on arrival at AFP headquarters. He welcomes me with his broad smile and a double hand shake. Mick Keelty is an iconic Australian—the 'real deal', frank, honest and practical. My job will be to minister to Federal and State police officers from forensic units who will be undertaking disaster victim identification. They are being activated from all over Australia and sent off on short notice to a developing and uncertain situation. I can see he places great value in Chaplaincy.

Swearing in by AFP Commissioner Mick Keelty

It's hard to believe all this is happening so fast. As we finish a cup of tea, Commissioner Keelty swears me in as a Special Member of the AFP, and then two duffel bags arrive with my AFP uniforms in them. Roger then advises that I have to keep moving, as my plane to Thailand departs at 7:00 p.m. and there are still a few other things to do, like getting an AFP Identification Card, and filling in a host of AFP forms. He then whisks me to his home in Weston where his wife, Cora, has a warm meal prepared for us, and then on to Canberra airport for transit via Melbourne and Bangkok to Phuket. Phew!

Intriguingly, my years of hyper-activity and hyper-arousal enable me to cope very well with frenetic activity. I am used to doing many things at once in multiple unusual situations. Sitting in Melbourne airport just prior to boarding for Thailand I write in my journal:

> Dear God, I just can't believe this is happening so fast. There are so many things that I will need to know in operating with the AFP. Guide me in this journey ... (I pause to listen for what God might be wanting to say to me. I write down the following thoughts that come into my mind) ... Gary I have been preparing you for this all of your life. You did not choose to come on this mission, I have chosen you. You have all the skills needed for this mission. Fear not for I am with you. Be not afraid—I am your God and will be with you wherever you go.

There is clarity in this communication that I truly believe is from God. I have been practising this spiritual technique of journalling for some years now, and the responses are wonderful. Whilst this might seem strange to some, it is a normal condition within Catholic spirituality. Whilst it might seem extraordinary to be hearing messages from God, what is actually happening to me is extraordinary to say the least. The Commissioner has skirted a whole raft of procedures to appoint me in the AFP and send me on a mission immediately. Government departments just don't do that. In bureaucratic terms they are taking an enormous risk with me. But the reality that this is happening just reinforces my strong belief that God is at work in and through me, in this amazing development in my life.

Even though I am in civilian clothes, at the airport, AFP officers enroute to the mission identify themselves to me. I'm not sure how they do this, but I guess they are trained to pick people out in a crowd! It is 6 am the following morning when we arrive at Phuket. The hotel bus transfers us to the Sheraton Hotel, where the AFP has set up its forward command post. This whole situation is starting to feel quite surreal to me. A beehive of activity is unfolding in front of me as the AFP set up their headquarters. Once again I reflect again on the past 24 hours, I start to feel a little apprehensive of what's to come.

The PTSD demon in my brain is trying to dislodge the peace of God that I have in my soul. For a start, I don't know any of the people that I am to be ministering to, and I know very little about the AFP or how they expect me to work. I am also conscious that we are dealing with a disaster of enormous proportions, with thousands of victims. I am also very conscious that this could trigger some nasty PTSD reactions, either during or after this mission. I hope I will not let anyone down. But, this is a moment in history. If Mick Keelty has personally asked me to help out, I will do my best until I can do no more.

I've found that God always has a way of letting us know that he is present and in support. On this day, His surprise to me is being spotted by a man in the hotel foyer who I recognize from my army days-former Army physical training instructor Bill Slape, dressed in an AFP uniform.

He calls out loudly to the other AFP officers present, 'Hey guys. This is Gary Stone, who's going to be our chaplain. He's a good guy. Welcome to the team!' My fears of having to break the ice are at once dissipated, thanks to Bill.

Shortly afterwards, I meet the AFP commander, Carl Kent, who arranges for me to be taken on a reconnaissance of the local area, where people have died. The extent of the tragedy is still unfolding. As we travel along the coastline, the devastation I observe is unbelievable.

North of Phuket, where there is a wide coastal plain, the tsunami waves have penetrated several kilometres inland. We pass a naval patrol boat that is aground more than 1 km inland from the beach. Everywhere you look there is destruction. Countless holiday resorts have been ripped apart. The ground is stripped bare in most places, and the debris is piled high in areas where an immovable object has been in the path of the wave. The only things to survive the tsunami are the palm trees.

We arrive at a Buddhist temple that is being used for the collection of bodies. The smell of death is overpowering. The bodies lie everywhere. There are piles of them. There is no refrigeration for them to be preserved in. The bodies are black and distended. Maggots and flies are all over them. Many have their bellies burst open from the heat. Bodily fluids are dripping from the tarps or sheets that they have been collected in. Crowds of people are gathered around looking for their loved ones. Most of the deceased are European holidaymakers. Their relatives are arriving from around the world to look for them. The whole scene is chaotic and distressing.

We return to the hotel for a wash and a planning meeting. Already, the smell of death has infected/permeated the clothes I am wearing. I have a long hot shower, and go down to dinner with the AFP staff. I discover that some of these people already have experience from the Bali bombing. Of course I have had my experiences of dead bodies in Iran, but none of us have had experience on this scale. To my absolute delight, I run into an army officer that I know. It is Paddy Ford, who went through Duntroon with my son Michael in 1999, and had participated in our Christian ministry training. Paddy has been activated, along with half a dozen other Defence linguists, to assist the AFP in communicating with the local people. We have a great chat, having not seen each other for a few years. This is yet another sign to me that God is with us.

In the morning, Commander Carl Kent invites me to go with him to a press conference in the Town Hall. Thousands of relatives and interested parties choke the grounds. By agreement with the Thai government, the AFP commander is given overall responsibility for all victim identification. The mission expands before our eyes as reports come in all day of bodies being discovered on remote beach areas and islands along hundreds of kilometres of coastline. Two more mortuaries are to be set up to start processing these bodies. The rough estimate at this stage is that there are 10,000 people missing and feared drowned on this section of coast and at least 2,500 bodies have surfaced and have been collected.

We return to the command post at the hotel, where more staff are arriving. After lunch I take some time out to pray and reflect how I can best assist. I decide I need to advertise and plan for some Sunday services for the staff, as well as plan a larger national memorial service to coincide with a National Day of prayer that is to be celebrated in Australia. I am conscious too that I need to establish a regular program of visits to all the mortuary sites, and to maintain regular contact with all our Australian staff. To do this I will need to visit them in their workplaces. We call this 'Ministry of presence.'

My first impressions of working with the AFP are very positive. Clearly they are all very competent individuals, who are accustomed to coming in to a new situation on very short notice and adapting to the tasks that are needed. It is not as if this is a pre-trained team that has come here, but rather a disparate group of individuals from all over Australia, who have just been streamed in to a location and are establishing themselves as they arrive. Unlike the military, there does not seem to be a very definite rank structure. There is a commander and he has appointed team leaders, but they are all on first name terms. Unlike the very precise orders and directions and planning that the army goes through, it appears from the sidelines that there is plenty of group thinking going on, with individuals suggesting ideas and then being told to go implement them.

As Day two dawns, I jump on the bus with the Disaster Victim Identification (DVI) teams heading out to the mortuary area north of Phuket. Overnight, many more bodies have been brought into the site. There are hundreds of them in a massive pile. They are loosely wrapped in tarps and sheets and blankets. Again, the stench is overpowering. I wander around the site, checking with the various team members as they go about their difficult task. I briefly introduce myself to each AFP member and tell them I am available to help them in whatever way that they may desire. Generally they are happy to stop what they're doing for a moment to have a chat, and distract themselves from the very unpleasant task they are doing. They normally ask me where I am from, and what denomination I belong to. A common comment is, 'Great to have you on board.' In reality I think all of us are still coming to grips with the extent of the task we have been given, and are uncertain how this is going to affect us.

Words cannot describe the unpleasantness that is involved in identifying decomposing bodies. This would have to be one of the worst tasks that a human being could be asked to do. This is how it works. We are all in white coveralls from head to toe, with masks and gloves on as well to try to avoid catching any illness. There is a production line of sorts set up. A team member lifts and carries a body from the pile and places it on a table for fingerprints to be taken. In the advanced state of decay in the tropical heat, the skin on the hands comes away from the bones like a glove. So the first action is peeling the skin off the fingers and pressing the fingertips onto a pad to make fingerprint impressions. The print is then scanned into a laptop. The team member who is responsible for finger printing carries the body to the next table where another team member is examining bodies for their dental features. This process involves positioning the head of the corpse and x-raying the upper and lower jaws. These x-rays and any notes about the corpse's teeth are also scanned into a laptop. The final team takes a DNA sample and photographs clothing, jewellery and any other items belonging to the deceased. The body is then placed in a heavy plastic body bag, tagged and placed in a refrigerated shipping container.

All of us working in the mortuary area must remain suited up in the coveralls, gloves and masks. It is oppressively hot and there is no air conditioning. We are dripping constantly with sweat. Every 45 minutes, the teams need a break to rehydrate and recover. We have major concerns about the outbreak of disease.

Apart from the identification teams, various members have been appointed as liaison officers, engaging with friends and relatives of the dead and missing. They have a very difficult job of dealing with the massive number of individuals that are desperate for information. A constant stream of people, both Thai and foreign, are coming up to the liaison staff, and at their request I assist them in communicating a standard pitch, along the lines of, 'We are in the early stages of identification, and will post pictures of the bodies that we have located on the noticeboards outside. Please be patient. We are working as fast as we can.' Of course I try to say this in a compassionate and empathetic way. I listen to their grief and their stories and gently touch them on the arm or shoulder when it seems appropriate. After a while I realise that this can only be a secondary role for me, as I must have sufficient energy for my primary role of supporting the AFP staff.

After about eight hours on-site, the teams halt for the day and return to the hotel for debrief, clean-up and a meal. I'm very conscious that the relaxation time of an evening is perhaps my most important time for ministry. At first, nobody wants to talk about the day's work. Now is a time for distraction from that. We spend time getting to know each other, and hearing about our lives up to this point. As always, people are interested to hear why I became a chaplain. I share some of my experiences from Iran, Timor and Bougainville. Some of the AFP have been to these places. I finish my evenings with a stroll along the beach. It's hard to imagine this same place was the scene of so much death and devastation-just a few days before.

Next day, at the mortuary site, Paddy asks me, 'Could you spend some time with a German girl called Nadine? She is very distressed and has been coming every day looking for and hoping she could find her fiancé.'

I meet her outside in the throng of people poring over a wall of photographs of the most recent bodies that have been brought in. I don't know of a more ghastly sight. There are thousands of bodies in the worst stages of decay. Nadine tells me:

'On the morning of the tsunami, my fiancé Johann and I were asleep in a hut near the beach. I am awoken by the walls crashing in and a flood of water engulfing us. We are swept away in the torrent of water and debris. Hundreds of metres later I grab a palm tree, but there is no sign of Johann. I search frantically for him for days, but I cannot find him.'

She is in despair and seemingly inconsolable. I am stumped. What can I say? She keeps asking to look among the bodies for him. But her emotional state wouldn't improve by searching through the decomposing bodies we have. Most already are unrecognisable. And there are thousands of them.

The only thing I have to offer her is faith. I ask her, 'Do you have any religious background or affiliation?'

She thinks for a moment and then says, 'I was baptised Catholic, but in Germany if you declare a religion, the government takes a percentage of your wages, and gives it to the church. I'm embarrassed to say my family haven't been involved in church for many years.'

She is pre-occupied with finding her fiancé's body so I ask her, 'What did you learn in your youth about a person's soul at the time of death.'

She thinks for a while and then responds, 'Their soul would go to God in heaven.'

I ask her, 'Do you think your fiancé's soul, his real essence, would still be among these decomposing bodies?'

A light seems to come on in her head. She replies, 'No he would not be here among this ghastly scene.'

I offer to pray for her and him. I place my hand gently on her shoulder. 'Lord, bless Nadine and give her peace. Bless her whole family at this time. Bless too Johann. We thank you for his life and entrust his soul to you ...'

She embraces me tightly and thanks me. Her mood changes dramatically. This is a moment of grace. I invite Paddy over and we spend some more time with her just sharing something of our lives. She agrees that maybe she should return home to Germany and the support of friends there.

We exchange email addresses and agree to keep in touch. (The following year she immigrates to Australia, and she eventually marries Paddy in Melbourne!)

Gradually we do start to get positive identifications of victims and we commence repatriation of their bodies. I am called to assist in ceremonies at the airport as the bodies are loaded on aircraft. I say some prayers and some words of appreciation to the staff involved, and some satisfaction is felt by all that we have done our bit to help grieving families.

One day, outside the mortuary in the humidity and putrid stench that we cannot get used to, I am asked the inevitable question by one of the AFP officers. 'Padre, where is God in all of this? How could God allow this to happen? Indeed what sort of God would allow this to happen?'

Blessing the body of an Australian who died in the Tsunami.

I respond, 'Scott, have you got time to sit down under the mango tree, while I share with you my thoughts on this.' He replies, 'Please Padre, I'm intrigued to hear what you have to say.'

I say, 'You have asked an understandable question. I don't want to palm you off with some textbook religious response. The question of why do bad things happen to good people has presented itself to me many times during my life. Additionally, whilst studying at the seminary, we were required to write a 6000 word paper on this topic. I have to say I don't have a simple or comprehensive answer. This is the most extraordinary tragic event that I have ever witnessed, and my heart goes out to everyone who is suffering as a result. I would not want any words of mine to diminish the sadness and loss that so many are experiencing.

But I do have some thoughts that have developed over time. I think I can provide some partial explanations, but admit that I don't have all the answers to your question.

Firstly in this case we are dealing with nature. I believe that God created the earth and nature, and that nature has its own rhythm of life, and that involves floods and fires, earthquakes and droughts, and humanity has to expect that these things will happen from time to time and take measures to accommodate them. Tragically some of these people died, because they were living in areas subject to flooding even without a tsunami. This is also a known earthquake zone, and many of the buildings that people were living in were not constructed adequately.

Tragically some of these people died by misadventure. They did not heed the warnings that were provided, nor take actions quick enough to evacuate themselves from danger zones.

But for the most part, I just have to say I don't know why this happened. But I do know from so many other life experiences that God loves us. God loves all humanity. God would not want any suffering to be happening here. God would not have wanted a single person to have been killed or injured. God would be weeping more than us.

Part of God's design was that humanity would have free will. God doesn't play 'grand puppeteer' orchestrating activity all over the world. He has given us life, and he has given us a world to live in, and generally speaking he leaves us to manage our lives, without interference from him. I certainly appreciate that free will to be able to make choices in my life. I would hope that a tragedy like this never happens again, and that the people who want to continue to live here, will be able to take measures to avert a future disaster, even should another tsunami approach this coast.'

After listening intently, Scott says to me, 'Thanks Padre, I really appreciate your insights. And I thank you for being so candid and honest with me. I don't know that anyone can adequately answer the question that I have asked. Actually I don't blame God for this. This is a natural disaster. By the way, the officers really appreciate you travelling around and visiting everyone. There is something mysterious about your presence that reminds us that we will get through this somehow. You won't find many of the AFP people talking about God, but don't let that put you off. I am sure that most of us have some sense of God, and your physical presence along with your welcoming smile reminds us that the 'big fella' is out there somewhere.'

I am to have a number of similar conversations with AFP officers over the coming days. Always a person of hope, I keep encouraging them to see the goodness that flows in the aftermath of this disaster. We get to introduce a spiritual dimension to our memories, our sadness and our hope, in a formal public service we hold on the beach at Phuket at dawn on 16 January. On this day in Australia, services of mourning are being held throughout the country, and the Australian Ambassador to Thailand asks me to plan a service to be held here as well. I am to be in charge, indeed there are no other Christian religious representatives in the area that I am able to locate. The service is to be relayed live to Australia.

About 150 people, mostly Australians and New Zealanders, gather on Pattong Beach at 6:00am. After a programme of scripture,

We remember and pray for Tsunami victims on Pattong beach.

preaching and prayer, I invite people to take off their shoes, and we carry a massive wreath down into the water. I propose that we do this because my training and experience has taught me that symbolic actions help people find new meaning and the ability to move on. After blessing the wreath, on this quiet, still morning, with only the gentlest lapping of the water onto the shore, the wreath somehow takes off out into the bay and sits about 100 metres off shore. This is another poignant moment of Grace. Tears flow freely from all the staff who have somehow taken a detached business-like approach to their duties over the previous days. For them, this experience allows them to release their own emotions as I and the Australian Ambassador, name, acknowledge and thank them for their efforts.

A few days later, the Thai authorities organise a massive inter-religious memorial service at a major sports stadium some two hours drive to the north, to which we are invited. Many thousands participate, with formal prayers offered by Buddhists, Hindus, Moslems, and Christian leaders. The service concludes with thousands of Chinese lanterns being lit, which take off up into the night sky. The scene is just amazing as I look up and see so many lights penetrating the darkness. I ponder how God must delight in us coming together in unity. I leave there even more strongly conscious that we are, I am, one with all of humanity. These are all my brothers and sisters. My life must continue to celebrate this.

After 16 days on this mission, AFP Chaplain Dave Cockram arrives to relieve me. Dave and I have known each other for 20 years, as he too was both soldier and Army Chaplain. Bodies are still being found, but all the staff are being rotated to minimise distress. Dave tells me the AFP would like me to continue on a part-time basis in Brisbane, as well as being available to serve on other short stints overseas. As with the military chaplaincy, I will care for AFP members and their families, as well as assist other Australian government officials in missions. The AFP is becoming a popular choice for the Government to deploy on short notice in our region. The AFP established the International Deployment Group to cope with its new regional and international outreach on behalf of the nation, and they would like my skills and experience to assist it. A new chapter in my ministry is being started.

Upon my return to Brisbane, I start one day a week at the Brisbane office of the AFP. There are several hundred Federal Agents in the city investigating organised crime, fraud, and terrorism, whilst out at Brisbane Airport there are airport police, air marshals and further counter-terrorism officers. I initiate a programme to get around and visit as many people as I can as soon as I can. Within a few months they increase my hours to two days a week, and then ask me to start visits of from one to two weeks to offshore missions.

Operation 'Helpem Hand' in the Solomon Islands

On 5 May 2005, I have my first visit to the Australian mission in the Solomon Islands. AFP Chaplain Roger O'Donnell accompanies me as we fly into Henderson Air Field. It's great to be mentored by Roger, who was one of the first Catholic Deacons ordained, and is about 8 years my senior. I look out the porthole, searching for signs of the US Marines' bloody battles to hold this airfield during World War II. To my surprise, the area is quite open and grassy. I identify a number of memorials on small ridgelines around the field and then spot the high grass-covered mountain overlooking Honiara that was the scene for the movie *The Thin Red Line*. Alighting from the plane, we are immediately hit by intense humidity. The mission welfare officer, Meredith Finn, greets us with a warm handshake and a bottle of cool water and we head down nearby 'Ramsi St' through lush tropical jungle to the joint AFP/ADF base. The street has been named after the mission acronym RAMSI—Regional Assistance Mission to the Solomon Islands, but also in a deliberate pun to reflect the complex interpersonal relationships that transpire on the popular TV show *Neighbours* in their Ramsay St!

In July 2003, a large ADF force with a smaller number of AFP, and overall led by DFAT head of mission Nick Warner, came into this country at a time of anarchy and civil war. They quickly disarmed rival militias and set about restoring services. Within a year the ADF numbers reduced to a rifle company of about 150 soldiers in support of a Policing mission, with 350 police officers involved in cleaning up and re-training a Solomon's police force. Thirteen Pacific countries now contribute to the mission.

At the former Guadalcanal Beach Resort, ('GBR' in AFP acronym-speak), I see a sprawling garrison village with additional temporary huts for the police, and tent lines for the soldiers. By Army standards, the base is luxury, nestling among palm trees. After a brief orientation at GBR, Roger and I head the ten kilometres into downtown Honiara.

Driving along the road, I see scenes reminiscent of Bougainville, but in much better repair. There are lots of 'leaf-huts' with palm frond roofs, built up on stilts, and many people walking slowly along the road in thongs and tee-shirts. Many carry long grass knives. Rubbish is everywhere, including burned-out vehicles, and in the downtown area there are many local youths 'hanging around', no doubt unemployed.

Our first stop is to meet Archbishop Adrian Smith, an Irish-born cleric from the Marist order of missionaries, who were the first Christian group to come to the area, over 100 years ago. Adrian has been here 40 years. In a beautiful Irish brogue he says, 'Welcome to Paradise! I've heard you were coming. The Marist bush telegraph is very good you know! How's my good friend Seamus Mc Mahon (our parish priest in Brisbane)?'

Adrian is very welcoming, and shows us his 360-degree, open-air Cathedral and the ornate carved altar, tabernacle and cross. A steep-sided roof sits above an area of some 100 metres square. There is bench seating for about 800 people, and there are no walls, allowing the crowd to spill out into the surrounding grounds. Wood carvings on the Cathedral furniture display the Middle Eastern bible images in the local culture. For example, the lectern from which the Scriptures are read, is carved in the shape of a canoe, indicating that the Bible has been brought to them from another island. In church-speak this is called 'enculturation'—a reinterpretation of the Christian story in this local context.

Adrian then shares with us the many current challenges he has in this divided community, where Christian values can easily be put aside when there are clan and family feuds to be resolved. He tells us that the transition from British colonial rule to independence in 1975 did not go well. Corruption in government and the police led to a breakdown of law and order that required international intervention. Adrian tells us about the social disintegration which fostered rival groups and culminated in anarchy and looting. The primary tension recently has involved violence between the original Guadalcanal residents and the migrants from the neighbouring island of Malaita, who have, over time got most of the better-paying jobs in town.

Resentful of the migrants, a local militia formed, calling itself the Guadalcanal Freedom Fighters, to terrorise the Malaitans into leaving. An opposing militia group formed to resist this intimidation—the Malaitan Eagle Force (MEF)—and took control of the town. The Malaitan-dominated police force condoned the MEF, and law and order broke down. The church had a major part in negotiating ceasefires and appealing for regional intervention. Bishop Adrian tells us that there is a long way to go, but 'slowly' they are making progress. I reflect how this same post-colonial tension is playing out across the South Pacific region. The fundamental problem is that local politicians expected independence to make them rich and powerful. What they really need to accept is their greater need for inter-dependence where they all contribute to each other's future. The concept of broad social responsibility is slow to catch on for people who for centuries have been content to conduct subsistence, while expatriates organised and maintained infrastructure that could enable economic development and improved standards of living.

From the Cathedral we go to Police HQ at Rove to meet the Solomon Islands Police Commissioner, Shane Castles. Shane is a former AFP officer, and is warm and welcoming. He outlines the delicate situation he has in developing the Royal Solomon Islands Police Force. A fundamental problem he faces is that ethnic loyalty supersedes all others. Police officers will not arrest people from their own clan, and will be quite violent in dealing with those from other clans. Those in places of authority will do 'favours' for members of their tribe that are blatantly illegal, including the embezzlement of government money. What we see as corruption is considered as looking after your extended family!

Downtown Honiara is in relatively better shape than anything in Bougainville, and we have a milkshake at a café called 'The Banana Lounge' where we catch up with Police officers off-duty, shopping in town. We go then to various Police stations in town, visit the prison, and return to a Friday night 'happy hour' at GBR. There are plenty of happy people, plenty of drinks flowing, and my first impressions are that this country and this mission are way ahead of others I have visited. We conclude the visit with some helicopter flights to remote island police stations, where our staff seem to be living in a tropical paradise, albeit without some of the technological comforts of home.

I return to the Solomon's again in September and November 2005, and February 2006 and generally, all appears to be going well. The AFP commander at the time, Will Jamieson, tells me that the AFP see this as a very long term mission, possibly in the order of 10 to 20 years. On each visit I also go to see Archbishop Adrian Smith. He certainly hopes that the regional policing mission can stay for a very long time. I sense he has concerns that troubles will break out again.

On Sundays I lead worship for the multinational group at GBR—a true example of the fraternity of humanity that Jesus hopes for. The harmonic singing of the Pacific Islanders is just wonderful. This is joyful ministry for me.

An interesting dimension to this mission for me is to see how the staff from police, defence and foreign affairs backgrounds integrate and work together. It is a new experience for all concerned and it certainly makes sense to be utilising a range of disciplines to promote and sustain peace and stability.

Gathered with representatives of RAMSI's 13 nations in the Solomons after church service, December 2007

My greatest enjoyment comes from interaction with the local community. The mission has a small community engagement team called, 'Helpem Fren (friend)', and on each visit they ask me to come with them to local schools and community gatherings, where I am invited to talk about peacemaking from a Christian perspective. I am also invited to be interviewed and to speak on the Catholic Church's community radio whenever I visit. The great thing about this is that it gets relayed throughout all of the hundreds of islands of the Solomon's, into places that I could never possibly visit. I offer them always a simple message, along the lines that God loves us all, and desires that we live in peace and harmony as brothers and sisters in one human family. I have heard it said that a good preacher just keeps reminding people of the fundamental truths that they need to believe, that may have been overlooked in all the 'clutter' and confusion that life overwhelms us with these days. As a Deacon my mission is to proclaim the good news of Jesus Christ, and that is what I try to do, by focusing on God's love, and his call that we should love our neighbours as we love ourselves.

Unfortunately, I am to be reminded of how little I really understand about what is going on here when, to the great surprise of everyone in the mission, in April 2006, protests and riots break out in the city following the election of a Prime Minister who is unpopular with a segment of society. In a bizarre twist, on the suspicion that Chinese businessmen had tried to influence the election, most of Chinatown is looted and burned to the ground, and numerous local police and AFP members are injured. Hundreds of military and police reinforcements are flown in, and our tropical paradise is now a place of fear and trepidation. From a chaplaincy perspective, Roger responds to the immediate crisis and I follow several weeks later.

The destruction I witness on arriving is just insane. Numerous islanders have lost their jobs, and foreign investment stops. Just as I have seen in Timor, complex tribal rivalries, unresolved disputes, and personal trauma from the past, not visible on the surface of people, can erupt without notice, with devastating results. I visit Adrian Smith, and he breaks down in tears, as he shares his exasperation over what has happened.

I am to spend much of my time on this visit listening to the trauma of the police officers who were overwhelmed by the thousands of machete wielding, rock throwing rioters, who went on a rampage in downtown Honiara. At one stage about 30 officers withdrew into a hotel, which was subsequently set alight and burned to the ground. Fortunately, reinforcements arrived, firing gas and rubber bullets and pushed the rioters back before anyone died.

I receive wonderful affirmation from the AFP officers, for my patience and understanding in listening to their stories after this crisis. They appreciate sharing with me because they know that I will keep their circumstances confidential. Indeed they comment that they did not feel comfortable sharing the same stories with the psychologists that come over because of the risk that they might be medically downgraded or sent home. From my own experience in dealing with trauma, I can empathise with them over this same dilemma. Indeed I share some of my own story with them when it seems appropriate. Certainly at this time in both the AFP and the ADF, people feel themselves to be in this 'Catch-22' dilemma. You are 'damned if you do, and damned if you don't' share your story with some people in the system.

Don't mess with us—Solomons 2009

I continue with a number of other short visits to the Solomon's over the coming years. Most of the time things are stable, but just to remind us of the potential for quick change, on a 2009 visit, after a peaceful Police Remembrance Day service on 29 September—the feast of St Michael, patron saint of Police officers—a gang of 15 criminals raid the Police Commissioner's private residence at 2am, and he and his wife avoid being beaten to death by their fortuitous escape into a cyclone-proof vault! I visit them later in the day. The Commissioner is stoic, but it is clear his wife is traumatised. Of course I am just one of a host of other people offering them support, but I offer them my prayers, and hope that this can be received as a component of their healing.

This Peace mission continues, with no definite end date in sight. Certainly in the eyes of many of the local people I meet, a regional policing arrangement is a desirable option for them, for years to come.

Crisis in Timor

The April 2006 riots in the Solomon's are followed by May 2006 riots in Dili. The Timor crisis is massive and unrelenting. 150,000 people flee their homes in Dili and seek refuge in church grounds. More than 30 die and thousands are wounded as anarchy erupts following violent clashes between the Timorese police and military. Half of the military has already deserted, and the 5000-strong police force disintegrates. Thousands of police weapons mysteriously disappear. Australia immediately mounts an International Stabilisation Force of police and military, soon to be followed by thousands of UN police from around the world.

My heart aches for the Timorese people. Haven't they suffered enough? Inside I am angry that our decision-makers in Canberra chose to disengage as quickly as possible from the significant capacity development that was going to be needed here after the destruction of 1999. By 2006, United Nations police and military forces have been withdrawn, and our only official Australian presence is in the form of embassy staff and a twenty person military training team in which our son Michael is serving.

While I am in the Solomon's at this point, Roger deploys to Timor. Despite the massive surge of troops, the violence does not abate. Resentment of the government, unresolved land disputes, payback owing from Indonesian times and widespread poverty see tribal and gang fighting continue until November. My son Michael is in the forefront of peaceful intervention in this crisis. I get my first AFP deployment to Timor in July 2006 and many more follow.

Flying into Dili this time has greater significance to me than any other overseas trip I have had. My eldest son is going out daily onto the streets amidst brutal violence, and despite our almost daily phone contact in the weeks before, now I get the chance to be present with him in this challenging task of peacemaking.

As we circle Dili, ready to land, the blue-plastic-sheeted, internally displaced people (IDP) camps around Dili give us a tell-tale sign of the troubles on the ground. Michael's heroic efforts are already in the public domain, and an ABC *Australian Story* team led by producer, Kent Gordon is on the plane with me to record the events of the next fourteen days.

As I alight onto the tarmac, Michael comes over, and we hug. He then leads me through Customs and on to the AFP base set up in the 'Timor Lodge' accommodation compound (an old Indonesian military camp) quite close to Comoro Airport. Driving through the first roundabout, Michael points out opposing gangs holding rocks in their hands, yelling at one another. We've scarcely come a few hundred metres when Michael pulls over. We are into peacemaking! He quizzes one group what is happening and then goes over to the other. Apparently one group alleges the other has stolen some chickens from the opposite village. He introduces me as *Amu* 'holy man.' The boys see the crosses on my uniform and immediately change expression and look coy and embarrassed. He tells them in forceful Tetun that they should try to resolve this issue through the village chiefs—not through fighting. They step back apologetically. I tell them, *Ba ho Paz* 'Go in peace'.

Less than a minute later, we arrive at the AFP base, with a line of officers holding batons and shields by the front gate. Gang violence has gone up and down the main street throughout the day. Immediately I see officers I had known in the Solomon's who had been flown in as reinforcements. Unlike the Solomon's, where order was quickly restored, here the violence has escalated, as anarchy spreads. This is a deeply traumatised society which has experienced years of unresolved grief, anger and poverty. The local police and military have fractured. Some are fighting each other. Many have just deserted. There is opportunistic looting. This is a serious, serious situation; it will take significant time to be resolved.

About 350 Australian and New Zealand police are living in converted shipping containers in an area about 400m x 400m, and fenced in with two chain-link fences with barbed wire on top. The officers are tired from daily riot-control duties. Many are bruised and sore from very physical arrests of ringleaders. I become aware that they are talking of thousands of gang members all across Dili throwing rocks, firing darts, hacking with machetes. Broadly speaking, we *malae* 'foreigners' aren't the targets. This is sectarian infighting—old-fashioned gang warfare really.

Michael has been working closely with the AFP, helping them get to know 'who's who', who the bad guys are, and who the potential peacemakers are. The task is clearly beyond our resources at this time.

The Army commander, Brigadier Mick Slater, has Michael speaking on radio and TV every night, dispelling rumours and appealing for peace and unity. As I watch him one night in the studio, my pride in his people skills is immense.

I listen as he says in flawless Tetun, 'Our Australian soldiers are here to help you restore peace. But all Timorese must accept this as your responsibility too. I call upon parents to stop your children from getting involved in gang fights. I ask village chiefs to exercise your authority and rein in gang leaders. I ask police and military members to remember your responsibility to serve your nation. Reject violence. Embrace peace and unity. God demands this of you!'

Michael appealing for peace to community leaders.

He has become the voice of reason in this madness. Day by day people tell me that Michael is *the* 'Peacemaker.' (The ABC chooses that as the title for their programme).

I get about my normal chaplaincy routines—visiting the officers on and off duty, listening to their stories, and giving advice on people issues. As in the Solomon's, many of the police have been affected by the violence. They are bruised and cut and traumatised from having feared for their lives, in trying to break up the riots. The AFP and the ADF are trying to work collaboratively, but it will take some time for smooth working arrangements to be developed, and in the meantime, some misunderstandings will have to be dealt with. Many of my interactions involve giving the police officers some cultural understanding of how the military think and act, and appealing for their patience.

I take the AFP chief liaison officer to meet Bishop Alberto Ricardo Da Silva. He thanks us profusely for our efforts. I am conscious too that Police Remembrance Day is coming up, and I make plans for a service. I feel that gathering the officers together in a spiritual context might be a good circuit breaker for some of them to reimagine the positive side of what we are doing here. The beautiful white church on the waterfront, St Anthony's Motael would be a good venue, so I go there in search of the priest.

To my delight, I find Father Antonio Alves. He invites me into the presbytery and we have a great chat. He has spent many years in Sydney and speaks better English than my Tetun, so we are able to comfortably converse. He has two thousand IDPs in his church grounds.

He tells me, 'The situation is traumatic for me. Every day there are problems with people stealing others' food, and getting into fights ... I cannot possibly feed them.'

He says, 'Your son Michael is doing a great job with his broadcasts. He speaks better Tetun than I can.' We make plans for our September service and he invites me to drop in whenever I can. I take this offer up on many occasions.

The Australian Army now has about 1200 troops in town, and one of the chaplains with them is my friend Father Morgan Batt, who I had invited to join Army Chaplaincy in 2001. Morgan is a very tall, athletic man. His hobby is mountain climbing. He has been active in visiting local community groups, and invites me to come to a daily, early morning mass he celebrates for the Canossian nuns who run an orphanage at Balide, close to the Army HQ of Camp Phoenix. Mother Guilherminho normally has 300 girls there to look after, but at the moment there are 3000 IDPs crowded into her grounds. There are a small number of local Catholic priests in Dili, but nowhere near the number that is needed to provide pastoral care for so many traumatised people. The Bishop has told me that the addition of Morgan and me as Catholic Clergy in the mission is greatly appreciated.

As we arrive at the front gate I am shocked by the overcrowding. Every patch of ground is covered in people. We celebrate the mass, which hundreds attend. A seemingly never-ending line of people come forward to receive holy communion, and we then go to Sister Guillerminho's convent for a breakfast of coffee, bread rolls and jam. It reminds me of the many such breakfasts I have had in Atabae. The Sister is a very strong woman who doesn't hold back on blaming the crisis on the incompetence of the former government. She asks me if I can raise some money for beds, and I undertake to. Actually I give her some money on the spot. I've learned to come prepared and I sense this is a very worthy cause.

Later in the day I catch up with our Friends and Partners with East Timor (FPET) staff—David and Margaret Hall. They come to Timor Lodge and I get them a meal. What saints these folks are.

They report, 'All is well in Atabae—no troubles, no violence at all.' Of course I had sensed there wouldn't be—we have been helping them and they have no need to be looting. Once again, I muse over the short-sightedness of our Government and the UN in shutting down their operations years too early. There was never going to be peace in this traumatised society whilst such poverty remained and the government institutions were so immature. Even now it still seems that security in the minds of politicians and government advisers equates to having police and military on the streets. They are needed, of course, but security needs to be experienced in the hearts of the people who live in fear of starvation or violence from looters. This is a long process. It may take 30 years. That's the timeframe I am planning for, with Friends and Partners' support.

Over the next three years I deploy to Timor in an AFP role nine times. Slowly stability returns but the challenges remain immense. I get to travel by UN helicopter to AFP members at the remote outpost of the Oecussi Enclave, 300km west of Dili and surrounded by Indonesian territory, as well as to Baucau in the East and Maliana in the West. In each place, small teams of AFP officers, alongside police from 37 other countries are dealing with criminality as well as mentoring Timorese police. They live in the community, eating the local food and are most appreciative of a visit. Several have community projects needing funds which I source. I really enjoy these visits, and it seems the police in remote areas really enjoy them as well, as senior management rarely gets out of the national capital. I always make a point of personally thanking the officers for their service, and offer to make contact with their families back in Australia. In a world of mobile phones and e-mails, a personal visit, a warm handshake, and the opportunity to look someone in the eye, will always be the best way to provide some emotional and spiritual support.

At Baucau one day, a tall, trim and cheery AFP officer, Morag Mc Cabe, asks me, 'Every week I drop into a girls' orphanage at Venilale, one hour south of Baucau. They are beautiful children, but they are undernourished, just getting one bowl of rice a day and rarely any protein. Could you get help for them?'

I reply, 'Please take me down there. Let me see the situation and take some photographs.'

We drive to Venilale along winding rough roads, and arrive at the orphanage. Hundreds of girls stream out of the school and orphanage complex, smiling and cheering. Sister Maria Fortunado invites us in for coffee and shows us around the facilities. We go to the kitchen which is almost bare except for a few bags of rice and several dozen cobs of corn. In one corner some girls are pounding the corn to crush it into powder with which they will make a form of bread. Sister Maria tells me that they are at the point of starvation and no aid agency has been up this way to help out. They have their own rice fields and vegetable gardens which the girls tend to, but a plague of mice has devastated this year's crops. I immediately give her some cash and undertake to tell their story to a school in Australia.

On my return, I speak about the situation to a member of our parish, Julie Whitehouse who is a teacher at Sienna College. She subsequently invites me to the school to speak to the students. They immediately raise $3000. Another benefactor who wishes to remain anonymous gives $3000.

I take this back to Timor with me the following month. The nun is speechless at first when I hand over the money in cash. She hugs me and thanks me profusely:

'This get us much rice from market and also cows and goats, and medicines. Oh may God bless you Deacon Gary. You save us. We forever grateful.'

I reply, 'Sister Maria, I will pass your thanks on to the people who have given you this. I am but a messenger connecting people with each other. You are our neighbours.

We love you as sisters in Christ.'

Some may wonder why the Catholic Church is not providing for these orphans from some other source. The reality is that the church is not the completely centralised organisation that people may imagine, where Rome collects and disburses funds as it sees fit. Certainly there are some functions that are conducted centrally, but many aspects of church life are very localised. In matters of humanitarian relief, the church will never have sufficient funds to meet the needs of continuing developing crises around the world, and it relies on local and regional people of goodwill, to get on with the business of loving their neighbour. It was for this very reason that the Catholic Church re-introduced the Ministry of Deacon 60 years ago, to have people doing exactly what I am doing here in Timor, going around and identifying unmet needs and finding ways to meet them.

Deployed inland

My AFP Chaplaincy sees one further area of deployment—to the Northern Territory (NT). We are assisting the NT police in an intervention in Aboriginal communities that are in crisis. Whilst many Aboriginal people make a very positive contribution to Australian society, there are a number of rural communities where tribal elders, as well as other concerned citizens have asked for specific government intervention.

I'm able to start this visit by meeting up with the Superintendent in charge of Alice Springs, Sean Parnell. He is an Army Reservist and also significantly involved in lay ministry within the Catholic Church. I've met him quite a few times before and we have kept in regular contact. (I have a sense that one day he will be a deacon.) He takes me for a drive around town, starting with the 'town camps' of squatters around Alice Springs. Inebriated bodies sit or lie sprawled under trees among garbage heaps of empty beer bottles and takeaway food wrappers, and other small groups sit in the sandy creeks drinking beer from big bottles in the middle of the day.

Sean says, 'It takes white fellas a long time to understand black fellas.'

I reply, 'Is it OK to use those terms?'

He says, 'That's the way they describe themselves and us Gary—yes it's fine. There are some very good people among them, but many others are suffering from acute alcoholism. We have tried every strategy to help them, but they are dying through self-neglect.'

I'm stumped! I don't know how to reply.

After that quite shocking introduction I drive over a number of days in a 1000km circuit around Uluru,(Ayers Rock) Hermannsberg, Haarsts Bluff and numerous other towns, and I witness a social devastation unlike any I have seen overseas.

I am shocked, sick to the stomach actually, to see the disaster of entrenched alcoholism in these indigenous communities. The police are there to protect the children primarily. This is one situation where poverty is not a problem. Actually the Government has provided everything they might need—schools, clinics, houses, electricity. The towns, though, are like rubbish tips where filth abounds and all care and dignity is lost in the alcoholic haze. Despite bans on alcohol in most towns, people still get it in, get drunk, fight and damage property, and collapse all over the place. Some children are sniffing petrol. It damages their brains. But their parents are too drunk to supervise their kids. The 'demon drink' is demonic indeed. I pray each day for this tragic situation. I know not how this will end.

In one sense this tragic situation has also developed following the 'colonisation' of Australia. Our forebears clearly did not understand, nor may have cared how to integrate European and Aboriginal culture. Again I am drawn to study and promote cultural understanding and social cohesion as a key component of peace in our world.

Of course my mission here has been specifically to visit, support and affirm the police officers in maintaining law and order. But from a purely personal and emotional viewpoint this is one trip that seriously disturbs me afterwards. I keep getting flashbacks in my dreams at night of the social devastation. I talk it over with my Psychiatrist and my supervisor Father John Chalmers. There is little one can do to rationalise what is happening here. I know that it is not my role to find a solution to this situation. There are clergy in most of these communities from various denominations that have a calling to respond to this situation. But as a human being, I am concerned and distressed by this.

In the end, I realise that it is unhealthy for me to allow this situation to continue to distress me. I feel I have no other choice than to block all thoughts of this mission. Seeing the unnecessary neglect and suffering of children is just a 'bridge too far' for me.

Taking a break...

I feel that I have made a positive contribution to the AFP, but I have come to realise that there are limits to what I can reasonably cope with, and I have reached that limit.

The police are certainly a wonderful group of people, with a similar sense of service to our nation and community, but I can only stretch myself so far, and so after 7 years' service I retire from the AFP.

With the AFP I undertake nine deployments to Timor, nine to the crisis in the Solomon's, and one to the Intervention in the Northern Territory. It has been interesting seeing the ADF and AFP working together for the first time in our nation's history on significant overseas operations. I would like to think my experience with both organisations has in some small way helped in bridging the differences and helping with the synchronization needed between them.

The police show their appreciation for my efforts by investing me with the Humanitarian Overseas Service Medal for my ministry in the Tsunami, the Police Overseas Service Medal for my service in the Solomons, and the Australian Federal Police Operations Medal for service in Timor.

I am proud to have served concurrently in two great national institutions and wear these police medals, along with my military medals, as a sign of our unity.

One AFP visit to Timor is particularly significant, and deserves a chapter all on its own. Once again Michael and I just happen to be at the right place, at the right time, to make a positive difference.

Chapter 12
The President has been Shot Please Pray for Him!

The President has been Shot—Please Pray for Him!

You will lay hands on the sick and they will be healed.
Matthew 28.29

From 2007 to 2011, our son Michael, is President José Ramos Horta's Military Affairs Adviser—his 'Mr Fixit'—in Timor Leste. On Monday 11 February 2008 I'm at Michael's house in Dili at the tail end of a visit to the Federal Police contingent and about to have breakfast. Michael's phone rings and he puts it on speaker so we can continue making breakfast while he takes the call.

A frantic caller bellows out, 'The President has been shot ... what should I do?'

Stunned, we look at each other in disbelief. Maybe one of his guard's rifles has gone off accidentally?

'Michael, the President is bleeding everywhere, what should I do!'

Michael gathers himself quickly and then calmly but loudly, says,

'Paulo, you must stop the bleeding. Tear up your shirt and hold it over his wounds! Bring the President immediately to the Australian Defence medical facility at the heliport. I will meet you at the gate.'

Turning to me as he hurries to the door, he says, 'Dad, stay here for the time being. I'll let you know how you can help, once I have worked out what is going on.'

Immediately my heart starts thumping, and I sense that something awful is happening.

After arriving at the scene Michael rings me with an update. In a machine gun burst of words he reports, 'The President has been shot by rebels. He is critically wounded. I have just helped carry him out of the ambulance onto the operating table at the medical facility at Dili's heliport. Dad, his blood is all over the floor of the ambulance and me. I'm not sure if he will survive. He is scarcely breathing, and is limp and pale from blood loss. The military are organising an emergency airlift to Darwin. Please pray for him Dad—pray for Timor. We don't know who is behind this or how far this rebellion extends. Gotta go!'

Though stunned, I quickly reply,

'Take it easy, Michael. We'll get through this somehow.' Then he's gone.

My system is taking a hit. Adrenaline is surging through me. I must calm down. 'Calm down!' I say to myself. I sit on a bench at the back of Michael's house, gazing at the hills overlooking the city with my heart racing and nerves bristling. I start praying my default emergency prayers for crises.

'Our Father who art in Heaven hallowed be thy name, Thy Kingdom come, thy will be done ... Hail Mary full of grace, the Lord is with thee ... Glory be to the Father, the Son and the Holy Spirit ...'

Praying the Rosary quietens my racing heart a little, but my hyper-vigilant mind is in over-drive. This is a critical moment in Timorese history. José is critically wounded, and our son is once again in danger. I've got to keep it together. I need to be calm, cool and collected.

I'm so proud of my son. I muse that Divine Providence has brought me to be here at this time and for important reasons. Evil has been running amok in Timor for several years now. In 2006 Australia launched a strong military intervention after Timorese military renegades and police fought with each other in the streets of Dili, and this event could prompt another period of chaos. My mind now focuses on two people—Michael and Jose—my son and his boss, one of the most important men in Timor Leste. I have to provide whatever spiritual support I can muster. I must get control of my emotional responses as well. I will do my best to be part of a spiritual intervention and leave my compatriots to the military intervention.

What danger is Michael facing? He is the President's man—potentially another target. Whoever has shot José may be after Michael as well. I prayerfully entrust his life to God. Only a week before, a bomb detonated about one hundred metres from the Australian Defence Compound, near Michael's house while Michael and I were sitting outside in this very same spot where I am sitting now. After the shockwave blew over us, we both immediately thought of Alfredo Reinado, a rebel leader and former military officer, who has been on the run since the rebellion in 2006. We wonder if this explosion was probably his work. Investigation did not reveal what this was about or who was responsible. Thinking now, it dawns on me that this explosion was a harbinger of worse things to come—or perhaps it was actually meant for us!

Since 2006 Alfredo had evaded capture despite the best efforts of Timorese, Australian and New Zealand military and police units, as well as Australian Special Forces scouring the countryside for him. He has become a romanticised Timorese Scarlett Pimpernel who is enjoying the support of locals throughout the country, foolishly attracted to his brash rebelliousness and swagger during media interviews. A month ago, Michael had accompanied José to a secret meeting with Alfredo in the mountain village of Maubisse. José offered him an amnesty if he would lay down his arms. Alfredo refused to do so and the meeting broke up acrimoniously. Michael was at José's elbow during these meetings and is very much part of the security apparatus here. He must be a target. I pray, 'Protect him please Lord.'

It's just seems so surreal that this is all happening. 'Lord may I be an instrument of your peace.'

Michael rings again and asks me to fly to Darwin to support the President and his family as he undergoes emergency surgery. In some ways I'd rather be with Michael and be on hand for the inevitable influx of Australian Federal Police as well. I ring my boss, the AFP commander in Dili, who agrees that I should help the President first. We are at a strategically important moment in both Timor Leste's and Australia's history. Should José die, opposition groups will scramble for power and violence is likely. In so many ways, José's personal leadership has held this fractured society together. Yes! My mission today is to minister to the President.

Dili is in shock. I look out from the back of the car taking me to the airport and see unusually quiet streets. Soldiers and police are buttoning the city down with road blocks and have begun looking for rebels. One hour after two bullets smashed into José Ramos Horta's lower chest, sounds of gunfire echo out from the hills at Dare immediately inland from Dili. A second rebel assassination squad ambushes a convoy of vehicles escorting Prime Minister Xanana Gusmão. He survives, miraculously untouched after rebels pepper his convoy's vehicles with bullet holes. The Australian military response is swift. Black Hawk helicopters filled with snipers take to the skies over Dili.

Sitting in the airport departure lounge at 8.30am my phone rings.

The President has been Shot—Please Pray for Him! 275

'Hi Gary, it's Kent Gordon here from the ABC *Australian Story* programme, just ringing to check that you and Michael are OK.'

Kent had recorded the 2007 episode that focused on Michael and me during the 2006 troubles. I reply briefly, 'Kent, I can't say much over the phone, but we are in the thick of this. Please pray for us. Things are really serious.' My gosh, how do the ABC in Brisbane know about this so quickly?

After arrival at Darwin an hour later, Federal Police officers meet me and take me to John Carrascalao, José's nephew, who is at his home with José's mother, who was about to go to Dili that day to visit Jose. Madeleina is in great distress, having already lost three children to violence during the Indonesian occupation, as well as José's father who died from a stress induced stroke. He, one brother and two sisters survive the attempted extermination of his family. Dear God, this family has suffered so much. Other relatives arrive. I pray with them and then lead them all to Darwin Hospital to await Jose, who is fighting for his life, in an inbound medical evacuation aircraft from Dili. I feel both honoured as well as humbled before God to be given this responsibility.

Sitting in the emergency waiting room, just before the medical evacuation flight arrives, we see TV reports of separate attacks made upon Prime Minister Xanana Gusmão and his wife, Kirsty. The Australian Government has ordered an emergency deployment of more troops and police to Timor Leste.

I ring Michael to report that I am with José's family at Darwin Hospital. After dispatching José to Darwin, he is now coordinating the swearing-in of an Interim President, arranging armed protection for other key government leaders, and advising where troops and police should deploy to pursue the assassins. Wow! I am so proud of him. Things couldn't get much worse. He is coordinating responses superbly. I am consciously calming myself so that I can support the President and his family and give Michael one less thing to deal with.

I tell Michael, 'I'll look after the President for now—you look after yourself and focus on the situation in Timor.'

I sense Michael is already grieving deeply for the President. We had discussed his concerns about the President's personal security several times, but José always over-ruled Michael's desire for extra precautions because he felt that the President must engender confidence by not having a bevy of armed guards surrounding him like a US President. Michael still hasn't recovered from the extreme dangers of the outbreak of violence and killings in 2006. I have long held concerns that he may also have PTSD because of his hyper-vigilance and hyper-activity. Both these conditions are helping him now in another crisis, but may deepen the longer term impact on him through an inevitable burn-out.

I know he will give his best, but everyone has limits. I hope that Michael has the insight to pace himself now so that he does not break down when he is needed most. I'm pacing myself with slow deep breaths and more decades of the Rosary prayed under my breath when no one is noticing.

José's mother Madeleina weeps and cries out. She looks me in the eye and pleads with me, 'Why, why, why is this happening? José has given his all for Timor.'

I can't find words of consolation. I just hug her and weep with her. My mind is racing and heart thumping. I am trying to make sense of these sudden tragic events. The attacks don't make sense. Once more my mind travels back three weeks to when Michael and President José met secretly with Alfredo at Maubisse. Alfredo must know that José desperately wanted to resolve this ongoing dissent peacefully. His offer of amnesty was more than reasonable. The country could then move on. It would seem Alfredo has decided again to use violence to get his way.

Anxiety pulses in my head in moments of silence—deep breath, deep breath, deep breath. It is a complex situation. How do Alfredo and his men afford to be so well armed and equipped? Other powerbrokers in the country must be supporting them? Is this attempted assassination the beginning of a military coup? Is more violence on the way? So many people, including me, are still haunted and troubled by the trauma of seven months of violent civil strife in 2006. Thankfully, while my mind is in over-drive, a simple message comes through from God,

'Put the past behind you, and be present to this grieving family, and love them.'

We are not long at the hospital when a Federal policeman alerts us to José's imminent arrival. I guide the family to a private waiting area inside the emergency casualty area like a shepherd herding his sheep with arms out, soothing words, gentle touches and gestures. Like a scene out of the movies or a reality TV show, ambulance medics pull José out on a gurney and wheel him into the triage area. José's nephew, John Carrascalao, who is also an Australian Army medic, asks the doctors to allow me to pray over him before they operate. John says to the Hospital Director, 'Please let Padre Gary pray for him before anyone does anything else. We are a Catholic family and we believe in the power of prayer as well as medicine.'

The Director says, 'Certainly, no worries. I'm happy with that.'

I accompany José lying on his gurney into the operating theatre. He is comatose and on life support, with tubes coming out of mouth and nose, drips in both arms. Time to concentrate and be intentionally present . I lay my hand on his head and bless him. I read some scripture and prayers from our Catholic ritual for ministering to the sick, and then pray for the staff hovering around that they might do their job well. I bless them all with the sign of the Cross.

I get through the ritual in serious but calm 'ministry mode', but as I step back and at least a dozen staff swarm around him to prepare him for major surgery, emotion grabs me and tears flow from my eyes. I listen to a doctor reading out the report sent from Dili. He has been shot in the torso with at least two rounds, one of which has punctured a lung. X rays show that one bullet is still inside him, about a millimetre from his spinal cord.

I compose myself, switch back into 'ministry mode', and go back to the family in the private waiting room, reassuring them and praying with them again. I lead them in the Lord's Prayer in Tetun, '*Ami Aman* …' I offer them Holy Communion, which the hospital chaplain brings me from the Reserved Sacrament Tabernacle located in the hospital chapel. I know they are comforted to remember that God is present. Much of ministry is like this-helping people remember what they already know; reminding them again of the rituals that connect them to God. We sit down and comfort each other. I am grieving too, of course. I go for a short walk down the corridor where no-one can see me, and burst out crying again. Their grief and my grief flows out in these tears.

Walking back and still struggling to control my own emotions, I run into Doctor Andrew Burke, who I had last seen in Bougainville some seven years before. Indeed he was the one who brought Cornelius into the PMG hospital with a gunshot wound to the head. An eyewitness to a miracle. We have a brief chat and undertake to catch up later. He says, 'The President could have no better support than having you here.' I am reminded of the miracle in Bougainville and marvel at the coincidence of meeting Andrew right now when I am again under extreme emotional pressure.

I have seen this man José many times, always inspired by his commitment and courage. But now, for the first time, I see him with all his charisma and power stripped away. He is lying naked and gaunt on a gurney, unable to move or talk. The tragedy of this situation reminds me of Jesus on the cross. But I also call to mind that, in his weakest moment, Jesus also redeemed the world. I have a feeling—perhaps an intuition within me or a hint from God—José will live through this. He must!

Doctors eventually come out and brief the family on the extent of his injuries. As expected, they are clinical and professional. Well in control of their emotions, they show the trajectory of the two bullets and the specific tissue damage, but baulk at predicting an outcome, warning that the first 24 hours are critical to survival. His body has had the most violent of shocks. His vital organs were starved of blood for a period that should have killed him. Doctors in Dili infuse nine units of blood into him to replace what had gushed from his chest—almost a total blood transfusion. There is now a high risk of infection. A betting man would say, 'He has no hope of survival.'

I ask to go in and be with him. They agree. I stand holding José's hand in mine and resting my other hand upon his head. I can see tubes draining away blood from his punctured lung so he can breathe. I pray and pray and pray that God will miraculously deliver him from the jaws of death.

Later I would find out that his assailant shot him in the torso with two SS109 5.56mm high-velocity rounds at a range of ten metres. He bled for thirty minutes before he received any treatment whilst a gun battle raged. Realistically he cannot survive, but I keep praying. He is in a coma, but I keep talking to him through the night. I try to pour my life energy into him. I leave him for a while to go out to comfort his mother and family members. They cling to me for hope. I pray with them too. In Timor Leste everything is up for grabs. Should he die, the country will return to the horrible sectarian violence of 2006.

When the flurry of medical emergency activity abates, I am invited to accompany family members into the intensive care room, one by one. They cry, stagger and wail as I have to hold some of them upright. I pray with each one, and they grip me firmly. It's like they are drawing energy from me. Indeed, I feel the energy move between us.

I ring Michael to report that José is being well looked after, and that I am looking after the family. He tells me he has dashed out to the President's house and identified the bodies of Alfredo Reinado and his deputy, Leopoldino, lying dead in pools of blood in the grounds of José's traditional, thatch roofed villa in the semi rural area between Dili and the imposing statue of Christo Rei (Christ the King). Michael is in overdrive, his words coming out like a gale force wind. I urge him to get some rest.

'I'll be right Dad.' he replies. I pray, 'Please, please God, look after him.'

The hours tick over without us noticing the time passing. Near and distant family members arrive and connect emotionally with those already there. I chat with José's son, Nino, who has been living in Singapore, his surviving brother, Arsenio, and sisters Rosa and Imelda. Various dignitaries come and go as well. Staff arrive from Dili to manage the messages of support that are arriving in increasing numbers from around the world.

Australian Foreign Minister Stephen Smith arrives. A government staff member introduces me to him as 'Mick Stone's Dad.' I cheekily respond that, 'I am the Adviser to the Adviser to the President!' He retorts that, 'Our Government is very happy with the quality of advice they have been getting from Michael.'

The Minister says to the family, 'We want to offer you any support you need and that our government can provide.'

Sister Rosa calls out, 'Thank you, but Gary has been looking after us just fine!'

For three days José fights for his life. Periodically I sit beside his bed and hold his hand and pray. Short in stature, like most Timorese, and with stubble invariably on his face, he appears so lifeless before me— near death. I plead with God to take energy from me and give it to him. Hopeful that he might hear me in the coma, I talk to him a lot. I remind him of God's love for him. I sing songs of hope and praise for him. I pray that energy will flow from my body into his. It certainly seems to, as after each session with him, I feel drained and exhausted.

On the third day after the shooting, the doctors declare that he is still in a serious condition but is stable and on his way to recovery. I am exhausted and I decide its time to return home to my family. It seems almost like an Easter story. Dying on Friday but rising again on Sunday. But I need a break. There are others who can play their part, and I ask my friend and local Darwin Army Chaplain, Morgan Batt to support the family in my absence.

Weeks later, José shares with me that even in the coma he was aware of God's presence. He felt Him holding his hand and preventing him from falling into the darkness of death. He remembers some of the words I had been saying to him *verbatim*, although he describes them as the voice of God telling evil ones to go away and reassuring

At José's residence as he recovers from the assassination attempt.

him. I'm sure God was putting thoughts and words into his head, but I think God was also using me to do the same.

José was shot at close range in the torso by two killer bullets. Alfredo Reinado and his deputy, Leopoldino, died instantly from single bullets of the same calibre also fired at close range. Do I think that José's survival was a miracle? Of course I do! José does too. He gives thanks to God for sparing his life.

In my own reflections with God after these dramatic events, I marvel at the providential nature of both Michael and I being there and available to help immediately in response to this crisis. After his recovery, José awards Michael the Presidential Medal of Merit for his efforts and confers on me the Timorese Solidarity Medal. Our citations reflect his profound gratitude.

About a month after the assassination attempt, Michael returns briefly to Australia to attend his brother Paul's graduation as a Lieutenant in the Army Reserve. He is able finally to tell us the full story of the attack. Several car-loads of rebels turned up at the President's villa, located close to the beach in a sparsely populated area ten kilometres east of Dili, at dawn. A gun battle ensued between the rebels and loyal soldiers on guard. José was out on a pre-dawn fitness walk to the massive statue of Jesus, called Christo Rei, accompanied by two armed policemen. He heard the gunfire and called his brother, Arsenio, who was at the villa with about six other family members, including young nieces, lying on the floor with bullets flying over their heads.

With more courage than good judgement, José ran back to the villa, concerned for his family. About ten metres from the front gate, a rebel gunman shot him at point blank range with a burst of bullets, knocking him to the ground. Subsequently, inside the compound, a loyal soldier eventually hit Alfredo and his deputy, killing both of them instantly. With the rebel leaders down and dead, and possibly presuming that José was also dead, the remaining rebels disengaged and drove off into the hills. A staff member at the house then rang Michael, who took charge of mobilising medical, police and military support.

It would seem that Alfredo wanted to overthrow the government by killing José and Xanana Gusmão. He had been evading capture for over two years, and had developed something of a cult following. He and his band had been involved in several dawn attacks, moving into position under cover of darkness and then launching in the gloomy first light as targets could be seen. He adopted these tactics for his early morning assassination attempts against José, Xanana Gusmão and Gusmão's wife.

The ABC *Australian Story* team thought the events of 2008 were pretty amazing too. Kent Gordon developed a whole new episode with Michael once again thrust into national prominence in Australia and in Timor Leste. José whimsically reflects in the programme that he now needs me as his personal pastor, so that I can be constantly praying for God's forgiveness of his sins.

Since his ordeal in 2008 I have come to know José Ramos Horta better. I had first met him during the 2006 crisis, when he took a liking to Michael's efforts as an adviser to the Timorese Defence Force in negotiating peace with antagonists. In August 2006, the Chief of the Australian Defence Force awarded Michael one of his Commendations for Michael's significant role in bringing peace to Timor during that crisis. Michael then returned to Australia in March 2007 to take up a job as Adjutant of 8/9 RAR in Brisbane. Three months later José wrote to Prime Minister John Howard and received approval for Michael to return to work for him as his Military Adviser in October 2007.

I had spent the two days prior to the shooting with José and Michael touring the Bobonaro district where José met the staff of our humanitarian organisation, Friends and Partners with East Timor. He saw and heard first-hand of our work there over the previous eight years. We shared meals together and reflected on the way forward for his struggling country.

During every one of my visits to Timor Leste since the dramatic events in 2008, José has invited me to his home for a meal and I have got to know him well. He loves joking with me, introducing me as 'Bishop' to others. I am impressed by his confidence, pragmatism and hope. His faith taught him that justice would eventually come for his people, as long as he could summon the courage to continue to speak out about their suffering under Indonesian occupation. I muse, 'Oh, that the world could have more politicians with such moral courage!' He always thanks me for helping his people. I reflect that I have simply fulfilled the Lord's command-to love my neighbour.

On the first anniversary of the shooting, José comes to Brisbane and spends the night in our family home at The Gap in Brisbane. It is an honour for us and a surprise to our neighbours to have a Head of State on our patch. We now have a 'Presidential suite' in our home! With an entourage of 15 Timorese, we have people sleeping all over the place, and security guards camped outside. Lynne and I put on a good old Aussie BBQ for him and he is able to relax in the company of friends.

I begin to learn about how life experiences shaped this charismatic leader and learn a lot more when Lynne, Michael and I travel with José's entourage to Melbourne in August 2009 for the world premiere of the movie '*Balibo*', and attend a range of receptions and speaking engagements.

Balibo, the movie

Robert Connolly, an award-winning Australian documentary maker, led the Australian company that made *Balibo*. The movie depicts the events of 1975 when 25-year-old José invited an Australian news crew to visit East Timor in order to expose Indonesian plans to invade. José directed Michael to assist with the making of this movie. Unexpectedly, Robert Connolly invited Michael to act in the movie. He rang me to ask advice on whether he should accept the offer.

I said, 'Yes, of course, but don't ask permission of Defence or DFAT [Department of Foreign Affairs and Trade] to do so! Just do it. The truth needs to get out!'

Whilst government officials in Canberra would choke over Michael's involvement, I am proud that Michael both facilitated the making of this movie and acted in it. He played an Australian government official interviewing a witness to the murder of Australian journalist, Roger East, at Dili wharf in 1975. His scenes were at the beginning and end of the movie. Roger East had been recruited by José to head up a news agency in Dili facilitating international reporting on developments in Timor after the Portuguese abandoned the country abruptly after a coup back in Portugal. After Indonesian Special Forces murdered five Australian journalists in the border town of Balibo (the 'Balibo Five'), Roger East remained in Dili to report on the invasion. Tragically, Indonesian soldiers murdered Roger on Dili wharf. José carried the great burden of guilt from these deaths. He was very happy that *Balibo* would set the record straight for the families of the Balibo Five and Roger East.

Successive Australian Governments had accommodated the official Indonesian military line that the Balibo Five were killed accidentally in crossfire between Timorese rebels and Indonesian forces. This was a disgraceful compromise of the truth in order to appease Indonesian sensibilities and maintain neighbourly relations. Australia ignored the testimony of numerous eyewitnesses to the callous shooting of the unarmed journalists.

At the conclusion of the premiere, José gets up on stage, and in sympathy with thirty or so members of the murdered journalists' families present, he shared his anguish over their loss. He described his feelings after the murder of one of his brothers and a sister during the same period. He lamented how Western governments ignored the plight of the Timorese at the time. Tears welled in my eyes as I contemplated his grieving over a lifetime of tragedy. His testimony inspires me to reaffirm my own emotional commitment to stand up and speak out against injustice and to challenge inaction by governments.

José's statesmanship is evident when he acknowledges that Indonesian governments had changed since 1975. He expresses his desire for Timor Leste and Indonesia to become the best of neighbours.

He puts out a renewed invitation to the Rudd Government in Australia to investigate the murders of Roger East and the Balibo Five. The perpetrators may never do jail time for their criminality, but Australia's honour and reputation would be enhanced if the truth was acknowledged. To date governments on both sides of politics have demurred.

In December 2009, José invites our whole family to join him for his 60th birthday celebrations. We have a great couple of weeks in Dili accompanying him to numerous activities and occasions. Then in September 2010, he invites us to stay at his villa for two weeks while Michael organises the 600km Tour de Timor mountain-bike race, part of his plan to bring some joy into the lives of rural Timorese. Such is the humility of the man, he drives us around town in his Presidential limousine, a ten year old open-air 'mini moke.' I am honoured to be a friend of José Ramos Horta. And it's just so hard to comprehend all this is happening to an ordinary Australian family.

Unbeknown at the time, God has other commissions for me including comforting other victims, and family members of lost loved ones. I will be challenged again to manage my emotions amidst death and suffering, but also to find strength in adversity, as well as to marvel again on how God works in the lives of those who mourn.

Chapter 13
Soldiering On

'I have come that you might have life in all its fullness.'
John 10:10

I hope after returning from Timor, that life might settle down, become more routine and less demanding. Perhaps God may now give me some rest after these recent dramatic overseas events. At a Christmas dinner with my RMC classmates, I find that some are taking the opportunity to access their accumulated superannuation funds and have retired or are about to.

While my doctors want me to retire, I just see a diverse range of ministry needs still to be met. I am on a mission from God. For me, life is to involve 'Soldiering On' in faith, hope and love, in whatever tasks God sets before me, with whatever capacity I can muster. My body and mind keep reminding me that I have range of disabilities that will limit the type of things I can do, but my soul reminds me that my disabilities are mysteriously a gift to help me minister to those similarly afflicted.

I help out in our local parish, preaching, baptising, marrying, and presiding at funerals. Lynne and I play in a mid-week tennis competition. We cherish regular family meals of a Sunday, with our children and our respective fathers. We play cards with friends, and walk daily with our clever dog, Charlie, a Cavalier King Charles. (Dogs provide wonderful therapy to those with health issues.) Lynne's mum, Marie, and my mum, Daphne, have gone to be with God, and we keep in weekly contact with our dads. We enjoy cycling and trips to the Gold Coast, staying at a unit my brother Craig has at Surfers Paradise.

Family in 2009

My military service continues part-time in the Army Reserve, and I'm now trying to influence the moral and spiritual attitudes of those I am entrusted to train. I'm invited to share my ideas through presentations on Courageous Leadership and The Spirituality of the Aussie Digger to almost every new Sergeant and many new Corporals in the Army as they come through their promotion course at either Canungra or Enoggera. The Army's Training Commander, Major General Richard Wilson awards me a Commendation Badge for my ministry.

A Defence sponsored Prince of Wales Fellowship Award facilitates a month's travel to the USA, researching ministry and mission in the US military, as well as studying their Diaconate programme. I meet Chaplaincy staff in the Pentagon in Washington, and spend time at the Army's Chaplaincy School in Columbus, South Carolina, as well as a week with Chaplains in units at the massive US Marine Corps Base of Camp Lejeune, North Carolina. I finish off the trip at a National Conference of Catholic Deacons at Baltimore, with 500 deacons. My horizons for what is possible in ministry widen and my hope in God's blessing is affirmed.

I become the Coordinating Chaplain for the 11th Brigade embracing all of the Army Reserve units in Queensland, including the training schools. Our son Paul's experience is an example of the diversity of Army Reserve service available at this time. While working as a sales team leader with the Suncorp insurance company, Paul participates in Army Reserve training on Tuesday nights, many weekends, and in one or more two-week camps each year. After fourteen months in officer training at Queensland University Regiment, he takes command of an infantry rifle platoon in 25th/49th Battalion, The Royal Queensland Regiment.

The following year he completes all the qualifications required of a Regular Army Platoon Commander and takes a platoon to Butterworth Air Base, Malaysia, for three months duties as part of Australia's bi-lateral Defence Cooperation program (a task I had undertaken in 1974). In 2010 he comes onto full-time army service for twelve months and spends six months deployed in Timor Leste as Liaison Officer with the International Stabilisation Force. I assist in the preparation of this contingent with culture and language training. Michael, our older son, joins us in the 11th Brigade in March 2011 as commander of our High Readiness Reserve Company, after transferring out of the Regular Army. He subsequently takes command of Jacka Company at Queensland University Regiment, where he trains officer cadets for their first appointment as officers.

After a community Mass when visiting Paul in Timor in 2011.

I have become a 'subject matter expert' in teaching our officers and soldiers on how to work effectively with other cultures. I cover cultural awareness and competency for service in Solomon Islands, Timor Leste, and Afghanistan. I like starting presentations with a playlet where I dress up in tribal garments and start appealing to the audience in a tribal language, gesturing and elevating my voice in the frustration that I have seen so many locals show in other countries when our young men and women on peace support operations have not been able to communicate with them. I then show them extracts from the *Australian Story* demonstrating how Michael had developed local language competency to communicate and win trust. I keep challenging higher authorities about the importance of cultural and language training. I will keep preaching this gospel, in the hope that one day it will be embraced and more time made available for cross-cultural and language training before our troops deploy overseas.

Kokoda

In April 2008, with Duntroon classmates, Peter Keane, Richard Healy and Al Pearson, I walk the Kokoda Trail in Papua New Guinea.

This long winding trail through the jungle, up and down a series of mountain ranges, probably has a claim to have defined Australia and the Australian spirit as much as the Gallipoli Campaign. Our young men were defending their homeland by going forward to fight in one of the world's most demanding terrains and climates to stop the southern drive of Japanese forces to Port Moresby. From there, Japanese ships, aircraft and marines could have raided northern Queensland with impunity.

After months of hard physical training, we begin our quest in pouring rain, walking twenty kilometres from Port Moresby on a muddy road, just to get to the start of the Trail at Ower's Crossing. Steeply we descend into the lush jungle surrounding the fast-flowing Goldie River, where we camp the night. In the pre-dawn darkness, we strike camp and commence 9 days of scrambling up and down hillsides across the Owen Stanley Ranges on a muddy footpad that frequently has us falling on our backsides or careening forward onto our knees.

Even after months of physical conditioning in the hot Brisbane climate, we drip with sweat, and our legs quiver with exhaustion on this back-breaking trek in the footsteps of our Second World War forbears. During my exertions I ponder the difficulties that faced our under-trained and under-equipped young men, many of them teenagers, as they fought to stop the all-conquering Japanese military. I am overwhelmed with admiration and occasionally emotional as I think of their courage, and physical and mental endurance, while our guide, Wayne Weatherall from Kokoda Spirit trekking company, describes scenes of battles.

On 24 April we arrive at Isurava, the scene of the bloodiest battle and now a National Memorial site. Four, man-sized marble blocks skirt the jungle amphitheatre, engraved with the words Courage,

Endurance, Sacrifice and Mateship. Some 800 trekkers walking from both the north and the south arrive for a dawn Anzac Day service.

Walking Kokoda with Duntroon mates Peter Keane, Richard Healy and Al Pearson at Isurava battle site, 25 April 2008.

By prior arrangement, the Department of Veterans Affairs has invited me to lead this service. This is a great privilege as the sun breaks through the mist. The haunting bugle notes of the Last Post, the silence, and then the uplifting tune of Reveille, sees us shed tears on this hallowed ground. We can see the outline of the airstrip at Kokoda, some 15 km down the mountain, as the sun rises and the mist clears. We mingle with other trekkers for a while after the service and then begin our trek down to Kokoda, arriving in joyous relief at about 3pm that afternoon.

Most days on the Trail I wonder if I am going to be able to get through the day without totally collapsing through exhaustion. There are many false crests in every ridge we climb. My legs shake like jelly. My heart pumps. On the steeper parts I walk ten metres and have to rest, puffing and blowing, another ten metres and have a rest, and so on. I find new depths of endurance in something harder than anything

I've done before. So it is with most things in life I realise. The body, mind and spirit can combine to get a person to unexpected and amazing levels. I won't stop or give up or ask for a longer rest because I am inspired by my forebears who fought along this muddy track against a dangerous enemy. There is minimal danger for me although the prospect of heart attack comes to mind! I am proud to finish and proud of my mates who also have to dig deep to do so.

Dealing with Sacrifice

Later in 2008, after the Kokoda Trail quest, and again in 2010 I am reminded of the blood sacrifice of our nation's youth in war and the devastating consequences for some families of sending our young people to troubled parts of the world. Two funerals I am to conduct, two years apart, arouse in me old feelings of frustration and sadness over the tragedy of campaigns like those in Iraq and Afghanistan where victory seems elusive.

Signaller Sean McCarthy and infantry Private Grant Kirby are both killed in Afghanistan, in July 2008 and in August 2010 respectively. Sean is killed when the vehicle he was in, drives over a mine while on patrol with the Special Air Service Regiment. Grant Kirby is killed by an Improvised Explosive Device while on foot. Sean had left a message in his will asking for me to conduct his funeral. I am uplifted to know that I had this impact on him and that he would trust me to comfort his family through a terrible emotional ordeal. Sean had been a student on one of the Junior Leaders Courses at Enoggera that I had addressed. I remember him well. He had stood out on the course as a cheerful young soldier, single, aged 25, who was confident in sharing that he had a Catholic Christian faith. Grant had also introduced himself to me on his Junior Leaders Course as a Catholic Christian, and had participated in the cultural competency training I had conducted for his company in 6 RAR before their deployment.

At Sean's funeral, I tell the congregation of how I recall Sean talking to me about life and death. He had been to Afghanistan before and knew the dangers of going back. Prime Minister Kevin Rudd attends his funeral at Sacred Heart Church in Surfers Paradise, along with Defence and Service Chiefs and 1000 other friends and family. I comment on Sean's courage and commitment and great compassion, and the solidarity of the Australian people in honouring their war dead.

I weep when I hear that Grant Kirby has been killed in 2010. He has been part of our local parish family in The Gap. He had married Edwina and had two beautiful girls, Isabella and Madeleine, who attend our parish school and are friends with our granddaughter Brianna. Words cannot adequately describe the anguish I feel in going to see this grieving family. What can you say? But say something I must, because, as with Sean's funeral, Grant's funeral is to be a nationally televised event. In the midst of a hung national election result, both Julia Gillard and Tony Abbott will be present, as will Queensland State Premier Anna Bligh, and numerous other dignitaries. There is a concern about security because we plan to celebrate the funeral in our parish church at The Gap.

The military have already had a welcome home ramp ceremony at RAAF Air Base Amberley, and a memorial service at Enoggera Barracks for all three soldiers killed in the week Grant died. In my opinion our parish funeral should be the family's farewell, not a media event for dignitaries to show sorrow on behalf of the nation that sent Grant and his mates to war. Grant's family really just want a simple community service. But Defence has offered them a big public service at our church with guard of honour, escorts, firing of volleys, and procession, to honour a brave soldier. The family have also asked for the celebration of a Catholic service rather than a blended interdenominational 'Army' service.

Basing my decision on family first, Army second and visiting dignitaries third, I offer the normal Catholic service including holy water, 'holy smoke' (incense) and Holy Communion, and a 'no holds barred' Christian homily. We Catholics have some uncompromising beliefs in God and eternal life. I am not going to water that down for anyone. The Catholic Leader subsequently publishes my homily (See extracts at the end of the book). The service goes really well and all those grieving are most affirming and appreciative of this ministry.

In an intriguing postscript, after the service, a very senior military officer complains up the chain of command about my insensitivity in preaching a pointedly Christian message when there are prominent Australians present at the funeral who are not Christians. I am amazed at his attitude. Of course, I too am grieving. I thank God for the faith I have received. It helps me deal with that grief, and manage my disappointment with this officer.

Camino

Coincidentally, and with perfect timing once again, Lynne and I then embark on a pre-planned quest of a lifetime that does much to soothe my soul, repair my bruised mind and equip me for the next part of my journey. Inspired by a terrific presentation Father Tony Doherty gives the year before at our National Catholic Deacons Conference, Lynne and I fly to Spain to attempt the famous Camino pilgrimage. In the same way as millions of pilgrims over the centuries, we are to walk to the Spanish city of Santiago, the burial place of St James, one of the original twelve who were sent to the ends of the earth to proclaim the Good News of Jesus.

The 'Camino' means the 'the Way' to Santiago from various places in Europe, that follow in the footsteps of St James. Pilgrims walk, cycle or run, from as little as 100km to as much as 2500 km, along 'the Way.' Hollywood actor, Martin Sheen starred in a movie/documentary of the same name that is released in 2012.

Lynne and I, accompanied by Peter and Rosemary Keane, decide to walk 350 km along the route from France. Packs on back, ponchos over the top, we head off at 6:30am in driving rain from León. This is a cold, wet start as opposed to the hot wet start along the Kokoda Trail. We follow scallop shells marking the way along a well-worn path through farms and villages across the hills and mountains of northern Spain. The rain keeps falling for four days until we climb so high in the mountains that it is freezing and is replaced by bone-chilling mist! What a stalwart wife I have in Lynne, who keeps going 20-25 km per day for fifteen days in really tough conditions.

With Lynne approaching Santiago July 2010.

Thousands of other pilgrims from all countries on earth are on the move at the same time. We share our evenings with them in 'Alburgues'—special pilgrims' hostels with bunk rooms, spaced all along the way. We are inspired by one middle-aged German lady who shares how she had felt that God had blessed her life so much, that walking the Camino all the way from Germany is her way of giving Him thanks and spending special time with Him. We visit and pray in many beautiful churches in every village along the way. We eat pilgrim's food—bread, cheese, ham, chips and numerous coffees, with a 'Grande Cerveza'—a large glass of local beer—or wine, to celebrate the end of each day's journey.

Spiritually, it is a wonderful time of tranquillity for prayer, at any moment of the day, especially during the long walking stretches along the way, marvelling at the grandeur of God's creation. We also enjoy 3 weeks' relief from phone calls, emails and driving. Daily journaling is an enjoyable task to relate the experiences on the way to the larger lessons of life. The Camino slows Lynne and I down mentally, and gives us the space and uninterrupted time to reflect on the important things in life. Here are some of my reflections and the messages that I felt God was sharing with me:

- Embrace your wife.
- Relax and be comfortable with silence.
- I liberate you from worry and fear—live in freedom.
- Let nothing bind you, but my command to love.
- People come and go in your life quickly—embrace them while you can—offer them all a compliment.
- Slow down, go steadily, find your pace—this is a long journey.
- See my constant love in the flowing stream—feel my warmth in the rays of My Son.
- Rejoice in your hope; be patient in tribulation; constant in prayer (*Romans* 12).

- Don't rush, you will miss the signs I leave to guide you.
- Get back to a simpler lifestyle—carry minimal baggage—get rid of the rubbish in your life.
- Leave your burdens at the foot of the cross—don't have them churning in your mind.
- Live, celebrate and enjoy the present moment—you can't get to my destination for you any faster.

The bottom line is that we have undisturbed time to get to know better the real Camino—Jesus of Nazareth.

At the end of our first week we reach the highest mountain peak, Cruz de Ferro, where a tall iron cross on a mast is surrounded by millions of stones left there by pilgrims over 1200 years. Each stone symbolises each pilgrim leaving their burdens at the foot of the cross of Christ.

The weather improves a little after the first week but remains overcast most of the way, until the sun shines brightly on us on arrival at Santiago. We participate in the midday Pilgrims' Mass and celebrate with our brothers and sisters of every race who were and are fellow pilgrims with us—companions on the journey of life.

I find the experience on this picturesque mountain in Spain cathartic. I leave a whole lot of burdens there—memories and hurts that have bugged me for years. I realise that with Jesus Christ front and centre in my life, they have no real power over me or the ability to hurt me anymore. I will continue my life liberated and freed, reminded that my life is in God's hands. I am free to serve my Lord, and not be burdened by the fear or worry that others may try to impose on me. I know I will still face injustices and obstacles, but like the mountain streams flowing down over rocks, with Lynne's help and love, I will just keep moving around them.

Soldiering On

After returning from the Camino, at a ceremony in Canberra in October 2010, the Chief of Army, Lieutenant General Ken Gillespie, honours my service with a 'Federation Star' to add to my Defence Long Service Medal, in recognition of over 40 years' service to the nation. It is a singular honour. Very few officers achieve this milestone.

General Gillespie hands me the Star saying, 'Gary, we thank you for an extraordinary career of service, both as an infantry officer and as a chaplain. You have been an inspiration to many people of all ranks through your dedication and commitment. I've personally witnessed your ministry as Chief of Army, and heard many positive stories about what you have done. Well done.'

In 2011, I get posted into the Queensland University Regiment, and return to a diverse training environment on a wide range of courses for Army Reserve soldiers, officer cadets and officers. I 'walk the walk,' joining them in physical training, at the rifle range, field exercises, and classroom instruction. To the surprise of some of the instructors, I ask to sleep in the field overnight with the students, getting wet and eating ration packs again, when I could be staying in staff huts. It's pure 'ministry of presence', and I love it! I remember one moment of humble pride at the example I am setting when, after giving a presentation to some new infantry soldiers on developing the character qualities required in a soldier, the duty instructor says to me, 'Padre, they might have taken the man (me) out of the infantry, but they have not taken the infantryman out of the man!'

Tour de Timor

Service in Timor Leste calls me again, but this time it involves Lynne and me, with Paul and Christy, travelling to Timor Leste to participate in the 2011 Tour de Timor bike race, along 600 kilometres of rough mountain roads. President José Ramos Horta has by now asked Michael to organise national events such as this, the world's toughest mountain-bike race, to promote peace and national unity. In 2010 Lynne and I had assisted as volunteer support staff for the race, assisting with meals and merchandise sales. But in 2011 Michael asks Paul and me to join him on the ride! No amount of hill training in Brisbane is sufficient to prepare us for the mountains of Timor.

At the start, President Horta invites me to bless the field of competitors, in front of the President's Palace in Dili. Several hundred riders then head out east and then south into the mountains. On day one, Paul and I get to 76 kilometres in fifty-degree heat, but are behind the pace required and must complete the trip in the back of a truck. Day two is just unbelievably steep and rough. I try to recapture the determination to finish that I summoned on the Kokoda Trail. But I am fated to lose control on slippery gravel, and go sliding down the road after about forty kilometres of gruelling riding, often in knee buckling low gear.

Grazed and bleeding all down my right side-leg, stomach, arm and shoulder, I have to painfully ride another twenty kilometres to an aid station for dressing, and then struggle on to the eighty kilometres post before the doctor insists I get in an ambulance for the rest of the journey that day. I am determined to continue and complete the race but I crash again on day three on another steep downhill, this time somersaulting over the handlebars. This time my head and shoulders take the brunt of the fall. Bruised and battered, with torn shoulder ligaments, I limp on cycling another ten kilometres until it's into the ambulance again.

I compete in, and complete the remaining three days with lots of sweat and a few scares, but without falling again. With tears of joy I cross the finish line on 16 September, the day before my 59th birthday, after an agonising 88 kilometres, 7.5 hour final day's ride, including eight kilometres through a loose gravel river bed. My satisfaction is that every kilometre of the journey, I have been greeting and blessing the thousands of Timorese who have lined our route in the most exciting event to ever visit the rural poor in this struggling country.

At the finish line where thousands have gathered to welcome in the riders, the President challenges Timorese youth, by telling them if a 59-year-old Padre can complete the Tour de Timor, then all of them should have a go. He then adds that he thinks God may have been helping me! Of course He was. I am proud that God was confident enough in me to inspire me to take on this challenge and that I have been able to meet it. Of course it also affirms that nothing is impossible when you put your trust in God. (*Proverbs* 3:5)

Paul and I conquer the Tour de Timor, 2012.

In 2012 I complete the Tour de Timor again—thankfully without incident—and this time riding through Indonesia as well. But an even bigger challenge awaits me on my return. I am diagnosed with cancer. It is present in my prostate gland and only surgery will tell if it has advanced any further.

Over my service, firstly as an infantryman, then as an Army Chaplain, I have received too many notices of veterans dying in mid-life, mostly from cancer. The early passing of these friends saddens me but I did not consider that much could be done about it.

The powerlessness of waiting for surgery and the fear that cancer could be growing in other places, prompts me to get to understand more of what is going on inside my body, and see what I can do to help myself.

A range of tests by Terry Hitske, a homeopath in our parish, identifies that my body is highly acidic, that my liver and kidneys are clogged with toxins, and that my body is deficient in a number of vitamins and minerals. He encourages me to embrace a 'Paleolithic' diet of fish, vegetables and fruit, and avoiding sugar, wheat and dairy, which works wonders. Another parishioner, Rob Vicary, is a remedial masseur and reflexologist. Rob gets my circulation and energy flow going better and releases tension from my muscles.

I also pray for God's guidance, and search the Internet for articles about cancer and its causes. I read numerous books, and meet cancer survivors who had utilised a range of complementary therapies. I become more aware of holistic (body, mind and soul) approaches to healthy living. This gives me hope, and lifts my spirits. I come to be aware that my PTSD has contributed to cancer. I sense I have now started on a new episode in my life to not just survive the long term effects of PTSD but to become somewhat of a 'specialist' in understanding, practicing, and promoting health in the veteran community.

What I don't expect is that I will have to fight another battle to survive Peritonitis as well as Cancer. Without the body, mind and soul preparation that I undertake leading up to surgery I probably would have been dead before the bowel specialist intervened. I vow to use my experience to educate others.

Chapter 14
Promoting Post Traumatic Growth and Maintaining Wellbeing

'Find rest for your souls.' Matthew 11:28.

Understanding Health and Wellbeing

The story of my hospital experience has been related in Chapter One. It is traumatic to say the least, but it provides me the impetus to really come to terms with the PTSD 'monster' that has challenged me for many years. I don't believe God caused the cancer or the peritonitis but, as with so many earlier trials, I surmise that God has got me through this latest challenge for His purpose. I am to continue to be a 'wounded healer', but now one with a sharper focus on helping other veterans with their myriad health issues.

In my research over the six months recovery period following surgery, I become more aware of how interconnected the body, mind and soul are, in terms of health. Following my initial diagnosis with PTSD from my service in the Iran-Iraq war, doctors prescribed medication and cognitive behaviour therapy. These helped manage symptoms of anxiety and depression, but did little to diminish hyper-vigilance and hyper-arousal. Anxiety attacks became a feature of my life. I also have a range of stomach, neck, and back problems that get worse whenever I am under stress.

I am to learn that my PTSD symptoms release Cortisol hormones into my body that immobilise my immune system, allowing cancer to grow. I come to realise that accumulated stress is killing me! At the same time, a diet with too much sugar, wheat and dairy products has been clogging up my digestive system causing me to put on weight and develop a range of other illnesses. Anxiety has caused me to be living with a 'battlefield in my mind' that spills over into my body and soul, and sees me react inappropriately at times.

Moreover, I realize my involvement with health care providers has been focused on 'treatments' for symptoms, with little emphasis on preventative health measures—promoting wellness for the future. I realize that a proactive, holistic approach to health is needed, starting by taking responsibility for my own part in rehabilitation and restoration of wellness.

Clearly I have prayed for God to help me in stressful situations and bring me peace. He does! In fact, whenever I get an attack of anxiety, I call on God to give me the strength to stay calm, and think clearly. I know that I am a child of God, and that God did a good job in making me the way I am. I know I can have hope and faith in God's deliverance from evil in this world, and the demons that occasionally chase me at night. I know that God can transform problems into opportunities.

I am resolved to continue to find ways to better health, and through testing complementary therapies, utilise what works best for me. Sometimes I can settle quickly through some focused breathing, a long walk and lots of self-talk. At other times I remind myself that an anxiety attack will pass, and I distract myself from anxious thoughts by attending to some work in another sphere of ministry. Many mental health conditions are episodic—they just grip us for a while when triggered by a stressor. I name them as transitory and start applying techniques to minimise their symptoms and return to normal.

Life is not meant to be a lone ranger activity. We all need to be open to the assistance of others. It may take some courage and the swallowing of some pride to be open to assistance, but my journey to restore health and to re-gain a life-giving disposition has had many people and practices help me. Let me acknowledge some of them.

Having an understanding General Practitioner has been foundational. I am grateful for the ongoing help of Dr Conrad Yoong, who has helped me with a multitude of issues and has understood the inter-relatedness of many dimensions to my health. On the specialised aspects of mental health I am assisted by Dr Malcolm Foxcroft, a psychiatrist who has seen many veterans and, when required, is able to prescribe medication that restores the appropriate chemical levels in my brain that get out of balance at times. I have come to realise that medication is essential at times to treat the acute symptoms of anxiety and depression. It pains me to see people who will not accept this treatment, or won't stay on their medication when they don't experience instant results, or experience some side effects. It will normally take at least two weeks before the medication 'kicks in' and there may need to be a change to different products if adverse side effects are experienced, but patience with this pays off. I have regular appointments to see Mal every six weeks as a 'safety net' to have him check me out, no matter how I feel I might have been travelling.

Counselling and advice is another normal component of both treatment and restoration. Over the years I use many counsellors, starting with Defence social worker Mary O'Gorman, and a range of psychologists. The Veterans and Veterans families Counselling

Service (VVCS) both in Brisbane and Canberra has provided outstanding individual and couple counselling to Lynne and me. More recently, the RSL sponsored Mates4Mates has been providing an excellent range of programmes for veterans.

Spiritually I have been blessed with a number of caring and wise Spiritual Directors, starting with Sister Monica Quilty, and including Father Bernie Patterson, Father Peter McHugh, Father Trevor Trotter and Bishop Joseph Oudeman. I see my spiritual director each month and he/she explores how I am travelling in my spiritual life. This provides me with a check and accountability that I have been faithful in prayer and scripture study. Of course Sunday mass is always nourishing for me, through the communion and fellowship of the people gathered, the teaching provided by the preacher, and the Holy Communion of receiving Jesus under the forms of consecrated bread and wine. An annual retreat where we go away and get some focussed life-giving inputs in a quiet setting is something I always look forward to. My morning prayer is something of a meditation, which is also a very healthy practice.

One of the disciplines of the spiritual life that has sustained many people over the centuries has been the practice of journaling. Sister Monica Quilty taught me that positive growth can come from detailing all the good moments of each day in a journal, and then re-reading them to remind myself of everything good in my life. I resolve from that point to be a 'good finder'. Further to that, I encourage others to be attentive to hearing what God might be saying to them in these times of reflection. I suggest that people should spend time each day reflecting on a scripture verse, reflecting on their experiences of the day past, and then writing down in a journal the messages that seem to be coming from God for them that day. Surely God wants us to listen to him—particularly through his Word.

Journaling has been the most significant tool that has helped me in restoring a positive perspective on life and limiting the negativity that those suffering PTSD struggle with daily. Some key journal reflections of mine are included in Appendix One.

Regular exercise is something I have always enjoyed and I come to realise it is highly recommended in the treatment of mental illnesses, due to the release of the 'feel good' endorphins and serotonin it produces. I start each day with a five kilometre walk humping a thirteen kilogramme backpack, followed by 100 sit ups and sixty push-ups. Some days I will also have a sixteen kilometre bike ride into the Army barracks and back. To top that all off, Lynne and I play in a mixed doubles tennis competition. I certainly don't plan on rusting out! We need to keep our joints moving.

Positive interactions with others are also life giving. The church provides many types of social interactions—dinners, barbecues, concerts, seminars—which we get involved in to get to know others. We have a monthly dinner group of friends from tennis which is great for encouraging each other. Both our circles of deacons and chaplains in Brisbane have monthly meetings to share developments and check on each other. I am active in our Royal Australian Regiment Association and local RSL sub-branch. The fellowship of other veterans is nourishing. Life is a journey to be shared.

This comprehensive regime of healthy practices may seem a lot, but for anyone who has to battle the demons of anxiety and depression, no less activity is going to be successful. I have built this regime up through trial and error over a number a years and feel I am in a good place with it. My heart goes out to those who struggle without such supports in place.

It's just not good enough to survive PTSD, depression or anxiety. It is most appropriate that we should still be able to have a joy-filled life.

In the gospel of *John* (10.10) Jesus says, 'I have come that you might have life—life in all its fullness.' I am determined that I am not to go through life as a victim, but I am going to make the most of life. This requires specific strategies and actions that nourish the soul as well as the body and mind.

Adopting a self-managed holistic programme I have dropped 16 kilogrammes, regaining a 'fighting' weight of 75 kilogrammes that I had as a thirty-year-old company commander. I have 're-balanced' and 're-created' a healthier lifestyle that involves less work, minimizes distress, and incorporates more self-care for my body, mind and soul. I have stopped being PTS 'Disordered' and am now into Post Traumatic Growth! Following surgery, I am now clear of cancer for the time being, but I am conscious that I must take 'intentional' steps to provide for my future health and avoid cancer appearing somewhere else.

A new future ministry

At times, life is quite challenging for any person, and there will be plenty of ups and downs, but I now know that we can endure the seemingly impossible, and with each new day there is a miracle and a gift called life that we can be thankful for. God invites us to live it to the full. I want to reframe the experiences I have had in the past, to shape a more positive future. I want to use my experiences and learnings for good. I will focus my attention on keeping things in perspective so that, now that I am better, I can to help show others the way to healing and restoration. There is also some satisfaction for me in being what Father Henri Nouwen termed a 'wounded healer'.

Providentially, I find myself listening to and counselling other traumatised people who are very grateful for my explanations of what this battlefield is all about. There is enormous satisfaction in seeing my experience help others. I know God didn't cause or will this condition on me, but He sure seems to be using it now for good. Increasingly, other chaplains start referring people to me for assistance with PTSD management.

One soldier says to me, 'Thank you for being so frank and honest about your own experience. That really made me feel better, to know that someone as experienced as you, could also have had this struggle. It's also good to know that you have found successful ways to manage the PTSD. I thought my whole life was stuffed. You've got me thinking now that I might be able to help other people too. Yeah, I'd really like to help others now. I've picked up a bunch of ideas from you to share with some of my mates.'

I look forward to the future with personal hope, and a hope that sharing this information might contribute to the improvement of health in other veterans.

As a result of my research, another 'Gospel' I am to preach is that we veterans need:
- to be educated on the nature of the health challenges we face, and the need to proactively embrace holistic wellbeing actions to achieve Post Traumatic Growth;
- to care for our bodies through good diet, exercise, rest and recreation;
- to care for our minds by minimising negative inputs and exposure to 'distressors'; and
- to care for our souls by embracing nourishing world views and spiritual practices.

To help soldiers and their families understand more about veterans' health, with the help of Tony Grlj I develop a website www.garystone.com.au. In it there are numerous articles and words of encouragement. Maybe it can help someone you know. I summarise a few of the recommendations it contains below.

A Wellbeing regime

I now manage distress and develop resilience, through a 'Wellbeing' regime.

My tested and proven 'Wellbeing' regime involves a range of components:

- Caring for the body
  - Exercise daily to release endorphins and produce more serotonin hormone.
  - Whenever distressed, reduce a runaway heart rate with deep slow breathing and meditation.
  - Eat regular and appropriate foods—particularly fresh fruit and vegetables, drink lots of water, and minimize alcohol and caffeine (which acts as a depressant in large quantities).
  - Avoid processed and fatty foods, and cut out sugar in all its forms.
  - See a doctor when you experience anxiety or depressive symptoms.
  - Be open to the complementary therapies of chiropractic, therapeutic massage and reflexology, to release tension and restore energy flow through the systems of the body.
  - Be open to taking medication. It is not addictive and helps in stabilising mood.
- Caring for the mind
  - Be open to learning cognitive behaviour therapy.
  - Recognise and avoid all unnecessary negative inputs to your life.
  - Remove yourself from persistently stressful environments and individuals.
  - Be a 'good finder'—name daily all the good things you see in life (journaling is helpful).
  - Read uplifting and nourishing stories and teachings.

- Learn to relax muscles and breathe deeply, to re-engage frontal cortex logical thinking.
- Become attentive and 'mindful' of the present moment and pleasant and safe surroundings.

- Caring for the soul
  - Find and embrace a spirituality or 'World view ' that is life giving.
  - Be open to the advice of wise teachers/mentors.
  - Be open to discovering and trusting in a 'higher power' to assist you in life.
  - Share your experiences with friends and be open to mutual support.
  - Invest significant time in key relationships. Become a better 'lover'.
  - Engage in team/group activities—e.g. sporting clubs, interest groups.
  - Practice meditation to get in touch with your soul.
  - Treat yourself to soothing music that will nurture your soul.
  - Identify a new 'Life Purpose' and plan to be a 'wounded healer'.

Choosing to be healthy and having sustained commitment

Restoring health, like desiring to lose weight, is easier said than done. We may need a coach or mentor, to help us get onto, and stay on, a healthy pathway. Research indicates that it takes from at least 28 days to many months, to change behaviours, and my experience is that with persistence, we will in time see measurable results, like loss of excess weight, better sleep and a calmer mind. I now feel liberated after twenty years of struggle, to enjoy the remainder of my life.

We get sick and 'dis-eased' because we have chosen or let stressful or toxic environments affect our body, mind and soul. Rather than just react to sickness when it occurs, a better way to live life is through a wellness model where we intentionally promote healthy living practices to avoid disease and achieve Post Traumatic Growth.

Reflection

Once again I have seen God replay the Easter story in my life. From the agony of Good Friday has come the new life of Easter Sunday. Though the crucible of experience I am equipped for a new mission.

Epilogue
The Way Ahead

The military has helped me to develop skills in many areas to deal with issues of importance in life's journey. I will now adapt them for the next phase of life. I hope to continue to be an 'Ambassador for Christ', and especially assist the disadvantaged and particularly ex-service veterans struggling with their disabilities, through speaking, coaching and opportunities I receive on media, and through publishing articles on various experiences I have had. We are all called to share good news. By doing so together, we can make the world a better place.

January 2015 will mark 45 years of service in uniform for me. More than thirty service chaplains in South Queensland now minister to people in uniform, but there are a massive number of ex-service people living in the region, including thousands of recent veterans of Afghanistan, Iraq, and Timor who are struggling with PTSD and adjustment difficulties in their families. There are no chaplaincy arrangements for them. I feel it is time to respond to this need by transferring out of uniform after 45 years continuous service and, with the blessing of Archbishop Mark Coleridge, I am about to build an integrated 'Body Mind and Soul' ministry to veterans, that I'm calling 'Veterans Care'. I will continue to develop my website www.garystone.com.au to provide resources to assist veterans, and hope to collaborate with others interested in promoting health and wellbeing.

Lynne and I have embarked on this quest together. We have bought a ten acre block of land on the eastern slopes of Mt Tamborine, in the Gold Coast hinterland, where we will build a new home. A new chapter in a new book is opening for us, and we look forward in faith and confidence to a continuing journey of service.

We are loved immeasurably by God. May all our journeys in life be blessed in following the real Camino—the way, truth and life, of Jesus. May God fulfil the destiny He has in mind for you.

Gary Stone
Brisbane, July 2014

Three veterans from one family, Anzac Day 2013

Epilogue—The Way Ahead

Appendix 1
Listening to God

Christians believe that the Holy Spirit dwells within them. Indeed it is through the Spirit's presence that we are enabled to hear the words of God for us. These do not come as audible sounds—but rather as 'Ah Ha' moments in our prayer, as we ask the Lord for guidance and we imagine what God's response would be. Quite often the inspiration the Spirit reveals is couched in the language of a scripture verse, or it may have more specific connection to a life experience you are dealing with. These are a small sample of the inspirations and revelations I have received in my journaling over recent years. Perhaps some of these messages may resonate with what the Spirit would have been saying to you.

2004
- Your daily prayer is more important than your physical training.
- Christian music is food for your soul—gets your music playing.
- A vibrant, hope-filled spirituality is the foundation of everything we do.
- This faith you have has been initiated by God.
- Be comfortable in the chaos—I am there too.
- Holy Orders give you an immediate relationship to Christ that entails certain autonomy and responsibility that others in the church must respect.

- I need energised people who ooze God's love and joy and peace.
- May your smiling countenance be a blessing to others.
- In *Acts* 2 we read of a community of believers, totally devoted to God and radically committed to each other. They prayed boldly, and signs and wonders resulted. We need that replicated now!
- Your life may be the only gospel some people will ever read.

2005

- You have been called and chosen to bring a sea of tranquillity into people's lives.
- You have responded to a personal call from me.
- You are not 'owned' by the Church or the Army—your first responsibility is to me.
- I have provided you with extra so that you might experience the joy of giving.
- Yours may not be an easy mission, but it is the mission I have given you.
- Have a good word for everyone and every situation.
- Help people remember their experiences of God. I have been at work in them before you.
- The same power of the Holy Spirit that sustained Jesus is in you.
- No handbook or resource will match a personally inspirational, enthusiastic witness.
- You are a living sacrament by witnessing to the grace I have given you.
- The Spirit is already at work in people before you meet them—awaiting your sharing of Good News.

2006

- This life is not about fame or fortune, but relationships. Your mission is to nurture the relationships between God, people and each other.

- I will guide and shape your life for my purposes. You don't have to orchestrate it. Your future is in my hands.
- Above all, be a man of prayer, nourished by my word, filled with my spirit.
- You are to embody me, the presence of God, and show people that God is active in their lives.
- Keep the vision of God at your core—that all people may grow in the love of God and each other.
- You are my representative in the world, reminding people of my love for them.
- Christian leadership involves expressing a vision and then influencing others to embrace that vision.
- In speaking to others, contemplate the outcome God would want to achieve.
- Reflect daily on the good news and blessings you see happening around you.
- Look at situations through the eyes and mind of Jesus.
- We change things best by inspiration rather than force.
- I will honour your commitment—my grace will be upon you—my protection around you.
- Your value is not dependent on your efforts—you enjoy my favour.
- At every stage in the life of the church, things have seemed disastrous, but God has prevailed.

2007

- 'Do not be afraid' appears 365 times in the Bible—so do not be afraid!
- The power I give you is stronger than the anxiety and fear you struggle with.
- People may obstruct you, but they will not defeat you.
- I did not come to make you 25% alive or 50% alive, but fully alive.

- Don't wait for others to lead—do what needs to be done.
- I set you free from obedience to unjust use of power and authority.
- You are free to live your faith in accordance with the conscience I gave you.
- I will make a difference in the world through your presence.
- Your best ministry will be marked by your peace, joy, hope and confidence.
- Like St Francis and Mary McKillop, when ignored or rejected, just keep working for the Lord.
- I have given you a mission as a Prophet. You will take hits like all prophets do. But have confidence that you are in my will and I will sustain you.

2008

- You don't need to orchestrate your future—the Spirit will lead you into God's plan for you.
- Keep smiling. No one can take the joy of the Lord away from you.
- Be optimistic, unrestrained, irrepressible, enthusiastic, joyful, engaged with the world.
- Be pre-occupied with people who will carry out my mission.
- At the apex of Jesus' ministry he was nailed to a cross, unable to move or speak and from that place he saved us all. Never underestimate my ability to transform the darkness.
- I will prevail in and through you. Evil will not be successful against you.
- I need your tranquillity and contentment. Fear no-one.
- My power within you is always more powerful than those who will oppose you.
- Your deepest heart's desire should be to do the will of God.
- Expect opposition, drama and misunderstanding—we are at war!

2009

- There will always be chaos—but I will sanctify it.
- When I need you to do something new, I will make it happen.
- Be satisfied that I am working in your life—I delight in you.
- Remind people of the grace within them.
- We are part of the greatest story ever told.
- There is no greater love, joy or hope than that offered by Jesus.
- You are a prophet and prophets speak out courageously.
- Live in the present, with hope in the future.
- Your future is one of Hope—bathed in my abiding presence.
- Display humility in conduct, justice in action, mercy in deeds, and discipline in morals.
- Despite all tribulations, nothing will separate us from the love of God.
- 90% of your success in relating to people will come from your respectful and inclusive initial engagement with them.
- Be contented with your present circumstances—this is my will for you.
- You are a witness in a barren land, and it's because of the barrenness that I have put you there.
- Always know that my justice will prevail. Do not submit to unjust control over you.
- When you are feeling weak and vulnerable, you will also feel my protection over you.
- With Christ within you, who should you fear?
- Be audience-centred. Focus on how you can help others understand God's message for them.
- You have the gifts of the Spirit within you—use them.
- Be like the smokers at work—take frequent breaks to pray with me.
- You are a work in progress making the world a better place.

- Remind the world of its obligations to the poor it does not see.
- You have the DNA of Jesus in you—his character should shape your behaviour.

2010

- Contentment is your birthright—be contented!
- I am a big God. I can handle all the issues you worry about.
- Even though people fight against you—no one shall overcome you.
- Guard yourself from everything that is displeasing to God.
- My grace is at work in you. Don't worry about the future.
- I have gone ahead of you and sorted it out!
- You are in the world to speak the truth, and truth lovers will be attentive to you.
- You will afflict the comfortable when you comfort the afflicted, so expect opposition.
- As a tall tree, you will catch the turbulent winds—flex and recover.
- You will cope, you will recover, and nothing will overcome you.
- You will be judged on one criterion—how did you treat the poor and needy?
- Someone plants, someone waters, but God makes for the growth.
- God doesn't give us a detailed plan—he gives us a landscape to explore.
- Have faith and live one day at a time.

2011

- You will always be more effective through tranquillity and peacefulness.
- Don't fear the future—your future is in God's hands.
- Crises can be boundary events—moving us in to new phases of life.

- Your life has developed as it has, so that mighty works of God can be revealed.
- God gives us more than what we need, so that we can share with others.
- Give your answers with courtesy, respect and good conscience.
- Decide to live peaceably with disagreeable people.
- God made you for a purpose—to live life to the fullest.
- You are custom-made for the things God wants you to do.
- Be hopeful, have faith, be fearless and unstoppable.
- Be like a sweet fragrance, blessing all those around you.
- I will use your life as an example of how I will prevail.

2012

- The most strategic use of your time is to invest it in nurturing others, who in turn will invest their time in nurturing others.
- Your best ministry will come from a place of contentment.
- Flow around obstructions like the mountain stream flowing ever onwards.
- Do everything, and greet everyone with a joy-filled smile.
- Knowing that there will always be some people who oppose you, stand up and do what is needed.
- Realise that most troubles are short lived—do not be afraid.
- Savour the present moment, name the goodness with you now.
- The deeper the commitment, the deeper the joy.
- Your presence is sufficient to change lives.
- Before we Do anything, remember it's who we Are that really matters.

2013

- Let go of anything that drains you and embrace all that is life giving.
- Don't be a spectator in the stands—get out onto the court and play.

- Honour the intention of the law, but embrace the freedom of the spirit.
- Your deep roots will sustain you till healing is complete.
- You are the master of joy in your life—don't let others rob you of it.
- Take the risk to break the silence, and speak the truth in love.
- Help develop the imagination of others to see new possibilities.
- That which must give light, has to endure burning to do so.
- God's love is like electricity—but it has to pass through you to energise others.
- I have made you of tough stuff—there is nothing we can't handle together!

2014

- You are a messenger of life, ambassador of Christ, called to bring the gospel to the world
- Gracious words came from Jesus lips—may they come from yours as well.
- Show gratitude to everyone who helps you.
- Till your dying moment I will be working through your life to help others.
- Let go of your doubts and fears.
- Don't worry about ANYTHING!
- I do answer prayer. I will deliver you.
- Never grow tired of doing what is right
- May you allow yourself to be enveloped in love.
- Every year ahead of you will be even more fruitful.

Conclusion.

I have come to experience that we can trust in God's promises. They have been played out in my life and in the lives of many others. You can receive power when the Holy Spirit comes upon you. You can be God's witness to the ends of the earth. Jesus calls us to go out to the world and be good news to all creation. I believe that Jesus will empower us to lay hands on the sick and have the confidence that they can recover. God calls us to go out and bear fruit, fruit that will last. Indeed, I pray that you who are reading this can experience the Holy Spirit's power. Together we can make the world a better place.

For those that have not made that choice to receive God's Spirit into their hearts yet, know that God is no more than a prayer away, and is waiting for you to turn to him.

Appendix 2
Soldiers of Australia

The Australian Army hymn
Written by Chaplain Jim Cosgrove—to the tune of *Waltzing Matilda*

Soldiers of Australia gathered now to worship God, under the badge of the Rising Sun.
Giving thanks for our country, our families and freedom,
Let hearts and voices arise as one.

Chorus

God of salvation, Guide of our nation, you give us strength to follow your ways.
With the cross raised so high, shining bright across our southern skies,
We'll serve Australia through all our days.

Soldiers of Australia, ready to be called to serve,
Training together we strive for peace;
Whether home or away, through the darkest night or longest day,
We trust God's guidance will never cease.

Soldiers of Australia, gathered as Gods family.
Brothers and sisters stand side by side;
Through our God we are one, as we do the work that must be done,
Courage and friendship will be our pride.

Soldiers of Australia have bought our freedom with their lives,
They grow not old as we grow old
At the setting of the sun and also in the mo-o-orning
We shall remember their deeds so bold.

Appendix 3
Homily delivered on the occasion of the funeral of Private Grant Kirby

by Rev Gary Stone

Coming to terms with the death of a loved one or a mate is a great challenge to us all. Each of us here would have their own particular emotions today. With Grant's death coming as it did so unexpectedly, there may have been things unsaid or things yet to be done in your relationship with Grant, or even with each other. Now is the time that you can address that.

No words of mine can or should remove the sense of sorrow or separation you might be feeling at this time, but I would like to offer you a reflection based on our scriptures which I hope will help you to deal with this situation. Indeed my theme for this homily is Hope. One of our fundamental Christian beliefs is that nothing can separate us from the love of God. Nothing can separate us from the power of love—nothing in life and not even death. We have been gifted with each other. Indeed our love for each other can be strengthened at this time. Light can still shine in the darkness. Look around and see how many people Grant has brought together here today. We are companions on a journey, and we will all have grown a little closer to each other through Grant's life and death.

There are many things I would like to have talked about today, but since I know that many of you are Catholics, I know I have to keep myself to about ten minutes before you start to get restless! So I'll be brief.

I'd have liked to have said a little more about my involvement with Grant and his mates as they were preparing for this mission. In my role as Army Chaplain, I'd been invited by their CO, Jason Blain to talk to them about life and death, and soldiering on in adversity. Grant and his mates were conscious that some might be killed in action on this tour. Grant had even talked to me about it. I had already come to know Grant well through his attendance on a Junior Leaders Course in Enoggera last year. I talked to all the students in similar terms to what I will be saying to you today—how I have experienced that anything you do, can be strengthened by faith.

I'd have liked to have said a little more to you about the many symbols around you today: The light of Christ; living water; holy smoke (a little later); a living Jesus, representing life after death, who reaches out to embrace us; and our patron St Peter Chanel who, like Grant, was killed in action, and whose death led to the civilisation of a barbaric society.

I'd like to have said a little more about the last post, silence, the rouse and the firing of volleys—all powerful Christian symbols reminding us of how death leads to new life. But I'll let all those symbols speak for themselves.

I'd like to have said a little more about the Royal Australian Regiment's National Memorial Walk in Enoggera Barracks. There a tree will be dedicated as a living memorial to Grant—amongst a whole forest of trees dedicated to his many other comrades killed in the service of peace. Go there and check it out one day and be inspired by the spirituality of the place and the veterans who maintain it, who keep the spirit of the Regiment alive.

I'd like to share lots of things but I will home in on just one— HOPE.

In today's scriptures St Paul tells us, 'do not grieve like people who have no hope.' Comfort one another like people of hope. Even though you may be feeling sad and emotional today, just try to imagine how Grant would want you to be. I'm sure he wants this farewell to be a peaceful event where we knowledge his contribution to our lives. I'm sure he would want us all to grow closer together, to forgive each other, to be reconciled, to be freed of any burdens we've carried in relationships. I'm sure that Grant's spirit is with us right now, watching us, and is delighted to see so many friends and family gathered here.

Many years ago Grant's parents saw that he was baptised and confirmed, and receive a Christian education. I reaffirmed to Grant and his mates of our Christian belief that, at the point of death, our soul leaves our body and goes home to the God who created us. Grant and Edwina have baptised their children, Isabella and Madeleine, in that same belief in eternal life. I hope all of you can believe that too. That wonderful promise of eternal life is available to all those who believe in God, and desire to be part of this family of God. Today we have before us the remains of the body that Grant lived in, but the soul and spirit of Grant lives on. He awaits us to join him when one day we will walk through death's dark vale. I have one image of life and death that is a bit like the Olympic marathon. At the end of our race we go through this dark tunnel that leads us into a grandstand of people who have gone before us and have been awaiting our arrival, cheering us on, welcoming us home. Our race is yet to be completed. I'm sure Grant would want us to run the race well, and is looking forward to us joining him one day.

In a few moments we will have an opportunity for some prayer. There are some specific prayers we can pray together in the booklet. There might be some particular prayers you would like to pray and we'll have a quiet moment for you to do that. God answers prayers. I've seen it many times. I'm sure Grant is now praying for us!

Today some of us might even be challenged to reflect upon our lives, and we might be challenged to make our peace with God. It's a healthy thing to ask God for forgiveness and to put our life in his hands. I would like you all to have hope and peace and the courage that flows from faith. Imagine the freedom, the liberation, that can come from not being scared of death, and not having to worry about the future. If you haven't been involved with a faith community or church recently, I'd like to invite you to try it out. We have a big campaign in the Catholic Church at the moment to welcome people home.

But faith is not just about us. God calls us to love our neighbour. Like Grant, we need to be on a mission to make the world a better place. We can do that together. By way of example, I might add that, over the last ten years, this parish has raised over $850,000 for the people of East Timor, and saved many children's lives through health and education programmes we run there. There are a number of parishioners here that have had many more trips to Timor than our soldiers have. Loving God and loving our neighbour is our fundamental Christian mission.

In conclusion, right now, we can simply thank God for the gift of Grants life and honour his friendship and his service as a peacemaker.

Grant, you have run the race well. You have shown the greatest love that a person can show by being prepared to give your life in the service of peace. We salute you. We look forward to meeting you again in heaven.

As a little postscript I tried to imagine what Grant might have wanted to say to Bella and Maddy today. I think it might have been something like this:

> My beautiful children-I love you so very much.
> Don't be upset that that this has happened.
> I have passed through death to the peace of heaven.
> But I am never more than a prayer away from you.
> Speak to me like you always have. Play, smile, and be happy.
> Love, forgive, and help others.
> We have coped with separations before and you will cope now.
> My work on earth is complete. Yours is just starting. And I will be watching over you every day. When your work is completed, I will be at the doorway of heaven to welcome you home too. I will always love you, right now and forever.

Acknowledgements

Acknowledgements

I must first thank my family. Not many families have had the honour of being the subject of two episodes of the ABC *Australian Story*. The story of God's work through us is inextricably linked to us being a close-knit family. Little of my own story would have been possible without the loving support of our family—my wife, Lynne, and our wonderful children, Catherine, Michael, Christy and Paul, Christy's husband Mark Welldon and our granddaughter Brianna, all of whom keep me grounded in love, and remind me to practice what I preach. Thanks be to God for them all!

When Lynne and I celebrated the sacrament of marriage in 1974, we engaged the Holy Spirit of God in an intimate communion with us, which has had an effect in everything we have subsequently been engaged in. Lynne has been my constant companion throughout all these experiences, whether by my side, or in prayer from afar.

All the major decisions we have faced along the way have been made collaboratively, and have reflected also the promises we made to God at the children's baptisms that we would nurture and teach them to love God and love our neighbour. The children have all done that in their own way, in their own various contexts.

Clearly the media attention that Michael has received through his personal and sacrificial service in East Timor has blossomed out to embrace us all. He would be the first to acknowledge that the family team has been there with him in prayer and spirit, and that our almost daily engagement with each other, sharing life and seeking advice has been a feature of all we have achieved. Of course the call to love our Timorese brothers and sisters has been taken up by all of us, through visits, fundraising and volunteer work in Timor.

The family has also paid a heavy emotional price, dealing with a husband and father who has spent a lot of time away from them, and has brought his demons back with him from whatever mission he was on. Thank you family for being so understanding and patient.

Even now, with the children being adults and living independently, we have maintained a discipline of regular weekly family meals, and family holidays together. We love each other.

I thank and also acknowledge my extended family, especially my parents, Alf and Daphne Stone, my brother Craig and my many aunts, uncles, in-laws, cousins, nieces and nephews.

There are numerous other individuals I would like to acknowledge.

There have been many companions on the journey, too many to list here, but these are some that have made a particular impact upon me and helped me shape this journey.

(I list them in the chronological order of us working together):

Duntroon classmates

Mick Swan, Jim Wallace, Bob Breen, Peter de Haas, Peter Keane, Peter Maher, John Hands, Graham Huggins, Geoff Kaslar.

Military mates

Bill Parry, Terry Barnes, Stan Hannaford, Paul Green, Ted

Chitham, Glen and Pam Willmann, Peter Harrower, Peter and Lee Leahy, Richard and Pippa Dannatt (UK), Bruce and Sandy Barlow (USA), Jock Mackay, Peter Stammers, Tex Howarth, Pat Cullinan, Barry and Jo Gwyther, Ranald Scott, John and Wendy Stanford, David Smith, Phil Davies, Mike Corne, Tony White, Stephen Porter, Chris and Margaret Appleton, Bruce Scott, Mex Cernez, Mike Smith, Luke Foster, Peter and Trish Mc Kay, Paul O'Sullivan, Stu Cameron, Andy Leith, Geoff Hourn, Shane and Carol Caughey, Ross Parrott, Angus Houston, Fred Pfitzner, Bill Crews, Glen Stockton, John Cantwell, Vince and Peta Connolly, Paddy Ford, Steve Tulley, Frank and Jacqui Kenny, Jim and Anne Molan, Don and Margaret Cousins, Pat McIntosh, Brian Cox, Dorelle Hegarty, Leon and Trish Coad, Matt and Di Ponting, John Stripsky, Peter Walsh, Richard Niessl, Michael Bond, Mark Smith and Peter Jeffrey.

Chaplains

John Hoare, Les Thomson, Peter Dillon, John Tinkler, John Williams, Gerry Cudmore, Bishop Geoff Mayne, Austin Griffin (UK), Royce Thomson, Bob Maguire, Terry Bergin, Brian Rayner, Bishop Max Davis, Peter Quilty, Chris Reay, John Butler, John Quinlan, Bernie Hennessey, Greg Flynn, Peter Woodward, Len Eacott, Graeme and Di Ramsden, Mick and Rosie Lappin, Jim and Vicki Curtain, Mick Taylor, Martin Langron, Dave Cockram, Gordon Petersen, Andrew Sempell, Jim Cosgrove, Derm Casey, Chris Reay, David Niven, Phil Anderson, Phil Wylie, Peter Willis, Andrew McNeill, Kerry Bartlett, Ken Schmidt, Morgan Batt, Dan Bosshard, Lyall Cowell, Peter and Jo Devenish-Meares, Grant Dibden, Brenton and Genyese Fry, Garth Mayger, Grant Dibden, Steve Neuhaus, Bob McKennay, Michael Morrissey, Glynn Murphy,

Paul Goodland, Steve Neuhaus, Leo and Paula Orreal, Haydn Parsons, Damian Styles, Joel Vergara, Cameron West, Stephen Thomas and Mick Flew.

Civilian Clergy

Seamus McMahon, Michael Carroll, Ray Chapman, Bishop Michael Putney, John Chalmers, Frank Lourigan, Vince Hobbs, Joseph Sardie, John Barlow, Jack Soulsby, Bernie Patterson, Peter McHugh, Archbishop John Bathersby, Archbishop Mark Coleridge, Bishop Brian Finnegan, Bishop Joseph Oudeman, Bill O'Shea, John Dobson, Stephen Byrnes, Dave O'Connor, Peter Olsen, Ray Pardo, Des Neagle, Russ Nelson, Anthony Gooley, Tim Shanahan and Vu Dinh Tuong

Friends and Partners with East Timor

Peter and Angela de Haas, Jack and Rosemary Brady, Helen Murphy, Nick and Von Delaney, Jim Johnson, Mike Dooley, James Johnson, Marseluus Banoule, Alfredo Leite, Manuel Mendes, Sidonio Fontes, Jorge Leite, José Asaca, Serv Nascimento, Ann and Ron Eldridge, José Ramos Horta, Dan Murphy, Vi and Keith Hall, Joel Hodge, Mary Hodge, Eric Muir, John O'Hara, Lindsay Stokes, Anne Chapman, and Roger and Christine O'Halloran.

AFP confreres

Mick Keelty, Roger and Cora O'Donnell, Mick Travers, David Cockram, Gayl Mills, Grant Edwards, Dave Moore, Toni Christmas, Brett Swan and Ray Holder.

Other companions from various places and fields

Therese and Peter Knight, Mal Foxcroft, Conrad Yoong, Lisa Forbes, Rob Vicary, Terry Hitske, Tony Grlj, John Hull, Geoffrey Fry, Robert Falzon, Matthew Platz and Janice Johnston.

Assistance with the manuscript

A big thank you must go to Bob Breen, Ian Gordon, Peter Gamble, Kay Danes, and Sean Doyle who provided invaluable coaching to me in turning a bunch of facts and experiences into this readable story.

God has blessed my life through all of the people above and many others. It is my hope that through this book I can bring a blessing to you, or someone you love.

Glossary

1300hrs—Military time using 24-hour clock to designate 1.00pm (etc)

ADF—Australian Defence Force

AFP—Australian Federal Police

AK 47—Kalashnikov 7.62 mm assault rifle

Aussie—colloquial term for Australians, or Australian made

Archdiocese—a very large Diocese led by an Archbishop

Bpm—heart beats per minute

Battalion—group of about 850 soldiers, comprised of five or six companies

Brigade—Tactical group of about 5000 soldiers, comprised of six or seven battalions

CIMIC—Civil-Military Cooperation

C130—transport aircraft that carries up to 100 soldiers in fighting order

Catechist—lay leader/teacher in Catholic Church

Company—Tactical group of about 130 soldiers, comprised of 3 platoons

Counter-insurgency—operations against enemies hiding in the general population

Digger—colloquial term for Aussie soldier (from the digging of trenches in World War I)

Infantry—the combat soldiers that close with the enemy on foot

Lieutenant—Army rank where an officer commands a Platoon

Lieutenant Colonel—Army rank where an officer commands a Battalion or Unit

Major—Army rank where an officer commands a Company

Maverick—a strong willed, independent, man of action

No-Man's Land—the area between opposing forces on a battlefield

Pasdaran—colloquial Iranian term for Iranian Revolutionary Guards a fanatical militia group that ousted the US backed Shah, and took control of Iran

Platoon—Tactical group of 30-45 soldiers, comprised of three sections

RAR—Royal Australian Regiment—the Regular Army infantry Battalions

Rosary—a traditional Catholic prayer based on *Luke* 1:42

Section—the smallest army tactical group, of about 10 soldiers

UNMO—United Nations Military Observer

UXO—Unexploded Ordnance

Veiled speech—conversation where participants speak in code words

Wontok—Melanesian concept of brotherhood

Diocese—a grouping of parishes led by a Bishop

Division—Tactical grouping of about 15,000 soldiers comprised of three brigades

www.ingramcontent.com/pod-product-compliance
Lightning Source LLC
Chambersburg PA
CBHW061930220426
43662CB00012B/1861